Youth justice in practice
Making a difference

Bill Whyte

BASW
BRITISH ASSOCIATION
OF SOCIAL WORKERS

First published in Great Britain in 2009 by

The Policy Press
University of Bristol
Fourth Floor
Beacon House
Queen's Road
Bristol BS8 1QU
UK

Tel +44 (0)117 331 4054
Fax +44 (0)117 331 4093
e-mail tpp-info@bristol.ac.uk
www.policypress.org.uk

North American office:
The Policy Press
c/o International Specialized Books Services (ISBS)
920 NE 58th Avenue, Suite 300
Portland, OR 97213-3786, USA
Tel +1 503 287 3093
Fax +1 503 280 8832
e-mail info@isbs.com

© The Policy Press 2009

British Library Cataloguing in Publication Data
A catalogue record for this book is available from the British Library.

Library of Congress Cataloging-in-Publication Data
A catalog record for this book has been requested.

ISBN 978 1 86134 839 5 paperback
ISBN 978 1 86134 840 1 hardcover

The right of Bill Whyte to be identified as author of this work has been asserted by him
in accordance with the 1988 Copyright, Designs and Patents Act.

The statements and opinions contained within this publication are solely those of the
author and not of The University of Bristol, The Policy Press or The British Association
of Social Workers. The University of Bristol, The Policy Press and The British Association
of Social Workers disclaim responsibility for any injury to persons or property resulting
from any material published in this publication.

The Policy Press works to counter discrimination on grounds of gender, race, disability,
age and sexuality.

Cover design by The Policy Press.
Front cover: image kindly supplied by www.JohnBirdsall.co.uk
Printed and bound in Great Britain by MPG Books, Bodmin.

For Anna and Patrick

Contents

List of tables and figures   vi

Acknowledgements   vii

Preface   viii

one   Introduction: youth justice in the UK and Europe   1

two   Children, young people and crime   21

three   Directing principles of effective practice   45

four   Assessing needs and risks   71

five   Early intervention and restorative practice   99

six   Effective responses to reducing youth crime   123

seven   Intensive intervention   149

eight   Maintaining and evaluating the change   169

nine   Towards integrated community justice and welfare   187

References   207

Index   233

List of tables and figures

Tables

1.1	Supervision practice in four paradigms	16
1.2	A social education or integrative paradigm for youth justice	17
2.1	Levels of criminological theory	31
2.2	Schematic of criminological theories	32
3.1	Factors associated with youth crime	54
3.2	Prochaska and Di Clemente's model of change	61
4.1	ASSET domains	84
4.2	Summary action plan framework	93
5.1	Ranking of predictors at ages 6–11 and ages 12–14 of violent or serious delinquency at ages 15–25	102
9.1	Examples of case management tasks	196
9.2	Framework for case management	197

Figures

2.1	Problem analysis triangle	27
6.1	A model of change	131

Acknowledgements

I owe many debts in relation to this book, which are too many to acknowledge. The support of colleagues in the Criminal Justice Social Work Development Centre for Scotland has been critical both in enabling me to develop my research and scholarship in general and to commit time to the task of writing this book in particular. I am also very grateful to Viv Cree for her encouragement to undertake the project, to Steve Myers for his helpful comments on the typescript and to Linda Hutton for her assistance with vignettes. However, the responsibility for any errors and omissions is mine alone.

Preface

This text is intended for social work and other practitioners and students who work in the community with young people involved in offending. There has never been a more challenging time to be a practitioner in youth justice in the UK. In particular, the politicised nature of practice, ambivalence towards young people in general and the demonisation of those who break the law characterises the tensions that exist. These sit alongside increased demand for effective responses to reduce and prevent offending which may be viewed as genuine or simply as camouflaging deep-rooted demands for greater punishment as a means of achieving social control.

UK jurisdictions stand accused by the United Nations Committee on the Rights of the Child of poor child-centred approaches to youth crime, of high levels of criminalisation and detention of young people, many with public care backgrounds, and of an over-emphasis on punishment, control and surveillance over care, shared responsibility and children's rights.

Practitioners could be forgiven for describing their world as something of a minefield in which they operate in the crossfire between opposing ideologies and in a 'no-win' situation in which they are seen to fail from any or every perspective. There is no UK consensus from which to present practice theory, principles or methods, or to balance the value of evidence-led practice and the directionality provided by research on effectiveness with the equally strong case for radical changes in approach to practice that suggest youth justice is a counter-productive concept without meaningful childcare and social justice. Issues of power and powerlessness abound.

It is not the aim of this book to resolve these difficulties. It is simply a contribution to the development of knowledgeable and reflective practitioners and managers. It aims to assist them to operate in a critical manner within a system they cannot easily change but have responsibilities to challenge at all levels on behalf of young people and the victims of their crimes. It attempts to explore the balance between science and art in which sometimes doing nothing is better than well-intentioned but poorly focused intervention.

The United Nations Convention on the Rights of the Child (UNCRC) and its associated guidance provides international benchmarks for youth justice. These provide the organising framework for examining the available evidence base for practice in youth justice at present.

Structure of the book

The development of effective practice for reducing youth crime in the UK requires a political and professional commitment to the principles of the UNCRC and an investment in equipping the relevant frontline staff with the core skills required.

Each chapter of this book includes a practice vignette or case study to encourage the examination of different aspects of youth justice practice in the UK directed by UNCRC principles. The chapters start with a brief scenario which is developed within the chapter at key points to give readers the chance to reflect on their own experience and on what they have read. Each chapter concludes with review questions and a practice exercise.

Chapter One provides an analysis of the challenges currently faced by youth justice practitioners in the UK and possible future directions provided by the far-reaching vision of UNCRC principles and international guidance.

Chapter Two explores contemporary influences on responding to youth crime and provides a brief review of important theoretical frameworks impacting on current thinking and understanding of crime committed by children and young people. It also provides an examination of empirical data on the nature of youth crime and of paradigms for practice.

Chapter Three takes this examination further by exploring what does and what does not seem to work in practice aimed at reducing offending and promoting desistance.

Chapter Four examines the nature of social work assessment and the place of standardised approaches to assessing need and risk in formulating holistic and integrated action plans to meet the best interests of the young person and the community.

Chapter Five considers the practice implications of early intervention and restorative approaches in delivering child-centred provision that addresses anti-social and criminal behaviour and supports resilience.

Chapter Six returns to the theme of effective responses to youth crime. The discussion covers key aspects of intervention from engagement and relationship building, to effective methods and approaches for delivering services which best support young people in the development of their human capital (knowledge, skills and personal resources) and social capital to support better social integration.

Chapter Seven explores issues of graduating intervention to fit the needs, risks and circumstances of the young person and the nature of their offending, whether by human 'wraparound' or administrative and electronic means.

Chapter Eight considers the challenges of monitoring, maintaining and evaluating change as an essential ingredient of empirically based practice, supporting effective 'co-production' and measuring achievement.

Finally, Chapter Nine concludes that for youth justice practice to be effective, practitioners require skills in change management, and the policy and practice agenda needs to move towards the development of better integrated community justice and welfare provision, reflecting the importance of shared responsibility and social justice.

Introduction: youth justice in the UK and Europe

This introductory chapter is based on an assumption that professional practice in the UK should be directed by the framework of principles and standards provided by the United Nations Convention on the Rights of the Child (UNCRC) (1989).[1] The UNCRC is not directly enforceable in UK or Scottish legislation but it is the policy of the Scottish Executive to reflect the provisions of the Convention wherever possible in the development of policy and legislation and its associated guidance which sets the international benchmarks for youth justice systems and places international obligations on its signatories. This is not a straightforward assumption, however, as international reports suggest that practice in UK jurisdictions fails to meet many of the international commitments expected of signatories to the UNCRC (Harvey, 2002; EC, 2005).

Like parents trying to figure out how to raise their children, countries have, in recent years, wrestled with the question of how to respond to youths who break the law (Tonry and Doob, 2004, p 1).

Vignette: first-time offending

John is 12 years old. He has been caught stealing sweets, a music CD and a video game from Woolworths along with two friends. This is the first time he has come to the attention of the police.

We will ask questions relating to this vignette throughout this chapter.

Practice approaches to welfare and justice for young people

Approaches to dealing with children and young people who break the law vary much more widely in the UK and in Europe than the equivalent justice systems for adults. In addition to cultural and institutional differences, youth systems vary in their structures and age jurisdiction as well as in the normative and underlying assumptions of policy and practice. Some countries operate youth systems that are in effect criminal courts for young people while others have systems based on child welfare and social education, and some have a combination of both depending on the age threshold for criminal responsibility and the normal age of transition to criminal court.

However, the age of criminal responsibility is not in itself an indicator of a non-criminal approach to children and young people as recommended by the UNCRC. The system in England and Wales, with an age of criminal responsibility of 10, relies heavily on *diversion*,[2] but all children and young people aged 10-17 when dealt with formally or compulsorily for offending are likely to be dealt with in criminal youth courts. In Scotland, while the age of criminal responsibility is lower, at eight, few young people under 16 will appear in a criminal court compared with most other countries because of Scotland's Children's Hearing system. Two sets of transitions therefore have important implications for practice – the transition from non-criminal diversion to formal criminal approaches and the transition from youth to adult criminal systems.

Systems tend to be evaluated against ideal types of *welfare* or *justice*. The political push has often been for coherence of a single approach, rather than on one that best addresses the issues facing young people who offend, or one directed by theories based on empirical data. As one commentator suggested:

> ... it is perhaps misguided to try to attempt to squeeze the facts of childhood into a unified theory of justice. Any system dealing with young people who offend needs to be sufficiently flexible to accommodate conflicting theories to achieve justice for children, instead of denying the conflicts of childhood to achieve a coherent philosophy. (Adler, 1985, p 2)

The terms 'welfare' and 'justice' have more than one distinct meaning although they are interconnected. Sometimes the terms are used descriptively to refer to agencies and decision-making bodies that deal with care and protection issues (*child welfare agencies*) or youth crime (*juvenile or youth justice agencies*). Welfare can be seen to denote a child's well-being and interests, while justice carries a wider sense of social and criminal justice as if somehow the two are mutually exclusive. In practice terms the contrast is reflected in jurisdictions that maintain a separation between systems dealing with the care and protection of children and young people (*child welfare*) and responses to offending by children and young people (*youth justice*).

Alongside statement of values, principles and standards for youth justice practice which vary in each UK jurisdiction, the British Association of Social Workers (BASW) promotes a definition of social work issued by the International Federation of Social Workers and the International Association of Schools of Social Work which applies to social work practitioners and educators in every region and country in the world.

> The social work profession promotes social change, problem solving in human relationships and the empowerment and liberation of people to enhance well-being. Utilising theories of human behaviour and social systems, social work intervenes at the points where people interact with their environments. Principles of human rights and social justice are fundamental to social work. (www.basw.co.uk)

BASW's code of ethics consists of five basic values and a set of practice principles associated with each basic value to guide ethical practice that should underpin professional practice. These are summarised as 'social work practice should both promote respect for *human dignity* and pursue *social justice*, through *service to humanity*, *integrity* and *competence* (1976, para 3, emphasis added).

> In the case of John, in what ways, if any, would a welfare or justice approach to practice differ in response to this behaviour?
>
> Whose interests should be considered and what ethical dilemmas are raised?

Children or offenders first?

Most mainland European jurisdictions deal with children who offend within a welfare system up to age of transition to (youth or adult) court systems, which is generally around 14 or 15 years old. UK jurisdictions, based on common law, vary much more widely. The near universal ratification of the UNCRC has placed importance on providing 'a level playing field' for all children through universal prevention and early social intervention measures. In all UK jurisdictions the 'reach' of children's legislation is the age of 18, yet many, if not most, young people involved in crime are 'criminalised' in some way long before that age, despite the evidence suggesting that early criminalisation is one of the best predictors of sustained criminality.

These circumstances present day-to-day challenges for practitioners concerned with effectiveness, values and ethical practice. They highlight dilemmas about practising in systems where obligations and duties under UNCRC and children's legislation seem underplayed and raise real questions about how the 'paramountcy' principle (the principle that the safety and welfare of the child must be the primary and paramount consideration in any proceedings or decision-making involving children) should operate in youth justice practice.

Many different models of youth justice exist; few are completely satisfactory and compromises abound. The manner in which different jurisdictions respond to children's needs and risks cannot be understood in isolation from their historical development, which makes comparison problematic. Few countries are comfortable with too rigid a distinction or separation between justice and welfare, with the result that there are many variations in the balance relating to prevention, early intervention, diversion, social interventions and sanctions or punishments incorporated within youth justice approaches. Ratification of the UNCRC has created pressure on many western countries to try and find a better balance and to construct a kind of synthesis or compromise between the two basic sets of 'principles' of justice and welfare, while at the same time recognising the importance of holistic strategies, cultural diversity and community involvement in decision making.

Despite the systematic difference between common law and continental law countries, many of the practice challenges facing child welfare and youth justice practitioners do not differ greatly between countries. In all states national legislation provides for a wide range of measures that allows for intervention, restriction and ultimately for removal from home of children and young people whether for welfare and behavioural or criminal difficulties.

In many cases local authorities will have had contact with the child and family in question for a considerable amount of time before formal proceedings relating to criminal behaviour begin, and will often have had responsibility for offering early voluntary assistance. Indeed many will have had 'care' responsibilities of some sort, for those who persist in their offending. Inadequacies in preventive welfare provision can create conflicts of interest when the main service provider is responsible for ensuring that children's 'best interests' and needs are met as well as the public interest. Too often young people in need seem to 'slip' too readily from 'care' status to 'criminal' status, re-labelling and re-processing them as 'offenders' as if by entering criminal processes they become 'former' or 'ex'-children.

There are few if any mechanisms to challenge service providers or to hold them to account for the quality of provision offered or for service failure to effect positive change in the lives of young people. While persistent and serious offending cannot be condoned or excused, there is little evidence to suggest that service failure is seriously factored into decision making. Criminal processes, in particular, have a tendency to 'translate' service failure into individual responsibility and young person or family failure.

Estimates are that in Scotland, between 50% and 75% of young people aged 16 and 17 entering Young Offender Institutions (YOI) via criminal courts have a public care background. Longitudinal studies have shown that as many as 9% of young people may have a conviction by the age of 19

(McAra and McVie, 2007). Criminal proceedings tend to deal with them as solely, individually and fully responsible for their criminal actions. This often serves to absolve service providers from accountability and any practical requirements for 'shared responsibility' intended by children's legislation and expected by UNCRC principles.

A major challenge facing most states and their practitioners is the UNCRC requirement to facilitate the participation of children and young people in legal proceedings and decision making. The position of young people in formal proceedings has been strengthened within recent decades in UK jurisdictions. Nonetheless there are still major deficits, particularly in the debate on the most appropriate forum for participative decision making and the suitability of adversarial criminal courts, whether these are designated 'youth' or otherwise. What constitutes 'a child' and 'a youth' varies between jurisdictions and with this the demarcations between those who are and those who are not deemed 'fully criminally responsible', and between those considered best dealt with in criminal proceedings and those not.

While young people who are heavily involved in crime often have substantial social welfare needs, no good comparative data exist across jurisdictions on when justice systems or welfare and protection systems are invoked when both could be seen as relevant. What is clear is that western jurisdictions have not arrived at a consensus on how best to respond to troubled and troublesome children and young people. There are, however, trends and changes in practice to support greater use of diversion from all criminal style proceedings, for example through the use of restorative practices, reparation and victim mediation. In New Zealand models of restorative practice and family group conferencing have been used to substantially reduce the numbers of young people going to court. At the same time restorative-type provisions are also being incorporated within criminal proceedings as forms of court disposal that may act to undermine diversion from formal proceedings.

Practitioners have to operate within the constraints set by their own jurisdiction. At the same time issues of professional integrity confront practitioners on a day-to-day basis with consequences both for children and young people who offend and for those who suffer as a result of their offences. If practice is to be evidence-led and effective, practitioners have a responsibility to operate in a principled and value-based manner even though this may create tensions between them and their organisational system (Hill et al, 2006). With regard to service failure and unmet need, this can place practitioners in a position of having to consider whether they should or could challenge and 'blow the whistle' on the system.

International guidance: benchmarks for practice

Most jurisdictions claim to be searching for new and more effective ways of dealing with troubled and troublesome children and young people without explicit reference to a common set of standards or principles against which to measure the appropriateness of their approach. UK jurisdictions have set national services standards that vary greatly and make little reference to the international standards that already exist which, in principle, should be reflected in practice approaches. This lack of consensus on what youth justice systems should be or what they are intended to achieve creates major challenges and ethical dilemmas for practitioners across the UK.

Benchmarks for practice have been set by international agreements and regulations including the European Convention on Human Rights (ECHR), formally entitled The European Convention for the Protection of Human Rights and Fundamental Freedoms, which was adopted by the Council of Europe on 4 November 1950 to protect human rights and fundamental freedoms. It was ratified and entered into force on 3 September 1953. All Council of Europe member states are party to the Convention and new members are expected to ratify the Convention at the earliest opportunity. The UK was an original signatory and ratified the Convention in 1959 but it was not until 1998 that it was incorporated into UK legislation and subsequently adopted by all the UK jurisdictions.

UNCRC and its associated international instruments and guidance

Article 3 of the UNCRC requires that 'in all actions concerning children, whether undertaken by public or private social welfare institutions, courts of law, administrative authorities or legislative bodies, the best interests of the child shall be a primary consideration'. The qualification of 'a' rather than 'the' primary consideration can find expression in quite different practices which invoke the public interest as overriding the interests of the child when it comes to criminal matters for relatively minor, even if persistent, offending.

Since the incorporation of the ECHR into law in UK jurisdictions in 1998, a number of practices have changed to comply with European court rulings. In the Bulger case (*Venables v Crown*) the European Court recognised that the ECHR had little to say about children involved in crime, and drew on UNCRC guidance for benchmark standards. In effect the European Court confirmed that the fulfilment of ECHR requires application of UNCRC principles. Yet no UK jurisdiction has fully incorporated the UNCRC within legislation, and practice remains some distance from the 'spirit' if not the obligations and requirements of being signatories.

The preamble to the UNCRC makes reference to the importance of the other international instruments. It stresses the dynamic nature of the framework set by UNCRC that it expects to be continually fleshed out and developed on the basis of research and practice-related evidence. A number of UN promulgations are of particular importance in providing directing principles for youth welfare and justice practice.

Key UN guidance for youth welfare and justice

- Standard Minimum Rules for the Administration of Juvenile Justice (Beijing Rules), 1985
- Directing Principles for the Prevention of Juvenile Delinquency (Riyadh Guidelines), 1990
- Rules for the Prevention of Juveniles Deprived of Liberty (Havana Rules), 1990
- Standard Minimum Rules for Non Custodial Measures (Tokyo Rules), 1990
- Economic and Social Council Guidelines for Action on Children in the Criminal Justice System (Vienna Guidelines), 1997.

The *Beijing Rules* set standards for the administration of justice, placing particular emphasis on children's rights, and stressing the importance of the well-being of the young person. They recommend that the age of criminal responsibility is based on 'emotional, mental and intellectual maturity' and that it should not be fixed too low. These standards stress the adoption of social educational responses to youth crime rather than punitive (criminal) ones. Rule 11 *requires* consideration of diversion from criminal proceedings with the young person's consent. The emphasis within these standards is, where possible, to avoid drawing young people unnecessarily into any formal processes and thus avoiding the amplifying and confirmatory effect (*net widening*) generally associated with criminalisation. At the same time they stress the importance of the young person's right to representation and the avoidance of deprivation of liberty unless the seriousness of the offence merits it and then only as a last resort.

Would your views about John be different if he was 10 or if he was 15?

The *Directing Principles of Riyadh* stress the value of child-centred early intervention, shared responsibility in the socialisation of young people and the promotion of non-criminogenic attitudes through multidisciplinary approaches to crime prevention. They focus on 'young persons who may or may not be in conflict with the law' and 'who are abandoned, neglected abused, exposed to drug abuse, in marginal circumstances and who are at general social risk' (Marshall, 2007, p 7). They promote a 'progressive universalism', signalling a major overlap between children and young people in adversity and for those in conflict with the law, and that meeting needs and building 'human capital' is a priority to avoid escalating offending trajectories and so reducing risks.

The *Havana Rules* stress the independence of prosecutors and their role in promoting diversion from criminal proceedings for young people up to 18. From existing practice evidence, this is not something that UK prosecutors seem to have shown much independent concern for. The *Tokyo Rules* are intended to promote greater community involvement and community-based responses to crime. They reflect a growing debate on the need to promote young people's 'social capital'. The *Vienna Guidelines* stress the indivisibility and interdependence of the rights of children outlined in the UNCRC. Guideline 11 specifically encourages the development of child-oriented youth justice systems. Guideline 15 explicitly supports prevention and the diversion from criminal systems and the importance of dealing with underlying social causes:

> ... one of the obvious tenets in juvenile delinquency prevention and juvenile justice is that long-term change is brought about ... when root causes are addressed. (Guideline 41)

The UNCRC sets out the terms in which children and young people 'by reason of ... physical and mental immaturity, need special safeguards and care, including appropriate legal protection'. It is the most widely ratified human rights treaty in the world. Yet many countries, including the UK, have entered reservations to its guiding principles. Nonetheless international law requires that none of these reservations compromise the spirit or principles of the Convention. Despite the existence of these important standards and the consistent practice philosophy running through them, it is difficult to argue from evidence on UK criminalisation and detention of young people under the age of 18 that the obligations implied by the UNCRC have featured greatly in the priority of youth justice policy makers, decision makers or practice agencies.

Key UNCRC principles relevant to youth welfare and justice

- ■ Article 1 recommends that young people under the age of 18 should be regarded as children, unless the local age of majority is lower
- ■ Article 2 promotes a non-discrimination principle that demands that all rights apply to all children without exception

■ Article 3(1) requires consideration of the 'best interests' of the young person in decision making: 'in all actions, concerning children, whether undertaken by public or private social welfare institutions, courts of law, administrative authorities or legislative bodies, the best interest of the child shall be a primary consideration'
■ Article 12 provides for the right of children to have their views heard in all decisions affecting them.

While these key principles are reflected in children's legislation in UK jurisdictions, in reality there are many situations in which they are overridden by criminal justice practices.

The UN Committee on the Rights of the Child monitors the application of the treaty and is due to report for a third time on the UK in 2007-08. This will make interesting reading for UK youth justice practitioners given the findings of the previous encounters. Representatives of the UK government first met with the Committee in 1995. The UK delegation was described as 'uncooperative and arrogant'. The UN Committee published a list of concerns and criticisms regarding the UK's performance, along with a comprehensive set of recommendations on how to better meet its obligations and protect children's rights. In revisiting these concerns in 2002 the Committee encountered 'a far more cooperative' UK delegation, who conceded that the UK's past performance had not been perfect, that concrete steps were being taken to implement children's rights and that the government was committed to making progress in the future. While recognising that significant steps had been taken, overall, the UN Committee remained highly critical of UK practices and expressed disappointment that the majority of the recommendations from the 1995 report had not been acted on. It concluded that the UK response was below what should be expected from a 'great country' and it lacked a child-centred and rights-based approach to youth justice. Concern was expressed about the punitive climate that had resulted in an increased use of detention for longer periods and for younger children (Harvey, 2002).

The UK delegation argued that the current low age of criminal responsibility allowed for early intervention while recognising children's responsibility for their crime. At the same time it maintained that the 1989 Children Act, although providing protection and guarantees of services for children up to the age of 18, did not apply to children in detention. Although technically the legislation refers only to England and Wales, it is to be assumed as a UK delegation this 'policy position' applied to all UK jurisdictions. On 29 November 2002 the Howard League for Penal Reform won a judicial review against the Home Office in a landmark decision in which the High Court held that the 1989 Children Act did apply to children held in custody.

The judge, Mr Justice Munby, said that the Howard League had 'performed a most useful service in bringing to the public attention matters which, on the face of it, ought to shock the conscience of every citizen' (*R v Secretary of State*, 29 November 2002; Case No CO/1806/2002, para 175).

In July 2007 the Howard League secured a further Court of Appeal decision in the case of J, who was 15 when she committed the offence leading to her detention. Three Law Lords confirmed that local authorities should provide her with the care due under section 20 of the 1989 Children Act. In effect local authorities have the same duties to children who leave custody as to children in need. This judgment highlighted that 'local authorities across the country are failing to provide proper assessments and care plans for vulnerable children' (Howard League for Penal Reform, Press release, 26 July 2007) entering and leaving detention, particularly where children are in danger of returning to precisely the same situations that led to their crimes and imprisonment in the first place. These young people are entitled to throughcare and aftercare support to ensure their personal and social integration and long-term desistance from crime. Giving expression to these duties in practice may be a difficult matter without coherent policy directives, joint protocols and shared resources between criminal justice, youth justice, children's services, housing, education and employment, leisure and health-related provision.

If UK practice standards remain ambivalent towards UNCRC benchmarks, it could be argued that this should be less so in the context of the ECHR that has been incorporated into all UK domestic legislation. The last report by the Commission of Human Rights (EC, 2005) praised the strong sense of individual liberty that characterises British society. It noted, however, that the UK had not been immune to a tendency, increasingly discernable across Europe, to consider human rights as excessively restricting the effective administration of justice and the protection of the public interest. Section IV (paras 81-98) of the report dealt specifically with youth justice matters including the introduction of a range of civil orders to combat low-level crime and anti-social behaviour. The report noted that many recent measures in tackling youth crime had been positive but that it was difficult to avoid the impression that 'juvenile trouble-makers are too rapidly drawn into the criminal justice system and young offenders too readily placed in detention, when greater attention to alternative forms of supervision and targeted early intervention would be more effective' (EC, 2005, para 81).

The report commented further that while there had been extensive programme development in the UK, policies appeared to have made little dent on the numbers of young people detained. The suggestion was that positive initiatives had possibly been 'undermined by the introduction of a series of civil orders aimed at reducing urban nuisance, but whose primary effect has been to bring a whole range of persons, predominantly the young, within the scope of the criminal justice system' (para 83). The report noted that the UK had among the highest rates of juvenile detention in western Europe, high rates of reconviction following the release of young people with troubled and disrupted childhoods, and an apparent lack of appropriate psychological care and inadequate education assistance for these young people. In commenting on the UK's ambition for young people in trouble, it suggested 'young adults should leave prison with something other than advanced degrees in criminality', and drew the conclusion that preventive intervention was 'minimal' in the UK (para 94).

While acknowledging the importance of taking positive steps to deal with anti-social behaviour, the report concluded that 'it is difficult to avoid the impression that the ASBO [Anti-Social Behaviour Order] is being touted as a miracle cure for urban nuisance' (para 113) and 'risks alienating and stigmatising children, thereby entrenching them in their errant behaviour' (para 119). Finally the report author noted that 'indiscriminate naming and shaming would, in my view, not only be counter-productive, but also a violation of Article 8 of the ECHR' (EC, 2005, para 120).

> **Does John deserve to be punished for his breach of the law?**
>
> **Would your views be different if he was already well known for offending?**

Converging practice in the UK

Practitioners have operated in a very turbulent environment in the first part of the 21st century. Despite the wide-ranging differences in principles and structures across the different UK jurisdictions, some commentators have suggested that there are similar pressures on practitioners and shared practice issues as a result of converging themes in all UK jurisdictions (Bottoms and Dignan, 2004).

Each jurisdiction shares a commitment to preventive as opposed to retributive goals in regard to youth crime. All emphasise the importance of multidisciplinary responses, although 'joined-up' approaches vary greatly in practice from area to area. The same strong emphasis on effectiveness and reduction of re-offending, standardised need–risk assessment and a growing emphasis on victims and the harm caused by criminal behaviour is pursued in contrasting ways. In Scotland the welfare-based system has a clear commitment to the paramountcy principle up to the age of 16 and to a lesser extent to 18. This is reflected in its unified response for children in need and those who offend and in the separation of the court's function in the adjudication of legal facts from Children's Hearings' decisions on how best to respond. In England and Wales the separation of family courts dealing with care and protection from youth courts could be argued to have reinforced correctional principles because of the strong emphasis on individual responsibility of offenders, parental irresponsibility, victim reparation and punishment.

Age thresholds represent the most significant formal entry and exit criteria to youth justice systems. In practice most jurisdictions have dual or parallel pathways through which more serious and persistent offenders, whose age is above the minimum entry threshold (age of criminal responsibility) but below the normal 'exit' age, can be 'transferred out' and dealt with in adult criminal processes. The rationale for 'passing up' a child normally relates to issues of symbolic censure and deterrence, public protection and the fact that punishments and sanctions available to adult proceedings are usually greater. How UNCRC principles and the Havana Rules are balanced against these pressures by prosecutors remains somewhat closed to public scrutiny in the UK.

There are inevitable tensions in all systems between having censure and 'consequences' for unacceptable and criminal behaviour and the need for positive assistance in the best interests of the young person and the community. In practice youth courts in the UK tend to operate as 'mini' adult criminal courts despite the potential for alternative responses. The reintroduction of youth courts in Scotland for those aged 16 and 17 is explicitly part of summary criminal justice and pays only lip-service to UNCRC principles, reinforcing a speedy exit from non-criminal processes at around the age of 16. This 'new' youth justice philosophy (Goldson, 2002a) is apparent, to varying degrees, in all UK jurisdictions. It reflects a struggle with the very difficult combination of trying to achieve a 'paramountcy' approach alongside and within judicial and criminal structures. Systems are constantly undergoing a great deal of political 'doctoring' to managing the 'mix' between social and protective measures, punitive responses and sanctions. Few practitioners can find much satisfaction in the compromises that abound.

Youth justice: future directions

The growing concern over improving children's services to tackle poverty, disadvantage and multiple difficulties, including offending, has found renewed expression in recent policy developments. The emphasis on multidisciplinary provision within integrated frameworks for delivering children's services, although not new, is a further step towards practice directed by UNCRC principles. *Every Child Matters* (ECM) (HM Treasury, 2003) and *Getting it Right for Every Child* (GIRFEC) (Scottish Executive, 2004) outline general concern about the welfare of children growing up in the care of local authorities. Many children in care have suffered abuse or neglect. Poor education achievement is a major issue for them when they are discharged from care or compulsory measures, usually still only in their mid teens. They are seldom supported adequately by positive family or social networks or well prepared to build stable and independent lives for themselves. The ambition to improve outcomes for troubled and troublesome children and young people is clearly reflected in the respective policies statements.

These restated childcare principles and policies re-establish responsibility for children in need or at risk, including those who offend, as a shared and corporate one. They recognised the requirements for a better integrated approach to provision, with less bureaucracy and greater freedom for practitioners to get on and deliver quality ('fit for purpose') services for children and families and for agencies to be held more accountable for their delivery and its outcome. The emphasis is on compulsory action as a last resort. Universal services should be progressive, providing information and guidance to engage parents in their child's development, alongside targeted mainstream provision and specialist support for parents and families including where parents are seen to be condoning a child's truancy, anti-social behaviour or offending.

The status of children varies in UK jurisdictions depending on the legal pathways they follow. In Scotland all young people subject to compulsory measures because of their offending are 'looked-after' children. The judicial review led by the Howard League (see above) has clarified that the principles of UK children's legislation should apply to young people irrespective of decision-making pathways. Whether comprehensive childcare provision is available to young people who offend may depend on how successful practitioners are at influencing decision-making pathways in the light of UNCRC principles and evidence-based approaches to practice.

The establishment of effective early intervention that does not further stigmatise disadvantaged children or reinforce and confirm anti-social and criminal identities will require major changes in (inter)professional culture and universal services that are more sensitive to signs of difficulties and problems before they become serious. Different ways of working are required to deliver effective preventive services at key 'pick-up points' through universal and mainstream provision, to get the right service, at the right time, in the right amount for their particular needs.

Children known to more than one specialist agency are expected to have access to one named professional to lead on their case. The success of lead professionals will depend on the 'clout' they have to coordinate the work of the different agencies and different disciplines, to operate as an advocate for young people, and if necessary to 'blow the whistle' on those, whatever their discipline, who 'fail' children. This is unlikely to be achievable without effective strategic community planning to ensure that one set of provisions, for example children's service practice, is not undermined by the action of the other, for example the police, youth justice or anti-social behaviour practices. The policy focus is intended to be on:

- *improving delivery* by reducing bureaucracy and ensuring effective arrangements for planning, sharing information and joint working;
- a *quality improvement framework* which will support the primary purpose of integrated children's services plans and a system for *assessment and information sharing* and support *coordinated action plans* for children;
- a need to concentrate more on *preventive educative programmes*;
- *mainstream services* (for example nurseries, schools, family centres, primary care services and youth centres) as frontline providers;
- compulsory measures only as a *last resort*;
- *intensive structured programmes* for children who face particular difficulties;
- *continuous improvement* across children's services by establishing an integrated system of inspection of services for children.

The landscape for practitioners involved with young people who offend is changing at a global and local level. UNCRC directing principles and developing children's services policies bring some optimism of a more meaningful and evidence-led approach to provision for troubled and troublesome young people. This renewed landscape demands, more than ever, robust practitioners who can combine practice expertise based on research evidence with the art of reaching children and young people who offend as children first, bringing together expertise on crime alongside expertise on effective children and family provision. Utilising the 'clout' attached to the lead professional role may provide a platform for ensuring more effective delivery and for exposing the pressures to 'filter out' young people who offend from their childhood into formal justice provision that is often counter-productive.

A paradigm for practice?

Youth justice directed by UNCRC principles requires a range of different models (multimodal) and approaches to practice. Policy makers promote the concepts of interdisciplinary, multidisciplinary and transdisciplinary practice as providing future directions. However, finding practice mechanisms which incorporate shared values and perspectives and link practitioners from different disciplines and service users or clients to meaningful planning activities (so-called 'joined-up' approaches) has proved difficult in all jurisdictions. Empirical evidence on interdisciplinary practice has not highlighted innovative practice solutions. The sense is of a number of disciplines exploring the same issues, largely unaware of the experience or research generated by other disciplines – 'each doing their own thing'.

Different perspectives influence practice. A funding (best value) perspective is concerned with the efficient and effective use of resources and the appropriate integration of youth justice practice with other services provision. Political concerns are often with appropriate access to services and the sharing and containment of costs for improved outcomes. From an individual practitioner perspective, issues of satisfaction with the process and with the working environment, professional fulfilment, the utilisation of skills and adequacy of remuneration all operate as influences on delivery. The professional and organisational perspective is concerned with intervention reliability, appropriate use of assessment, the effective and appropriate use of support services and the pivotal role of the practitioner and client in the planning and intervention system. From a service user or 'consumer' perspective, satisfaction with the process, problem resolution or clarification, transparent assessment with prediction or uncertainty clearly explained, intervention sequencing, intensity and duration clearly defined and access to integrated services are likely to be major concerns.

Integrating these multiple concerns requires a cultural shift that is often unrecognised as a key element of the change process. Most commentators recognise that the practice of using multiple methods and techniques has to be grounded in a comprehensive theoretical and evaluative framework. However, the integration of practice methods within a unified paradigm – a model or set of assumptions, concepts, values and practices that constitutes a way of viewing social reality – is itself not a straightforward matter. When moving across and between disciplines and methods, shifting from one paradigm to another, there needs to be an account of more than just the methods and techniques. Shifting paradigms means that there are inevitably differences in interpretations, explanations and values.

Despite the emphases on interdisciplinary practice, attempting to incorporate social, educational, health and behavioural sciences into service provision, client–professional relationships and interdisciplinary approaches have largely retained their discipline-based affiliations ('turf'). The growing interest in transdisciplinary approaches to service provision calls for a greater synthesis of practice at the stage of conceptualisation, design, analysis and interpretation through better integrated practice approaches.

The need to clarify the theoretical and practical issues involved in cross-boundary practice through the development of a more responsive or unifying paradigm for practice is not a new one. Two generations ago Bottoms and McWilliams (1979) sought to explore a non-treatment paradigm for probation practice. This was further developed in line with research developments on effective practice and on more recent research on desistance in adults. Table 1.1 summarises the contrasts between the constructions of practice implied by the non-treatment, revised, what works? and desistance paradigms. While these frameworks were not developed specifically for children and young people involved in crime, where the expectation of levels of self-efficacy, self-direction and individual responsibility are different, the conceptual development and associated debate have parallels.

Bottoms and McWilliams' influential 'non-treatment' paradigm attempted to redirect practice away from a correctionally driven 'treatment' and quasi-medical model to a model based on help and mutuality. This was revised to focus more specifically on empirical data on offending and its consequences (Raynor, 1985). Raynor and Vanstone (1994) examined the so-called 'what works?' paradigm that dominated probation practice from

TABLE 1.1: Supervision practice in four paradigms

Non-treatment paradigm	Revised paradigm	What works? paradigm	Desistance paradigm
Treatment becomes help	Help consistent with a commitment to the reduction of harm	Intervention required to reduce re-offending and protect the public	Help in navigating towards ending and reducing re-offending, to reduce harm and to make good to offenders and victims
Diagnosis becomes shared assessment	Explicit dialogue and negotiation offering opportunities for consensual change	Professional assessment of risk and need governed by structured assessment instruments	Explicit dialogue and negotiation assessing risks, needs, strengths and resources and offering opportunities to make good
Client's dependent need as the basis for action becomes a collaboratively defined task as the basis for action	Collaboratively defined task relevant to criminogenic needs and potentially effective in meeting them	Compulsory engagement in structured programmes and case management processes as required elements of legal orders imposed irrespective of consent	Collaboratively defined tasks which tackle risks, needs and obstacles to desistance by using and developing the offender's human and social capital

Source: Adapted from Bottoms and McWilliams (1979); Raynor (1985); Raynor and Vanstone (1994); McNeill (2006)

the mid-1990s in an attempt to build both the empirical and ethical case for the further development of earlier paradigms for practice. More recently, some commentators (for example, McNeill, 2006) recognise the potential impact of research on desistance on practice.

Meeting needs and addressing deeds through social education

The direction of the case for adults has applicability for youth justice. The relevance of key practice 'qualities' associated with engagement, compliance and effectiveness which cast practitioners as mediators between clients, victims and communities supports a rights-based approach to better personal and social integration. Table 1.2 proposes a refocusing of existing paradigms towards social welfare and social education practices as a means of achieving the same outcomes for children and young people who offend.

If ending offending or desistance is the intended outcome of intervention, then practice approaches need to be embedded in empirical understanding of how young people and adults desist. Effective practice should incorporate the connections between social structure, personal agency and identity. Practice is characterised as accommodating intervention to meet needs, reduce risks and (especially) to develop and exploit strengths and build resilience. Whatever form practice might take, it is likely to be worked out on an individualised basis with practitioners assisting young people in the context of their family

TABLE 1.2: A social education or integrative paradigm for youth justice

Help and intervention in acquiring and sustaining personal and social 'capital', building resilience and a positive personal identity to support change towards reducing and desisting from offending, reducing harm and making good to victims with the support of family

Explicit dialogue and negotiation with young people and their families through professional assessment of their social and developmental needs, risks, strengths and resources, assisted and directed by structured assessment instruments and explicit corporate planning to identify and direct opportunities for positive change

Collaboratively defined tasks through voluntary, or as a last resort compulsory, engagement which tackle risks, needs and obstacles to change by using structured approaches, relational and case management processes as required to develop the young person's human and social capital and their personal and social integration; maintained change through community resources.

and community network, building their personal resources (human capital) and acting as an advocate for social resources (social capital).

This requires more from practitioners than the technical management of social education and offence-focused programmes and the disciplined management of compulsory orders as the key to engagement. The paradigm places a high premium on collaboration and involving young people and their families or 'communities of interest' in the process of establishing shared objectives and co-designing interventions to meet these. A necessary ethical and practical corollary is that interventions should be equally preoccupied with making good to young people to enable them to achieve better personal and social integration and inclusion and with it the progressive and positive reframing of their identities essential to personal maturation, social integration and maintaining desistance from crime.

Youth justice in the UK has struggled to find a satisfactory unifying conceptual or practice framework for work with children, youth and families in trouble with the law. The UNCRC sets the standards and benchmarks against which any system of youth justice should operate and be evaluated. This stresses social education principles as the practice philosophy, reflected in a longstanding European tradition of social education or social pedagogy in its widest sense of social well-being and cohesion. Social education principles underpin effective social work practice in Europe in ways that are often missing in Anglo-American traditions. The term 'pedagogy' or 'educator', if used at all in the UK, is mostly used in the science of teaching and learning, locating education within the cognitive domain of the school, while care, by contrast, is something that happens within the confines of the family (Petrie, 2001, p 23). This is apparent in the downplaying of the role of universal and mainstream welfare provision and the move towards the targeting of problem families and children detached from universal provision (Parton, 1996). This ideological shift has seen the focus change from the needs and social integration of those who offend to a greater emphasis on individual responsibility, punishment and community safety.

Social and education perspectives are rooted in education and social sciences respectively, which in coming together can provide a better integrated theoretical framework for youth justice practice directed by UNCRC principles, children's services and children's rights (Hämäläinen, 2003). The language of social education, if somewhat underdeveloped, has found its way into children's policy discourses (Moss and Petrie, 2002; Cameron, 2004; Petrie, 2004). The approach has the potential to incorporate the integration of the individual within society as part of personal development and the promotion of social functioning, inclusion, participation, identity and competence as members of society with shared responsibilities to that society. It offers a shared practice language for promoting social welfare and justice for children and communities.

Social education, in this European sense, is grounded in opposition to individualistic approaches that fail to consider the social dimensions of human existence (Smith and Whyte, 2008), and is consistent with ecological and social learning theories. It offers possibilities for the development of practice methods within an integrative approach to social well-being consistent with research on desistance from crime, without over-focusing on the young person as an offender. Social education provides a positive alternative to deficit-based and/or correctional models of practice that often serve only to highlight tensions in philosophies of justice and welfare.

Conclusion

The wider social context of behaviour and the impact of structural factors such as poverty and community fragmentation have become marginalised in social work and youth justice practice. The role of practitioners is to promote well-being and safety through broadly based social education strategies and to find education solutions to social problems (Hämäläinen, 2003). While practice is generally concerned with direct work with children and young people and their families, social education principles can be applied to wider questions of social integration in different phases of the lifespan. This is based on the belief that social circumstances and social change can be influenced through social education. This is not an alternative, but should complement political action to affect the external 'power' issues of society structures, institutions and legislation. Social education action aspires to change society by influencing the personal in society: people, morals and culture.

Notes

[1] The UK signed the Convention on 19 April 1990 and it came into force across the UK on 15 January 1992.
[2] 'Diversion' is usually used to refer to alternatives to prosecution or formal proceedings for children and young people – see Goldson, 2008, pp 147–9.

Key questions

(1) What case can be made for expecting John to take full responsibility for his actions or for viewing him as a child in need?
(2) If a decision is taken for formal action against John, what is the case for diversionary measures?

(3) What, if any, jurisdiction is there for dealing with John in a criminal court? What sources, nationally and internationally, would you draw on to justify your position?

(4) What are the practice challenges if young people like John are to achieve something other than advanced degrees in criminality?

(5) Why do approaches to dealing with children and young people who break the law vary much more widely in the UK and in Europe than the equivalent adult justice systems?

(6) What mechanisms, if any, are available to support, challenge, and 'blow the whistle' on the system with regard to service failure?

(7) In what ways, if any, do you think welfare and justice approaches are compatible?

Practice exercise

John is now just over 16 and has a difficult family background, with a history of domestic violence and parental separation. John is well known for his persistent offending, drug and alcohol misuse and depression. The outcome of his latest offending is detention. Identify practice issues that are likely to be raised by John's rights under the UNCRC or the ECHR. How might your practice take account of local authorities' legal duties under children's legislation?

Further reading and resources

⮕ UK Children's Commissioners (2008) *Report to the UN Committee on the Rights of the Child*, www.sccyp.org.uk/

⮕ CRAE (2005) *State of Rights in England*, London: Children's Rights Alliance for England, www.crae.org.uk/cms/dmdocuments/State%20of%20childrens%20rights%202005.pdf

⮕ Barry, M. (2005) *Youth Policy and Social Inclusion: Critical Debates with Young People*, London: Routledge.

2

Children, young people and crime

Introduction

There are variations in the way children and young people involved in crime are described, with terms such as 'youth crime', 'delinquency', 'youth disorder' and 'anti-social behaviour', and also in how these are defined and interpreted. There are also wide variations in transitions from childhood to adulthood and the nature and experience of adolescence is often culturally determined by a network of social forces (Erikson, 1995). The machinery of 'justice' is just one of the social 'vehicles' used to shape that experience and to influence the acceptance of and compliance with social norms by young people.

For practitioners absorbed in the delivery of youth justice services, theory may seem unimportant to day-to-day practice. Nonetheless, dominant theories of youth crime are likely to influence, at least in part, the use of language, understanding and responses to young people who offend. A crucial aspect of practice activity involves 'reflexivity', making and constructing meaning through interpretation of individual activities bound by the social and material context in which they exist (Pfohl, 1985, p 294). In the absence of good theoretical and empirical frameworks, choices can be shaped as much by cultural and political preferences as by evidence.

The first section of this chapter provides a brief summary of a selection of important theoretical perspectives that continue to influence current thinking and understanding of the nature of youth crime. No one theory can account for all forms of youth crime and there is no single criminology. Maruna (2000) has argued that few criminological theories have provided much in the way of specific assistance to practitioners as to what they should actually do to best assist people in stopping or desisting from crime or how best to sustain personal and social integration. Values remain crucial to shaping the nature of interventions and their effectiveness. At the same time critical criminological commentary can provide direction and operate as a valuable check on overly correctional, administrative and bureaucratic tendencies.

Vignette: difficult transition to adulthood

Steven is 16 years old and is charged with two incidents of burglary and one of assault. His drinking and misuse of alcohol has created difficulties for him with his mother and her partner. The situation has deteriorated recently as he has started using drugs. He has experienced disruption and relationship difficulties throughout his late childhood, particularly at school. He has now left school and is currently unemployed. He tends to sleep all day and go out with his friends at night, most of whom are involved in offending.

Theories of crime

Biogenetic theories

Biogenetic theories reflect a controversial but nonetheless important school of thought (Lahey et al, 2003). Early commentators tended to write about youth crime and delinquency as if the young people involved were a distinctive 'type' ('the born criminal') with clearly inherited genetic or biological features associated with tendencies to criminality (Emsley, 1997; Garland, 1997). Contemporary theories, recast in terms as diverse as biochemistry, evolutionary psychology and neuropsychology, offer insight into the link between personality and crime, based on the belief that the fundamentals of human personality can be expressed only in terms of a few significant dimensions, largely predetermined genetically. Robust studies show that the links between parent–child relationship quality and children's psychological adjustment are in part genetically mediated (Deater–Deckard and O'Connor, 2000).

The thrust of recent research using behavioural genetic methodology has been to examine *how* genetic factors may be involved in mediating psychosocial adjustment and psychosocial risk. Some commentators (Scarr, 1992) argue that apart from abusive parenting, most of the variability in children's outcomes is due to genetic factors, implying that, so long as parenting is 'good enough', differences in children's developmental trajectories will be due to inherent factors. Genetically driven temperamental characteristics impact on parent–child relations and on parenting style. Youth crime can be characterised as involving young people who have under-developed consciences and 'limited' moral reasoning because they are constitutionally poor at building up conditioned responses to parents or authority figures. While the evidence remains inconclusive, studies, for example of adopted children, suggest that crime may be more related to birth parents than adoptive parents, supporting those who argue that crime owes as much to biology as to social experience (Rowe, D., 2002).

Socioeconomic and ecological theories: control, disorganisation, reaction and strain

Youth crime can be viewed as a response to *inequality, social injustice and poverty*, and its consequences create social circumstances providing limited alternatives to crime. Modern theorists have moved a long way from simplistic association between material deprivation and criminal behaviour. It cannot be argued in any simplistic way that poverty 'causes' crime, which would suggest that only the poor and most of the poor would commit crime. Empirical data show that this is not the case. Periods of declining unemployment and improved standards of living and greater freedom have been accompanied by a growth in criminal activity in the western world since the Second World War (Wilson and Herrnstein, 1985). In the 1990s economic difficulties co-existed with a significant drop in reported youth crime. Nonetheless, the evidence suggests that most young people involved in formal systems for criminal behaviour are poor, disadvantaged and socially excluded.

> What do you find most striking about the background characteristics and needs of young people involved in criminal behaviour like Steven?

A variety of ecological theories have developed directly or indirectly from the work of the *Chicago School of Criminology* that examined the effects of industrialisation and urbanisation on behaviour in the 1920s and 1930s. Many draw on ideas associated with Tonnies (1912) on the nature of social relationships including family and neighbourhood bonds and associated feelings of 'togetherness' (*gemeinschaft*/'community') and on groups that are sustained more by instrumental goals (*gesellschaft*/'society'). The idea that informal social bonds tend to be weakened once groupings begin to develop in both size and number of social relationships was a key observation.

Social control theories suggest that people offend because their ties to the conventional order have broken down. Increased freedom and prosperity have created opportunities for crime in routine activities, particularly in communities lacking formal and informal social controls (Brantingham and Brantingham, 1991; Hudson, 1997). Conformity is normally ensured by family control, community identity and neighbourhood surveillance. When cultural ties are broken, informal social controls are replaced, often ineffectively, by the administrative machinery of crime control and by punishment (Christie, 1993). Contemporary theorists distinguish between the coercive, educative and normative elements of socail bonds. Gottfredson and Hirschi (1990) claim that coercive methods (criminal sanctions) tend only to work in so far as normative controls (social or self-control) are functioning well, that is sanctions tend to work best on those who 'need' them least. As social or self-control does not deteriorate over the life course early intervention can mitigate against criminality. Some theorists suggest that the strength of social bonds may help explain why most young people do not persist in their offending (Sampson and Laub, 1993). Crime may be higher in adolescence because young people are detaching themselves from childhood relationships that once bound them into a 'social fabric' but have not yet established adult attachments and so are only loosely 'integrated' with the rest of the community.

Social disorganisation theories emphasise the importance of social geography and the physical and spatial boundaries of crime, reflecting not just the physical environment but also the social organisation of communities that exists when residents are prevented from implementing and expressing their own values (Bottoms, 1994). Social disorganisation is characterised by high population turnover, consequent disruption of social networks and weak ties within communities, failure to establish shared non-delinquent values and an inability to maintain social controls. Such social circumstances present young people with conflicting standards and competing values, while generating few or no efforts to deal with their problems (Rock, 1997).

Some have argued that it is less the absence of deep-rooted social ties, as many poor neighbourhoods may well have close bonds, but the lack of sufficient resources that results in the failure to establish social control (Wilson, 1987). This questions any straightforward relationship between social control and community ties and proposes that order is maintained through 'collective efficacy' linking social cohesion with expectations of control. Others have argued that a range of positive neighbourhood characteristics are required to produce a social ethos or 'ecology' that will benefit all of the community and reduce crime (Sampson, 2004). It has also been suggested that social and physical disorder can escalate from minor urban difficulties and neglect, for example vandalism, poorly kept gardens and litter (the 'broken windows theory'), which results in local residents withdrawing from concern over their neighbourhood or having any sense of control over it, which in turn opens the way to more serious crime (Wilson and Kelling, 1982).

Environmental criminologists have developed the ideas of place and time as important dimensions to understanding crime. While the focus has often been on land usage, traffic pattern and street design, more emphasis has been placed in recent years on the daily activities and movements of people who offend and their victims (Brantingham and Brantingham, 1991). The development of *social 'maps'* allows for the examination of crime patterns in communities, and modern technology has allowed multidimensional 'geomapping' to identify crime 'hot spots' and 'social localities'.

Social reaction theories link stigmatisation and labelling with offending in an attempt to understand why some people seem to become 'locked into' offending (Matsueda and Braithwaite, 2000). Surveillance by police or social workers and the public attribution of deviant labels is viewed as confirming and amplifying deviance, by reinforcing the label and reducing non-deviant options. More recent commentaries argue against crude and simplistic use of labelling theories, while characterising the criminal justice system as deliberately stigmatising. Individuals in the process of being caught, shamed and punished change or confirm their view of themselves that in turn reinforces the adoption of a criminal lifestyle and associations and confirms their criminality. This view supports the idea that offending is consolidated through social networks in schools, neighbourhoods and associations such as gangs, and ultimately is reinforced and confirmed by system responses, particularly formal and criminal processes.

Social strain theories locate crime in the separation between 'culturally prescribed goals' and the 'institutionally available means' of achieving them (Merton, 1957). The concept of 'anomie' (a lack of social regulation and/or a confusion/breakdown of moral norms resulting in deviant behaviour) is somewhat loosely borrowed from Durkheim. People trapped in lower structures of society are encouraged to achieve socially valued material goals but denied the legitimate opportunity to do so (Cloward and Ohlin, 1960). Legitimate desires cannot be achieved by socially acceptable behaviour, resulting in those in the lower social classes offending. Cohen (1985) has argued that middle-class values are applied to all children in schools. Poor children are ill prepared for the resulting competition for status achievement and 'assessment' by rules that disadvantage them. Unable to compete, they respond by entering a delinquent subculture. These developments in macro and locally based theories gave rise to the development of ecological and differential opportunity theories.

There is still little theoretical direction to suggest the precise mechanisms between the characteristics of neighbourhoods and young people's perception of them as a force behind delinquent behaviour. Nonetheless, ecological 'influences' are re-emerging through the concept of building social capital and the importance of social cohesion in restorative practices. The relevance of neighbourhood and community is a recurrent theme in contemporary policy discourses, recognising the interplay between urban and rural regeneration, community identity and meaningful responses to anti-social behaviour and youth crime.

Psychodynamic, rational choice and social learning theories

Psychodynamic theories suggest that anything that prevents children from developing in healthy ways brings about patterns of emotional disturbance that are at the root of anti-social and criminal behaviour (Hollins, 2002). Freud's theory of conscience development did not focus on offending behaviour as such, but has influenced many early childhood theorists and their understanding of anti-social behaviour, concepts of personality differentiation, instinctual urges and control mechanisms and parent–child interactions. Children learn to separate good and bad feelings, which in turn lead to good and bad internal images, initially of their parents. This is the context within which a sense of self develops. These theories recognise that adolescence, the process of maturation, individuation and emotional development, is the same for both the 'offender' and the 'non-offender' but has been experienced differently. They support the case that what is significant for later life is not necessarily specific childhood events, but the general quality of family relationships and parenting style, none of which are irreversible.

> What kinds of life experiences in adolescence assisted you in developing and perhaps altering your own identity?

Rational choice theory (RCT) and its many variants attempts to show how sharing, cooperation, or social norms emerge. Starting from the viewpoint of the individual as an actor whose initial concern is only about him or herself and his or her welfare, RCT is intended to provide an analytical bridge between individual social actions and their structural outcomes. It has been argued that RCT provides the only overall explanation of social systems and society, and the only solid basis for progress towards a unified social theory (Coleman, 1988). The rational choice perspective assumes that people who offend seek to benefit in some way from their offending behaviour and portrays them as active decision makers who undertake some kind of 'cost-benefit analysis' of crime opportunities. RCT views offending behaviour as involving decision making and choices, which are constrained by time, information and cognitive ability, resulting in 'limited' rather than 'normal' rationality. The premise is that factors that affect decision making vary greatly at different stages of an offence and between different offences. Cornish and Clarke (1998) stress the importance of being crime-specific when analysing decision making and choice selection, and of treating separately decisions relating to the various stages of involvement in offences.

Situational crime prevention theories such as *routine activity theory* (RAT) develop aspects of environmental criminology and have links to cognitive behavioural theories (Felson, 1998). RAT was developed to explain predatory crime and to examine changes in technology and organisation on a societal scale. It suggests that for a predatory crime to occur, three elements must be present at the same time in the same space: a suitable target (as opposed to victim) is available, lack of a capable 'guardian' (human presence, but not the police) to prevent the crime and a motivated offender. These are depicted as the *problem analysis triangle* (PAT) (see Figure 2.1).

Much offending takes place in groups, yet young people who offend are often rejected by pro-social adolescents. *Sub-cultural delinquency* theories view crime at its most frequent in circumscribed social groupings. Individuals, with particular sets of difficulties, particularly young people with difficulties at home and school, seek alternative groups in which they can gain standing and self-esteem. Sutherland's theory of differential association (Sutherland and Cressey, 1970) attempts to account for this and views criminal activity as simply one form of normal learned behaviour, whereby the conditions and situation in which a young person grows up increase or lessen the chances of opportunities to participate in pro-social or delinquent activity. While criminal affiliation may simply reflect the normal habits of adolescents, there is evidence to suggest that criminality in the family and anti-social peer associations also play an important role in reinforcing delinquency (Rutter et al, 1998).

Developmental or *life course theories* (Loeber and LeBlanc, 1990) have become very influential on practice thinking in recent years and attempt to disentangle the different and complex pathways to offending careers. These have provided important insights into onset, escalation and desistance as different stages of development, each with distinctive associated risk factors. Probably one of the most important influences on practice thinking has been

FIGURE 2.1: **Problem analysis triangle**

Motivated
offender
Motive

Crime

Suitable target   Lack of capable guardian

Opportunity

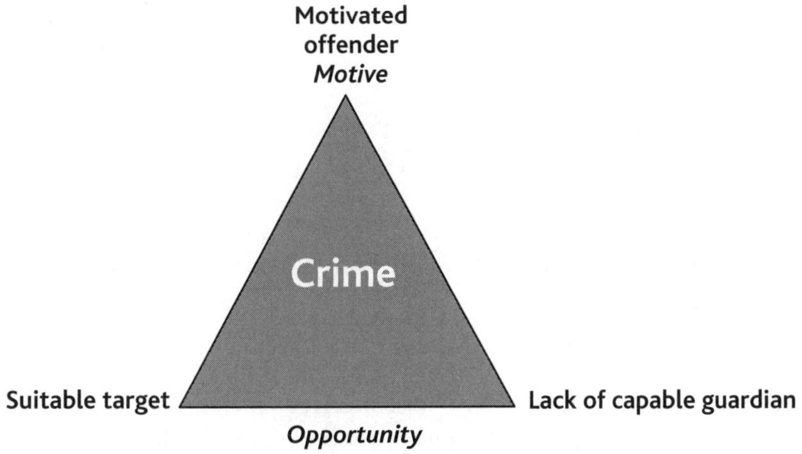

the work of Moffitt (1993) and Patterson (1996) who distinguish between 'early onset' or 'life course' and 'late onset' or 'adolescent only' groups. While these two 'types' are hard to distinguish during adolescence in terms of their offending patterns, they are said to be different in their earlier offending histories and in adult behaviour.

The adolescent or late onset group are characterised as transitional; they start later (in adolescence), are involved in less serious offending and tend to desist before adulthood. Those persistent in their offending are characterised as a small group involved in frequent and serious offending, whose difficulties start early in life and who tend to progress into adulthood continuing to offend long after adolescent-limited offenders have stopped. It is not the contention that early offending necessarily 'locks' these young people into a cycle of re-offending; rather it is that early onset of offending in some children is indicative of a range of other characteristics that adversely influence their development and their behaviour (Smith, 2002). While some studies suggest that adolescence-limited offenders may evidence some of the same sorts of factors that account for persistent offending, they do so to a much lesser degree. The distinction between the two types may not be as clear-cut as it appears:

> … life-course persistent anti-social behaviour starts very early and continues throughout life, but the forms in which it is expressed and the ways it is perceived and described, and the social reactions to it, change at different stages of the life cycle. By contrast, adolescence-limited anti-social behaviour increases rapidly in early adolescence, then declines rapidly after the peak age at around eighteen. (Smith, 2002, p 734)

The value of this work for practitioners is its attempt to identify developmental factors that better explain different pathways through crime. Research has highlighted a wide range of distinctive groups rather than simplistically two distinct groups (Ayers et al, 1999).

From what we know of Steven, do you think he is likely to become a persistent offender?

In what ways, if any, are those involved in persistent offending likely to be somewhat different from others?

Critical criminologists would maintain that the search for 'risk factors' and 'offender types' is fundamentally misconceived and warn that it runs the risk of 'pathologising' by focusing on the individual as the main unit of analysis. Developmental perspectives, by under-emphasising the importance of social-structural factors, may misdirect practice attention towards the individual-level impact of these factors, rather than emphasising that crime, criminality and criminalisation are social constructs governed by wider economic, structural, cultural and political forces. This stresses the 'inherent difficulties in predicting crime prospectively over the life course' (Laub and Sampson, 2003, p 290). The suggestion is that the 'risk factor paradigm' should be avoided as findings show that boys with very similar risk profiles turn out to have very divergent lives. In practice it is almost impossible to predict which children with similar characteristics will become offenders and which will not – an argument for progressive and staged universal approaches to services provision.

Social learning theories share many of the principles discussed above. Involvement in crime is seen as the product of a complex set of learning experiences both in terms of life changes and acquired attitude and behaviours (Bandura, 1977). Social education and cognitive behavioural theory highlight an interrelated link between thinking, feeling and doing as key to understanding youth criminality in its social context. Each of these three interlocking dimensions in turn has three dimensions – intensity (experienced 'strength'), frequency (how often it occurred) and duration (time lapse since first occurrence).

Cognitive development can be defined on three levels:

1. *Pre-conventional*: moral rules are not fully understood, and conformity is often associated with fear, punishment and reward.
2. *Conventional*: conformity to society's rules and expectations because it preserves social relationships.
3. *Post-conventional or principled, ethical behaviour*: awareness of the need for a social contract involving rules and cultural norms (Kohlberg, 1981).

Behaviour, cognition, other personal factors and environmental events are seen to interact as determinants or causes of criminality. While young people who offend do not differ fundamentally from young people who do not offend, it is more likely that they may justify their offending through a series of techniques that neutralise their guilt, such as denying responsibility or denying there is a victim.

Hirschi's (1969) *social bonding* theory includes four key elements. Three focus on adolescents' relations with their immediate social environment including family and school; the fourth is an attitudinal concept. The elements are:

1.   *Attachment*: sensitivity to others' opinions.
2.   *Commitment*: the extent to which social rewards are tied to conformity.
3.   *Involvement*: level of engagement in conventional activities.
4.   *Belief*: the extent of internalised conventional norms.

Adolescents who score high on these four elements are likely to exhibit low levels of deviance because they are constrained by their close relationships with conventional surroundings and their positive attitude toward the moral value of social rules. Studies, whether cross-sectional or longitudinal, tend to provide empirical support for social learning theory suggesting that adolescent associations with deviant peers tend to increase deviance.

Ethnicity

Most criminological theorists do not consider ethnicity as a causal factor of crime; rather, that racial predictors reflect environmental and socioeconomic factors as well as child-rearing conditions (Smith, 1997). There is evidence of bias towards people from minority ethnic backgrounds at different stages of the criminal justice process. However, this offers only a partial explanation of the differences in crime rates, particularly in studies of white and non-white populations from the UK and the US. The disproportionately high representation of people from minority ethnic groups dealt with by the criminal justice system may reflect discrimination towards black or other minority ethnic people and/or result from the associations of poverty and disadvantaged neighbourhoods and crime. People from minority ethnic backgrounds are equally over-represented among those experiencing social and economic disadvantage.

> What assumptions have you made about Steven's ethnicity?
>
> Would you think differently about Steven's case if you knew he was black, or white, or Asian?

Gender

Most theories have tended to neglect gender differences until relatively recently (Heidensohn, 2002). In general males offend more frequently and more seriously than females, and data on which theoretical perspectives are based tend to relate to male offending. Feminist theories of criminology developed as a reaction against gender distortions and stereotyping within traditional criminology. Females have tended to be viewed as offending because of their gender or because of some individual difficulty perceived as 'abnormal' and subject to more intrusive intervention. Feminist theories have raised important critical questions about social roles, gender identities and biological sex characteristics. These cut across conventional academic disciplines and emphasise the importance of women as full social actors in their social world and of recognising the difference between sex as biologically ascribed and gender as socially constructed. As gender role expectations tend to define acceptable behaviour and attitude, they are powerful forms of social control maintained through formal and informal mechanisms.

In many countries the differences in the rate of offending between the sexes has narrowed over the past 50 years and may vary according to age, ethnicity and seriousness of offence. Criminality in males is often understood in terms of peer group activity or of adolescence, as a stage in life which most will grow out of. Theories of female offending have generally lacked this age and social group perspective. Smith and McAra (2004, p 6) found the same explanatory model applied, for the most part, to boys and girls aged 15 in relation to a broad range of crimes. Offences were seen to arise out of situational opportunities in leisure time activities and the social circles in which they moved. In relation to serious offending, they identified a much stronger association with gender, suggesting that possibly a different explanatory model may apply to boys and girls. Recent studies of the distinctive process of female desistance from crime (Rumgay, 2004) continue to add to our understanding of female criminality. For practitioners key concepts may apply to males and females, but female narratives are likely to differ, requiring distinctive service responses.

A helpful schematic (Table 2.1) represents criminological theory as operating on five discrete but interconnected levels (McGuire, 2000).

TABLE 2.1: Levels of criminological theory

Level 1	Macro explanations
Level 2	Locality-based accounts
Level 3	Lifestyle, rational choice and routine activities
Level 4	Socialisation and group influence
Level 5	Self-definitional

This schematic is expanded in Table 2.2.

TABLE 2.2: Schematic of criminological theories

Level	Explanatory focus	Objective	Illustrative theory
1	Society	Explain crime as a large-scale phenomenon	Conflict, strain, control; feminist
2	Localised area – community	Account for geographical variation in crime	Ecological
3	Proximate social group	Understand role of socialisation and social influence through family, school and peer group	Sub-cultural, differential association, social learning
4	Individual criminal acts	Analyse and account for patterns and types of crimes	Rational choice, routine activity
5	Individual offenders	Examine intra-individual factors	Cognitive social learning, neutralisation, psychological control

Source: After McGuire (2000, p 32)

> What theoretical approaches would help to influence how the youth justice system should respond to Steven?
>
> What about young people:
>
> involved in minor and first offences?
> who are persistent offenders?
> involved in serious offences?
> at different ages?
> in relation to gender or 'race'?

Integrated theories: social development and desistance

Given the diversity of behaviours that come to be defined as 'criminal', some have argued that it may be fundamentally misguided to seek to develop general theories of offending (Gelsthorpe, 2003). The modern trend has been towards multifactorial models. Social development theories draw on earlier theories of crime, relating structural factors such as poor housing and poor socioeconomic conditions to individual factors, including conscience development.

Integrated theories attempt to examine the interplay between the two and provide important meaning for practice. Farrington's (2002) integrative theory of male offending and anti-social behaviour draws on strain, control, social learning, rational choice and labelling theories to account for both the development of 'anti-social tendencies' and the occurrence of anti-social acts. He suggests that offending is the result of a four-stage process involving:

1. *Energising*: motivations develop which may lead to offending.
2. *Directing*: criminal methods for satisfying those motivations come to be chosen as a matter of habit.
3. *Inhibiting*: beliefs, values and socialisation may inhibit offending.
4. *Decision making*: situational opportunities, calculations about costs and benefits, the subjective probabilities of different outcomes of offending and social factors that inform decisions about offending.

The consequences of offending may then reinforce anti-social tendencies, and the stigmatisation and labelling that often accompanies criminalisation may also encourage further offending by diminishing the individual's prospects of satisfying their needs and wants by legal means.

'Realist' criminology recognises the interplay between both structural and individual factors as relevant to understanding, preventing or reducing crime. Young (1994) identified four overlapping and influential paradigms of 'left idealism', 'new administrative criminology', 'right realism' and 'left realism'. *Left realism*, for example, developed as a critique to earlier criminological theories that provide only a partial and one-sided view of the possible causes of crime. Left realism rejects the extremism of earlier theories that suggest that absolute deprivation alone causes crime and those which suggest total determinism or mechanistic causation.

The central aim of left realism is to provide a synthesis of competing ideas. The importance of the social context is emphasised, including the development of criminal behaviour in time and space. All crime has a spatial dimension and the social geography of crime varies. Some types of crime have a national or international dimension. Some relate to one estate in one town. It is argued that those concerned with reducing offending among young people must develop an understanding of the nature and form of crime itself as a social phenomenon, taking account of:

■ the background causes
■ the social and moral context of crime
■ direction through time
■ enactment in time and space
■ detection of crime
■ response to the offender
■ response to the victim.

Left realism points to the interaction between the police, other agencies of formal social control, the offender and the victim as the four definitional elements of crime referred to as the 'square of crime'. Crime rates are generated not merely by the interplay of these four elements, but by the social relationships between various points on the 'square'. As a consequence crime responses should be 'multiagency' and coordinated to address all points of the 'square'. This is a 'realistic' attempt to identify what can actually be done about crime while recognising the limitations of current knowledge in tackling the root causes of crime. Neither left nor right realism underplays the value of social interventions even where they show only marginal gains in reducing offending, nor do they discount the search for utopian or ideal solutions to the problem of crime. Both emphasise the need to learn from closely monitored interventions and evaluative research and that these can make a cost-effective contribution to crime reduction strategies.

Earlier theories such as the Chicago School's emphasis on issues of social cohesion and the importance of social capital sit well alongside realist theories. They provide a platform for developments in desistance and integrated practice theory aimed at explaining how and why people reduce and stop their offending by achieving better personal and social integration. While there is now a considerable body of research on effective interventions, much less attention has been paid to the 'black box' questions of 'how' as well as 'why' the process of personal and social integration works (Lin, 2000).

Maruna (2001) places importance on three broad theoretical perspectives relevant to desistance that articulate well with practice considerations in youth justice. These are drawn from theories discussed above: maturational change, social bonds and narrative theory. Maturational change theories focus on the established links between age and certain criminal behaviours. The *age–crime curve* remains the most robust and yet the least understood empirical observation in criminology (Moffitt, 1993). Social bonds theory suggests that ties to family and education or employment programmes in early adulthood can assist explanations of changes in criminal behaviour across the life course. Where these ties exist, they create a reason to 'go straight'. Where they are absent, people who offend have less to lose from continuing to offend. Narrative theories have a long tradition in qualitative research and stress the significance of subjective changes in the person's sense of self-identity, personal and social 'connectedness' or integration, which in turn are reflected in changing motivations, greater concern for others and consideration of the future.

These theories draw on empirical findings that stress the importance of the relationships between 'objective' changes in a person's life and 'subjective' assessment of the value or significance of these changes (Farrall, 2002). They support the argument for more holistic responses aimed at crime reduction and suggest that the 'key' to stopping offending is likely to reside somewhere in the interface between developing personal maturity, changing social bonds associated with life transitions and individual subjective narrative constructions built around key events, transitions and changes. It is not simply the events and changes that matter, but what these mean to the young people involved.

Attempts at integrated practice theory recognise that stopping offending is not an event or straightforward outcome from a programme of intervention but is part of a developmental process that is necessarily 'offence-focused', that is, about reducing and ceasing offending, but it is not in any simplistic way or exclusively 'offence-led'. It requires taking steps to refrain from offending over an extended period in ways that are associated with personal maturation and social development. Drawing on integrated theory should assist youth justice practitioners in avoiding the trap of over-exaggerating the importance of cognitive 'within' person changes which need not always be sufficient to accompany desistance (Laub and Sampson, 2003). Practice directed towards reducing offending will also give attention to supporting resilience and sustaining personal and social integration.

The nature of youth crime

It is important that practice methods and approaches are based on and directed by theories and strategies developed from empirical data on the nature of youth crime. Graham and Bowling (1995) found that among young people aged 14-24 in England, 55% of young males and 31% of young females admitted committing at least one of a list of 23 offences at some time in their lives. Most only admitted one or two offences but a small proportion accounted for a wholly disproportionate amount of crime (3% of the young people were responsible for 26% of the offences). The most commonly admitted crimes for both males and females involved dishonesty, in particular theft and handling stolen goods. Most studies since then have produced quite similar findings.

Anderson et al (1994) found no major differences relating to geography and, by implication, socioeconomic or class background of young people who admitted offending in different socioeconomic neighbourhoods, and concluded:

> In no sense … can 'delinquency' be regarded as the preserve of any particular group or section of young people. On the contrary, rule breaking and petty crime would seem to be very much a normal feature of young people's lives, wherever they come from and whichever school they go to. (Anderson et al, 1994, p 164)

Early sweeps of the *Edinburgh Study of Youth Transitions and Crime* (Smith et al, 2001) paint a similar picture of delinquency at the age of 12 or 13. Well over half of respondents admitted to two or more kinds of delinquency within the previous 12 months; 12% or 13% of respondents accounted for half of the incidents, which were overwhelmingly group activities. There was a marked tendency for children who had been in public care to have higher rates of delinquency and victimisation than others. The study concluded that being a victim of crime could be one of the most important predictors of delinquency (Smith et al, 2001, p 63). Delinquency was significantly related to family controls, relationships and activities, with particularly strong association between delinquency and lower levels of parental supervision (p 95), attitudes to school and relationships with teachers.

Jamieson et al (1999) explored desistance and persistence among three groups of young people aged 14–15 (the peak age for recruitment into offending for the boys); aged 18–19 (the peak age of offending); and aged 22–25 (the age by which many would be expected to grow out of crime). The study was based on interviews with a total of 75 'desisters' (43 male and 32 female) and 109 young people (59 male and 50 female) who were still offending or had done so recently. In the youngest age group, desistance for both boys and girls was associated with the real or potential consequences of offending and with growing recognition that offending was pointless or wrong. For young people in the middle age group, changing behaviour was associated with increasing maturity linked to the transition to adulthood and related events like securing a job or a place at college or university, or entering into a relationship with a partner or leaving home. For the oldest group, 'desistance was encouraged by the assumption of family responsibilities, especially among young women, or by a conscious lifestyle change' (McIvor et al, 2000, p 9).

Some gender differences were associated with ending offending. Females tended to offer moral as opposed to utilitarian reasons for stopping and were more likely to emphasise the importance of relational aspects of the process than males. For some young women parental responsibilities seemed to be linked to their decision to stop, while young men tended to emphasise personal choice and agency. Nonetheless age and, in particular, the transitions associated with it, seemed to be a more important determinant of desistance than gender. Among persisters, girls and young women were more often keen 'to be seen' as desisters, possibly reflecting societal disapproval of female offending.

Failure to desist among young men seemed to be best explained by three sets of risk factors: a high frequency of prior offending, continued contact with delinquent peers and heavy drinking and controlled drug use. Only two factors seemed to be positively associated with desistance for males in the 16–25 age range: their perception that their school work was above average, and continuing to live at home and spending less time with delinquent peers. Other studies have revealed that decisions about offending and stopping offending are often related to the need to feel included in a social world, through friendships in childhood and through wider commitments in adulthood. Young people from very disadvantaged backgrounds often have limited access to mainstream opportunities for social status because of their age and social circumstances and as a consequence have limited capacity for social recognition in terms of durable and legitimate means of acquiring 'capital' (Barry, 2006, pp 328-9).

Rumgay (2004) has suggested that female desistance from crime may be best understood as an opportunity to establish a pro-social identity during a period of 'readiness to change', subsequently sustained by resilient 'strategies for survival' in adverse circumstances. The concept of 'readiness to change' is as much socially as psychologically driven and is a more complete concept than traditional practice notions of motivation to change. In general, establishing readiness to change seems to be slower for young men than for young women. Graham and Bowling (1995) noted a clear association between the life transition from adolescence to adulthood and desistance from offending among young women aged 14-25. Young men, in contrast, were less likely to achieve independence, and those that did leave home, formed partnerships and had children were no more likely to desist than those who did not.

Findings from more recent studies (Flood-Page et al, 2000) have led to some revision of this conclusion, suggesting that probably similar processes of change do occur but for males they seem to take longer to take effect. The assumption of responsibilities, for example, in and through intimate personal relationships or through employment can make a difference but this tends to be more notable in men aged 25 and over. The suggestion is that young men take much longer than women to mobilise their personal and social resources for change and that this is likely to be well recognised by experienced practitioners. This has major practice implications for services provision and social network support on how to maintain and support change in young men, in particular, into their twenties, while avoiding the often damaging consequences of criminal justice responses in their late teens.

The focus of UK policy and practice in recent years has been on young people who persistently offend. The debate has often been hindered by the lack of any clear definition of persistence that allows a meaningful classification of those at highest risk. In one major UK study (Hagel and Newburn, 1994), from a sample of 531 10- to 16-year-olds who had been arrested at least three times (84% male and 16% female), three definitions of persistence (see below) were applied to identify the common characteristics of young people persistent in their offending. The definitions applied were:

- the top 10% of the young people arrested most frequently for offending in the previous year
- all known or alleged to have committed 10 or more offences in a single three-month period
- all aged 12–14 who had committed three or more imprisonable offences.

Only three young people in the 12–14 group were common to all definition groups and appeared as persistent and serious offenders. The researchers conclude that 'no two definitions of persistence will lead to the identification of the same individuals' (Hagel and Newburn, 1994, p 121). Those identified as committing offences most frequently were not those who committed many offences over a short period and were not the most serious offenders. The evidence suggests that any single definition if applied too rigidly is likely to miss out an equally important group of young people when targeting intervention and runs the risk of drawing minor offenders unnecessarily into the 'reach' of formal systems. When the characteristics common to these young people were examined, the commonality in the subgroups was less their offending and more their adverse personal and social circumstances. There was little evidence of criminal specialism; offences varied greatly. Patterns of offending were not continuous but tended to involve bursts of activity over short periods then stopping. The most common offences committed were traffic offences, theft from shops and car theft. Violent sexual offences and other serious violent crime were very rare in young people.

   Self-reported data from the group suggested that while these young people were involved in much undetected or unreported crime, a lot of it was of a minor nature. The vast majority of young people in each of the three groups were already known to social services and patterns of familial disruption, alcohol and drug misuse problems within their families were common, as was criminality within the family. Most had experience of being admitted to public care. Many of the young people had initially truanted and had then been excluded from school, subsequently leaving the education system permanently. They tended not to be involved in education, employment or training. Severe family disruption was common and the level of alcohol and drug use among this group of young people was high. Very few offended entirely on their own and usually did so with others they had met in public care or elsewhere in the local area.

   The consistent message from empirical research is that young people who get into trouble persistently are generally found to have an interrelated set of problems, differentiating them from those who get into trouble once or twice (Schumacher and Kurz, 2000). They are often well known to social work services for non-offence reasons, with many having a history of local authority care (Hagel and Newburn, 1994).

Families, schools and communities

Disrupted family life has been confirmed by all major longitudinal studies as associated with youth crime (Juby and Farrington, 2001). Reviews of family factors associated with youth crime report poor parental supervision, harsh and inconsistent discipline, parental conflict and parental rejection as important predictors; broken homes and early separations (both permanent and temporary) and criminality in the family are also commonly linked to youth crime (Farrington, 1996). There have been major changes in family structure over the last 25 years since these reviews were undertaken, and the high rate of family breakdown in the UK has resulted in large numbers of children now experiencing instability and disruption in their family life. As many as a fifth of households are now headed by a lone parent and one in eight children grow up in reconstituted families (NCH Scotland, 2002).

Findings support the view that children living with both natural parents are less likely to offend than those living with one parent or in a reconstituted family (Graham and Bowling, 1995). However, family structure seems to be less important than parenting style and parent–child attachment, including levels of parental supervision and involvement, family disruption and parental attitudes to crime. While much is known about parenting styles generally, parental practices and differences between types of households are not well understood. Young people from families where issues such as friendships, use of money, bedtime and behaviour are monitored carefully by parents are significantly less likely to be involved in delinquent activity (Laybourn, 1986).

Parental and family criminality is reported in research as an important factor in the lives of young people involved in persistent offending. Studies have found that men aged 18-23 with criminal fathers are nearly four times more likely to have committed serious or violent criminal acts than those with non-criminal fathers (Baker and Mednick, 1984). Boys who had a parent arrested before their tenth birthday are twice as likely to commit serious or violent crimes than those with non-criminal parents (Farrington, 1989). The evidence does not suggest that criminal parents necessarily directly involve or encourage their children to become offenders, but parental criminality may influence the family's approach to social control and parental supervision which, in turn, impacts on delinquency (Osborn and West, 1978).

Education problems have long been identified as an important component in a cluster of disadvantage experienced by children and young people who offend. Poor school performance and being seen as 'troublesome' in school at a young age are major crime-risk factors identified both by British and North American studies (Farrington, 1996). Links between disaffection at school and delinquency are well established, although it is less clear whether young people who dislike school are more likely to offend or simply that children and young people who offend come to dislike school (Graham, 1998). Features of schooling itself, such as relationships with teachers, rewards and sanctions, and systems of pupil support are thought to play a part in sustaining or reducing difficult behaviour. Less is known at what age these behaviours begin to predict offending at later ages (Rutter et al, 1998).

There is evidence to show that having relationships with criminal 'others' is associated with criminal behaviour (Sutherland and Cressey, 1970). Studies have suggested that boys identified as anti-social in childhood show poor-quality friendships at age 13-14 and that these boys are at risk of delinquent behaviour over the following two years (Poulin et al, 1999). Substance misuse is often a peer-related activity and using drugs has been found to be *the* predictor of serious or persistent offending among boys aged 12-17 (Flood-Page et al, 2000). There is also evidence that young people who are 'heavy' or 'binge' drinkers are more likely to be involved in violent offences (Honess et al, 2000). There is debate about the mechanisms through which offending associates influence one another and how they acquire networks that support criminal pathways. Positive social associates are likely to be an important factor in desistance from crime.

An important indicator as to the kind of neighbourhoods where young people who offend live is often the type of housing occupied by their families, in particular social housing. Studies examining data about patterns of offending, social composition of neighbourhoods and mechanisms of informal social control suggest that large neighbourhood differences in crime rates may be explained, in part, by differences in the functioning and composition of communities (Sampson et al, 1997). Relatively little is documented about the capacity of such neighbourhood communities to regulate themselves according to shared values or about the factors which most influence variation in a community's capacity to control its social environment by informal methods.

Risk and resilience

For some children and young people, early criminal or anti-social activity combined with multiple disadvantages provides a warning sign for later difficulties (Rutter et al, 1998). There is consistent evidence that persistent offending into late adolescence and adulthood, particularly violent behaviour, is strongly associated with early age of onset of criminality (Farrington, 1996). However, because children tend not to commit particularly serious or violent offences and because they usually have not acquired an extended pattern of criminal behaviour, they often receive limited appropriate attention for this behaviour by way of mainstream family, school and community services (see Chapter Five).

Children at risk of more serious or violent behaviour often exhibit behavioural 'markers' of violent activity in their earlier years, including:

- bullying other children or being the target of bullies
- exhibiting aggressive behaviour or being alternately aggressive and withdrawn
- truanting from school
- being arrested before the age of 14
- belonging to delinquent or violent peer groups
- abusing alcohol or other drugs
- engaging in anti-social behaviour, such as setting fires and treating animals cruelly (Loeber and Farrington, 1998).

Not all children and young people exposed to multiple risk factors become offenders, in the same way that not all children and young people who offend grow up in socioeconomic difficulty. It is simply not possible to predict prospectively with any accuracy which individual children are likely to become offenders on the basis of the level of risk to which they are exposed at an early age. For this reason, it is argued that programmes to prevent or reduce crime should be part of wider mainstream programmes to address difficulties such as school failure, substance misuse and social exclusion (Graham, 1998, p 8).

Many children are surprisingly resilient in the face of multiple adversity and have aspects of the lives that can protect them against risk. Studies suggest that many children appear to survive even serious risky experiences with no major developmental disruptions (Kirby and Fraser, 1998). Individual characteristics, such as having a resilient temperament or a positive social orientation, positive and warm relationships that promote close bonds with family members, teachers and other adults who encourage and recognise a young person's competence, as well as close friendships with peers, are all recognised as operating as protective factors that can reduce the impact of risks or change the way a child responds to them.

The evidence supports the value of targeted early years intervention as part of mainstream provision. It is questionable if a formal 'crime prevention' label is helpful because of the risk of confirmatory and net-widening practice, and early years work should not be a primary remit for youth justice or anti–social behaviour practitioners, although they may provide specialist assistance to mainstream providers.

Conclusion

Youth crime, in particular persistent and serious offending by young people, stands out as one of the most prominent social issues attracting the attention of the media, politicians and public alike in the UK. Research evidence highlights that young people who are persistent in their offending tend to display multiple and overlapping difficulties including problem drug misuse, mental health problems and school and family difficulties, and are often among the most socially disadvantaged of young people.

It is important for practitioners to understand crime as a social phenomenon and the social circumstances in which it exists, as well as understanding the young people who commit crime. The emphasis within practice policy on reducing re–offending and desistance is appropriate. However, simple reconviction or offence re–referral data are notoriously unreliable and problematic measures of the impact of interventions because they measure only the system's response to reported crime (Mair and May, 1997). There are risks that too exclusive a focus on desistance from crime may provide a lens through which the child or young person is viewed primarily as an offender.

It is clear from the evidence that interventions aimed at preventing and reducing persistent offending are likely to require multifaceted and multiagency approaches capable of affecting a broad range of need and risk and multiple difficulties and require good coordinated responses (Liddle and Solanki, 2002, p 6). It is important for practitioners to challenge dominant political views and to operate with integrity, particularly where it appears as if support for individualised practice solutions is based on the premise that it is cheaper to manage the individual reactions to an adverse environment than it is to mend the environment itself (Gray, 2007). The political climate in the UK stresses individual responsibility as if somehow reduction in re–offending and personal and social integration is the sole personal and moral responsibility of young people, with scant regard to structural barriers and broader social justice requirements of shared responsibility.

Key questions

(1) How would you define desistance from offending? What seems to motivate it?

(2) From experience, to what extent are the different types of desisters familiar to you?

(3) What are the limitations of focusing on desistance in practice with young people?

(4) What evidence, if any, or experience would make you consider that desistance is different for males and females? How important are age differences?

(5) What crime prevention or intervention methods can be adopted that are supported by theory?

(6) What is the evidence that formal youth justice systems can be counter-productive?

Practice exercise

Drawing on a case you are familiar with, what factors in this chapter are useful in understanding this young person's criminality? Identify possible practice approaches that might assist in their personal development, better social integration and desistance from crime.

Further reading and resources

- Garland, D. and Sparks, D. (eds) (2000) *Criminology and Social Theory*, Oxford: Oxford University Press.
- Gottfredson, M. and Hirschi, T. (1990) *A General Theory of Crime*, Palo Alto, CA: Stanford University Press.
- Mednick, S., Moffit, T. and Stack, S. (eds) (1987) *The Causes of Crime: New Biological Approaches*, Cambridge: Cambridge University Press.
- Saunders, B. (2005) *Youth Crime and Youth Culture in the Inner City*, London: Routledge.
- Maguire, M. Morgan, R. and Reiner, R. (eds) (2007) *The Oxford Handbook of Criminology* (4th edn), Oxford: Oxford University Press.

3

Directing principles of effective practice

Introduction

While youth justice has become highly politicised across the UK, it is not unreasonable in itself for politicians, the public and others to be concerned about evidence for the effectiveness of public services aimed at reducing youth crime. The political emphasis on 'what works?', however, often seems to be applied to complex social difficulties as if good outcomes can be achieved from relatively straightforward interventions. In reality the issue of effectiveness – 'what works?' – is a question to be addressed and explored, and not a formula that can be applied in any routinised way to individual children and young people.

Research findings have helped recover confidence, in a very punitive climate, that carefully directed social interventions can have a direct and positive effect on young people who offend. Existing evidence points to the importance of collaboration and cooperation across professional disciplines and the need for good strategic and integrated provision (see Morris, 2008). This chapter examines the directing principles of effective practice drawn from research. They provide a framework and context for practitioners to guide planning and delivery of planned interventions in partnership with young people, their families and with other relevant professionals and service providers, particularly child, youth, health and education providers.

Vignette: pre-16 persistent offending

Ali is a few months short of her 16th birthday. She is already subject to a statutory order and has been charged with further offences. Ali has been known to social work services since she was ten. At that time her parents were experiencing difficulties and there were unconfirmed reports of domestic violence. Ali had difficulties at primary school mainly related to behaviour problems and her being bullied. She has a poor attendance record at secondary school and has a reputation for physical aggression and bullying at school for which she has been excluded several times. Ali has been involved persistently in a range of minor offences including stealing from school and shops, vandalism and disruptive behaviour in the community.

Effective practice

Effective practice in this context is discussed in terms of an assumed goal of reducing or stopping re-offending, often referred to as desistance, which is neither a straightforward measure nor the only consideration in working with children and young people involved in offending. Other objectives around personal maturation, social development and the wider social and community context are equally important since 'social circumstances and relationships with others are both the object of the intervention and the medium through which change can be achieved' (Farrall, 2002, p 212) and maintained over time (McCulloch, 2005). Criminological commentaries seldom provide detailed guidance for practitioners on how best to help individual young people in desistance from crime, or on how to generate the social circumstances within which individual learning can be fulfilled and lead to personal and social integration. Practitioners have to find direction by marrying research with experience and the art of human engagement and motivation (Schon, 1987). Values and principles remain crucial to shaping the nature of human service interventions. At the same time, critical criminological commentary can provide a valuable check on over-rampant correctional tendencies sometimes associated with too strong an emphasis on structured programmed approaches or professional process solutions.

Criminal behaviour in young people cannot simply be tackled as an episode of individual criminality disassociated from the social context or from available child welfare, education, health, social and recreational provision. Research has identified a range of factors strongly associated with youth crime that can be grouped into four broad focus areas for intervention as:

- *Individual characteristics* including impulsivity, personal controls, anti-social attitudes, continued contact with delinquent peers and heavy drinking and controlled drug use.
- *Family factors* including poor parental supervision, parenting style, inconsistent and harsh discipline and criminality in the family.
- *School factors* including truancy, poor achievement, disaffection and aggressive behaviour.
- *Community factors* including disorganised neighbourhood, poor amenities, drug and alcohol availability.

Any discussion on effective practice must rest on a realistic understanding of the nature of the social sciences, and limitations in the scope for measurement in human service interventions. Many factors are unpredictable, in particular the social context, which changes with time and space. Effectiveness of intervention with children and young people, in particular, is often very individual. The same practice approach may work in different ways in different circumstances, and sometimes it will not work at all (Pawson and Tilley, 1997).

At the heart of an effective programme of supervision will be methods aimed at equipping young people with knowledge, skills and capabilities for new ways of thinking, feeling and behaving. Effective change requires a 'productive investment' in young people as a form of 'human capital' to make 'possible the achievement of certain ends that would not be attainable in its absence' (Coleman, 1994, p 302). Not all young people in trouble with the law will have the same requirements. They will range from those with capacities that can be strengthened in the context of their family or wider social network through to young people who have very limited personal and social resources other than those provided by the state through public care. While well-structured social interventions can build individual human capital, in terms of enhanced cognitive and social skills, in themselves these are unlikely to generate the necessary 'social capital' residing in social relationships and opportunities needed to facilitate or produce social participation and inclusion vital in maintaining desistance from offending.

Evidence-based practice

Evidence-based practice (EBP) has been defined as the integration of the best research evidence with professional expertise and client values in making practice decisions (McNeece and Thyer, 2004, p 8). Evidence-based practice can be viewed as an attempt at a systematic approach to making decisions that emphasises:

- generating answerable practice questions;
- locating, critically appraising and interpreting relevant evidence;
- applying best available evidence in consultation with clients; and
- evaluating the intervention.

The term 'evidence' has multiple meanings. While different 'weight' is often attributed to different kinds of scientific evidence, with *quantitative data* from *randomised controlled trials* often seen as a gold standard (see the Campbell Collaboration at www.campbellcollaboration.org on systematic reviews), there are many sources of 'respectable' data within the social sciences. These include interpretive data that are important for practitioners including client stories or *narrative* and other *qualitative data* that 'fill in' the details of the direction provided by quantitative evidence.

The knowledge, skills, values and experience that practitioners bring to bear on practice decision making is 'a different kind of evidence' from classical positivistic evidence (Epstein, 1999, p 834), but information generated by practitioners from interactions with clients and client narrative is equally valid and valuable evidence for practice. Indeed some commentators would argue that conventional science might not be the best way to arrive at social meaning. A central tenet of this critique is that knowledge of reality is *socially constructed* through language and human narrative and discourse (Heineman-Pieper, 1985; Witkin, 1991). Practitioners are, in many ways, experts in narrative discourse – at allowing individuals to speak and assisting them to 'make meaning' of their social worlds. They utilise information that emerges from interactions with clients as well as information derived from sources external to individual clients.

One danger of over-stressing social constructionism is that practitioners can over-rely on their interpretive skills and give no premium to any research evidence in their practice. This, in turn, can give rise to what has been described as professional 'quackery' in the human services, where 'fancied' or favoured methods of interventions are based neither on existing knowledge of crime nor on evidence of what is likely to assist individuals change their behaviour in a positive direction (Latessa et al, 2002). A clear example of this is the evidence which suggests that unstructured counselling can be counter-productive (Andrews et al 1991), yet a great deal of practitioner contact may add up to little more than unstructured conversations with young people and their families. It is equally important to note, notwithstanding the limitations of unstructured psychodynamic approaches, that in allied research, structured psychotherapeutic methods combined with other methods have shown positive results (Fortune and Reid, 1998).

Increasingly government is suggesting that only interventions that demonstrate efficacy or effectiveness should be supported financially and politicians have been quoted as saying 'it is what works that counts'. But this is oversimplifying things, and a commitment to putting evidence to use does not mean that practitioners can or should only make use of data from systematic reviews or meta-analyses in order to make practice decisions – if that were the case few practice decisions would ever be made. Randomised controlled trial studies in social work are still very rare in the UK, and most practice-related studies are at best comparative studies or quasi-experimental design (QED) or qualitative and interpretative studies. It is equally important to suggest that practitioners should be assisted to find out what guidance and direction can be obtained from all forms of evidence that presents itself including their own practice (McNeece and Thyer, 2004, p 12).

Despite the number of systematic reviews which have identified a sizeable body of demonstrably effective practice methods and a critical mass of tested intervention knowledge, there is still a great deal that we know little about in any systematic way. The case for EBP becomes rather aspirational if there isn't actually enough scientific evidence to provide direction for practice. The best evidence points to the use of action-oriented and social learning methods, particularly cognitive-behavioural ones which are key characteristics of a social educational approach. However, there has been little testing of ecological approaches that combine strategies for dealing with disadvantage alongside personal change strategies; issues of power are often unresolved. At the same time there is very little research in the justice field on how best to assist neighbourhoods to take responsibility for their difficult young people without excluding them further.

In the practice world of complex social issues where data can provide some assistance or direction, then it seems reasonable to attempt to utilise the best that is available and for agencies to endeavour to make this accessible to practitioners. Nonetheless practice decisions will continue to be heavily influenced by practice wisdom and values at best or idiosyncrasy and bias at worst.

Whatever the source of evidence directing practice, it not unreasonable for those who receive services or those who make important decisions in the lives of young people to expect practitioners to be able to make clear and explicit what the typical service response might be for certain kinds of difficulties; what evidence, knowledge or experience those responses are based on, if any; and what outcomes might reasonably be expected. Studies have suggested that the client or 'user' can have limited awareness of the likely impact of practice approaches, which is not consistent with the idea of empowerment and is likely to result in poor outcomes (Mayer and Timms, 1970). There are, therefore, growing ethical, professional and economic reasons for placing greater emphasis on transparency and the use of research in planning and delivering services; in sharing information with service users, carers, other relevant persons and communities; and in evaluating outcomes.

There are broadly two approaches in which practitioners can put evidence to use. One is to follow a scientific model in conducting professional activities. This 'science as method' is reflected, for example, in the use of standardised assessment tools such as ASSET or in the use of psychometric tools. The model involves using tests, systematic observation, forming judgements for action about individual need and risks, monitoring progress of delivery throughout the programme of supervision and evaluating results and changes at key moments of time, particularly before and after the intervention. The practitioner here is behaving as a social scientist with regard to the case or cases at hand using single case methods.

Another approach is to use scientific knowledge to inform and direct practice activities. In this 'science as knowledge' approach the practitioner applies research-based knowledge and evidence to improve understanding of the young person (assessment knowledge) and to assist them in tackling their problems (intervention knowledge). Evidence must be viewed with caution, however, as research may produce knowledge about the 'efficacy' of an intervention – that it works under certain defined or in nearly ideal conditions – but how often, if ever, these ideal conditions are replicated in real world situations is a debatable point. Social workers generally deal with people experiencing multiple and persistent difficulties, often with few social supports and with low motivation to be involved in change-directed activities.

Realistic questions to inform practice are:

What is likely to be effective in any given situation?

What seems to work, in some situations, with some people, some of the time?

What can be done ethically that will do no harm and may prove beneficial to individuals or to the community?

These approaches are not mutually exclusive. The most effective way of producing science as knowledge is for practitioners to be more rigorous in their professional activities, ensuring the integrity of interventions and doing what they say they intend to do, by having clear, explicit and measurable objectives, transparent methods and resources capable of achieving the objectives and 'measuring' and evaluating outputs and outcomes at least at case reviews.

What practice approaches could you use to help Ali to better understand her offending and its consequences for others, and to acquire skills and begin to change her behaviour?

There are 'no magic bullets' in terms of evidence-based practice and no definitive answers to the complex problems presented by young people in need or at risk. There are, however, a number of good reasons for trying to use different types of evidence in practice. These include:

- *Ethics*: there is nothing caring or professional about carrying out an intervention that does not work or that might cause harm. Using good evidence can help identify what interventions or approaches are likely to be effective.
- *Empowerment*: practitioners who explain to their clients that the path they are advocating is based on solid evidence may find a more open working alliance and relationship is possible. People using services who are informed about the options open to them and the strength of the evidence to support these different approaches may feel more engaged and positive about their programme or service or have reason to complain to politicians.
- *Economy*: with public expectations growing all the time and finite public resources, it is important that the public money is used on interventions that are likely to work.
- *Credence*: using evidence can strengthen and support practitioners' decision making, giving credence to their arguments about the services required for the people they are working with.
- *Credibility*: evaluating practice and being able to demonstrate effectiveness can enhance the credibility of services.

What works?

Cognitive behavioural and *social learning* methods are generally recognised as having a central role in effective personal change. Many questions remain unanswered and many ideas are still to be tested through local innovation. Considering the enormous number of young people who pass through youth justice systems in many jurisdictions, there are still a comparatively small number of evaluations of interventions. Most systematic reviews have been carried out in North America and may not 'translate' readily to UK practice. For example, Fortune and Reid's (1998) systematic review of social work practice across a range of areas showed positive findings for the overwhelming majority of the programmes (88%) on at least one major variable. Many types of methods were helpful but behavioural and cognitive approaches appeared to work better than the other techniques; in particular, action-oriented, social learning and cognitive behavioural methods, life skills and family work proved most effective across a wide range of practice.

Also, emerging principles and findings have tended to be formulated in regard to adults and young adults dealt with through formal criminal processes and need to be tested in their application to children and young people in diversionary and non-criminal processes as well as in criminal ones.

During the 1960s and 1970s research findings proved inconclusive about the effect of human service on re-offending. One particular group of reviewers emphasised the lack of statistical significance in much of the research and fed the view that 'nothing works' in terms of changing criminal behaviour (Martinson, 1974). Distilled from a larger co-authored research report, Martinson concluded from the results of an assessment of 231 evaluations of intervention programmes conducted between 1945 and 1967 that 'with few and isolated exceptions the rehabilitative efforts that have been reported so far have had no appreciable effect on recidivism' (1974, p 25). The predominantly negative conclusions drawn from this review were challenged by researchers (Palmer, 1974, 1992); Gendreau and Ross (1979, 1987) argued that the broad generalisations of the conclusions overlooked many positive instances of success. They argued that it was not that social intervention programmes had no potential to reduce re-offending, but simply that it was impossible to draw firm conclusions from the research because the methodologies were so often inadequate and few studies warranted unequivocal interpretations about their effectiveness.

The interventions studied were often so poorly implemented and delivered that they could not reasonably be expected to have a positive impact. This message 'lingers' as a challenge for practitioners today. Martinson (1979) subsequently rejected the conclusion and slogan 'nothing works'. Nonetheless the debate contributed to a loss of professional, public and political confidence in the idea of doing constructive work with people who offend aimed at reducing their re-offending. While relatively few intervention programmes have been evaluated well enough to generate scientific evidence to draw firm conclusions, there is enough evidence available to provide direction on what is likely to work, what is unlikely to work and what is promising (Sherman et al, 1997). Literature reviews and meta-analyses completed in the 1990s provided consistently promising evidence that social intervention programmes could be effective in assisting young people who offend in changing their behaviour (Lipsey, 1992).

The use of meta-analysis, a technique for encoding, analysing and summarising quantitative findings from research studies, has allowed small-scale studies to be aggregated in order to establish statistically significant findings. Meta-analysis is used to review, synthesise and interpret existing research on topics such as the effects of intervention, assessment of change, relationships between risk variables and subsequent behaviour, and the reliability and validity of measurement instruments. The results of meta-analyses can, of course, only be as good as the quality of the individual studies from which they derive their data, and concerns have been expressed that some of the most influential meta-analytic studies may overstate effectiveness rather than simply the directionality of 'what works?' measures (Smith,

2005). An over-reliance on reconviction data as the key outcome measure can be a limitation.

A further criticism of meta-analytic reviews is that such studies often fail to take account of potential selection effects caused by agency gate-keeping practices at earlier stages of the process, and the broader (and possibly cumulative) impact of being drawn into a formal system and moving from stage to stage. A number of studies have explored the longer-term (mostly damaging) impact of system (rather than individual programme) contact on young people (McAra and McVie, 2007). Early meta-analysis drew only on studies published in edited journals that included re-arrest, reconviction, re-incarceration or self-report of illegal behaviour as an outcome, and post-intervention follow-up with control group comparisons. In recognition of the risk of bias, in that only successful studies tend to get published, much wider sweeps of 'grey' literature have been included in recent reviews.

The use of meta-analysis in reviewing existing research, while not without limitations, has provided practitioners and policy makers with promising leads and positive direction in the challenging work of helping young people reduce their offending. Re-examination of existing reviews of literature has routinely found since the 1950s that between 47% and 86% of better-controlled evaluation studies report positive effects on re-offending (Andrews et al, 1990). Andrews et al reported the range of positive outcome evidence as: 75% (Kirby, 1954), 59% (Bailey, 1966), 50% (Logan, 1972), 48% (Palmer's (1974) re-working of studies reviewed by Martinson), 86% (Gendreau and Ross, 1979) and 47% (Lab and Whitehead, 1988). They concluded that 'this pattern of results strongly supports exploration of the idea that some service programs are working with at least some offenders under some circumstances' (Andrews et al, 1990, p 374).

Garrett (1985) surveyed 111 experimental studies carried out between 1960 and 1983, incorporating a total of more than 13,000 offenders. She found a significant overall positive effect of intervention on a variety of outcomes including re-offending – 'the change was modest in some cases, substantial in others, but overwhelmingly in a positive direction' (1985, p 293). The most powerful approaches were cognitive behavioural, life skills and family therapy. Palmer (1992) similarly reported many positive outcomes from a wide range of intervention approaches. These included:

- several types of systems of diversion incorporating structured interventions of various kinds;
- behavioural and skills training involving young people and their families;
- family crisis intervention strategies;
- 'buddy' or mentor approaches;
- peer-administered management programmes;

- youth counselling incorporating a range of cognitively oriented approaches;
- vocationally oriented psychotherapy;
- role rotation training, parent training, interpersonal problem-solving training and anti-criminal modelling.

Gendreau and Ross (1979, 1981) carried out a series of detailed literature reviews on studies between 1971 and 1981 and further reviewed over 300 studies published between 1981 and 1987 (Gendreau and Ross, 1987). They presented evidence that 'reduction in recidivism, sometimes as substantial as 80%, had been achieved in a considerable number of well controlled studies' (1987, p 350). One major review found broadly similar results in relation to youth crime as for all categories, with education achievement and anti-social attitudes and associates presenting stronger associations in young people (see Table 3.1).

TABLE 3.1: Factors associated with youth crime

All categories		Young people	
Lower class background	0.06	Lower-class background	0.05
Personal distress	0.08	Personal distress	0.07
Educational/vocational achievement	0.12	Parent/family factors	0.07
Parent/family factors	0.18	Poor parent–child relations	0.20
Temperament/behaviour/ personality	0.21	Educational/vocational achievement	0.28
Anti-social attitudes/ associates	0.22	Temperament/behaviour/ personality	0.38
		Anti-social attitudes/ associates	0.48

Source: Andrews and Bonta (1998, pp 42-3)

The authors argued that the sets of risk/need factors (in Table 3.1) are very robust across various types of subjects (differentiated by sex, gender, age and 'race') and across methodological variables (such as self-report versus recorded crime; longitudinal versus cross-sectional designs). They concluded that the 'big four' need–risk predictors for people involved in offending are anti-social attitudes (including values, beliefs, rationalisations, cognitive states), anti-social associates (including parents, siblings, peers and others), a history of anti-social behaviour (early involvement, habits, perceptions of criminal ability) and anti-social personality. An additional four predictors were added to establish a 'big eight' – family and marital situation, school and work, leisure, and substance misuse (Gendreau et al, 1996). Andrews et al (2001) summed up their 'big eight' empirically based associates for effective practice as practitioner relationship, anti-criminal modelling, differential re-enforcement, problem solving, structured learning skills, advocacy/brokerage, cognitive restructuring and the use of authority positively.

> **Which background features, characteristics and crime-related issues and needs are likely to be evident in Ali's life?**

These reviews highlight consistent practice features and it is difficult to do other than argue that the evidence should be utilised to direct the design, delivery and evaluation of service provision aimed specifically at helping young people reduce their criminality. A further major review (Lipsey, 1992), including around 40,000 young people, was based on 397 experimental outcome studies published between 1970 and 1988. It reported that 65% of the experiments showed positive effects in reducing re-offending. The type of intervention was important. Behavioural, skill-oriented approaches and, especially, combinations of ('multimodal') approaches showed the greatest effect. Deterrence or 'shock' approaches were associated with negative outcomes compared with control groups. When all types of programmes and outcomes were combined, re-offending averaged 9% to 12% lower than for control groups. For 'multimodal', behavioural and skill-oriented approaches, the re-offending rate was 20% to 32% lower than for control groups. Detailed critical analysis of meta-analytic reviews are complex and beyond the scope of this chapter. However, while the average effect sizes may not appear large given the volume of research carried out, an average effect size conceals a wide variation in outcomes and many studies showed much larger reductions in re-offending rates, and provide promising evidence of the value of the right kind of human service and practice. Most recent reviews confirm earlier findings and highlight positive outcomes for young people, particularly community supervision including direct victim reparation, aftercare and surveillance (Lipsey and Cullen, 2007).

There is no single way of helping an individual change his or her behaviour and precise knowledge about which methods are likely to work best with individuals or for specific kinds of offences remains limited. Youth justice practice is by its very nature explorative. In applying the principles and findings from research on the most effective approaches to intervention, every piece of work needs to be subjected to some kind of ongoing evaluation. Nonetheless, some clear trends are emerging from research concerning the content of intervention programmes with higher and lower levels of effectiveness in reducing offending.

What does not seem to work?

Meta-analysis has allowed some distinctions to be made between those approaches associated with positive outcomes and those that have very little or apparently negative effect. Some types of approaches seem less suitable for general use with young people involved in offending. Some therapeutic approaches involving loosely defined and unstructured models of counselling or support seem to be ineffective and in some cases counter-productive. Lipsey (1995) found that unstructured face-to-face counselling was associated with increased re-offending. Similarly programmes that were long term in nature and frequently employed psychotherapy or group therapy approaches have also been found to be ineffective.

These findings have been supported by contemporary reviews of social work effectiveness. Sheldon (1994, p 226), for example, while emphasising that counselling approaches in other fields of social work have produced positive gains, acknowledged 'that without undue pessimism ... rarely do we see offenders exposed to a therapeutic programme giving up criminal behaviour in large numbers in comparison with their control counterparts and maintaining these gains at two year follow up' (1994, p 226). An unstructured 'talking' approach has often been the mainstay of supervision in the past, and while this method may provide some support, help build a working relationship and fulfil certain monitoring requirements, it is unlikely to assist a young person change their behaviour on their own.

It is important to stress that these findings do not suggest that 'talking' or reflective approaches have no contribution to make – the opposite is actually the case – and other findings indicate that well-structured person-centred counselling and planning may be effective, particularly with more serious offenders (Lipsey, 1999). Counselling methods have been found to have a more positive effect when they are part of a 'multimodal' approach. Russell (1990) found that where evaluations were more encouraging, it was because more structured approaches, such as task-centred or behaviourally based methods, had been adopted within it. Andrews et al (1990, p 379) summarised 'inappropriate' service as:

- service delivery to lower-risk cases and/or mismatching according to a need/responsivity system;
- non-directive relationship, dependent and/or unstructured psychodynamic counselling;
- all milieu and group approaches with an emphasis on within-group communication without a clear plan for gaining control over pro-criminal modelling and reinforcement;
- non-directive or poorly targeted academic and vocational approaches;
- scared straight programmes.

In considering evidence of effectiveness, the thorny question of punishment for children and young people who offend cannot be ignored. It is a subject that is often avoided by practitioners who can find themselves caught in what seems like a dichotomous position of being seen to be 'for' or 'against' punishment. The normal expectation of society at large is that punishment for wrongdoing is morally justifiable and a moral necessity because of its communicative value, and, as such, is likely to be effective. However, no one has ever been able to show that punishment (inflicting pain) in itself reforms or leads to lasting positive change in children or young people subjected to it nor that young people are deterred by the example of its infliction. As with all human service practice the reality is complex and is better addressed from the context of evidence of effectiveness rather than its moral appropriateness.

Developments in the philosophy of punishment have attempted to explore the issue in a more up-front way. Penal philosophers (for example, Duff, 2001, 2003) argue that the concept of punishment should not be merely 'punitive', that is, concerned simply with the infliction of pain as a form of retribution. Rather, there are forms of 'constructive punishment' that inflict pain only in so far as this is an inevitable consequence of facing up to the impact and consequences of crime, for example as part of the process of reparation or restoration (Duff, 2003, p 181), where this is an obligation which ideally the young person imposes on himself or herself in the process of better personal and social integrity. From this standpoint the role of punishment (even including the infliction of pain) and sanctions is viewed as communicative: encouraging and supporting change and healing.

Certainly there is evidence that punishment can influence change. However, the conditions for success tend to be with subjects with little previous experience of punishment, where the response is consistent, immediate, reinforced by rewards and administered in the context of a positive relationship. Generally speaking the pre-conditions for effective punishment seldom exist with the clientele discussed here and it is almost impossible to replicate them through formal state punishments. It is perhaps within such a debate that practitioners have to find expression and 'meaning' for the practical concepts of discipline, sanctions, controls, consequences, compliance and restoration as morally meaningful and relevant practices, particularly where compulsory measures are in place.

Bottoms (2001) identified some important practice principles that characterise the qualities of an authoritative supervisor.

■ Representation – providing opportunity for young people to state their point and have their viewpoint taken into account; negotiation and linkage to other services.

■ Consistency – treating people the same over time, setting realistic expectations, minimising personal bias.

■ Accuracy – demonstrating ability to make high-quality decisions by being open about the nature of issues and using reliable information.

■ Correctability – reviewing and being willing to change decisions where necessary.

■ Ethicality – treating the person with respect and dignity.

Compliance theories highlight that a person may be compliant with different aspects of supervision for quite different reasons including:

■ instrumental (self-interested calculation);
■ normative (felt moral obligation);
■ constraint-based;
■ habit/routine-related compliance (Bottoms, 2001).

Some young people may be compliant with the technical elements of supervision requirements without engaging in personal change. For others, compliance can be a real sign of change but this may or may not be sustained in the long term. Nellis's typology of compliance (2004, pp 239-40) identifies different mechanisms including incentive-based, trust-based (creating working alliances and a sense of obligation), threat-based, surveillance-based and incapacitation-based compliance.

In a traditional criminal justice paradigm, communicative or constructive punishment is seldom easy to achieve and practitioners have to be aware that overly punitive approaches to compliance are likely to be counter-productive and induce resistance, resentment and strategies to avoid pain which will not necessarily be related to positive or sustained change.

What should direct practice?

Some encouraging trends are emerging from research concerning the content of intervention programmes with higher and lower levels of effectiveness in reducing offending. Developments particularly in behavioural and cognitive or social education group work practice alongside family-related and education provision have provided encouraging evidence that effective work can be undertaken to change attitudes, to boost self-esteem and self-efficacy and to support the acquisition of skills for making better decisions, for resisting pressures to commit offences and for self-management (Gendreau and Ross, 1987; Andrews et al, 1990; Lipsey, 1995).

Criticisms of 'what works?' principles relate not only to the limitations of meta-analysis as a method but also to the use to which the findings have been put, in particular to the somewhat over-optimistic assumptions about the value of specialist structured programmes, on their own, in terms of crime reduction. Even the best and most rigorously conducted meta-analytic studies only ever claimed that average re-offending rates could be reduced by modest amounts – on average around 10% (Lipsey, 1992). Lösel (cited in Smith, 2005, p 187), in a review drawing on the results of over 500 evaluations, found that the average effect size was equivalent to an average reduction of about 5% in comparison with control groups. This has not prevented policy makers from setting unrealistic targets for youth justice agencies for reductions in the number of persistent offenders. Similarly there has been a rather naive assumption that measures appearing to work in one jurisdiction can be successfully or simply transplanted into others, without any need to consider differences in the cultural and social contexts within which such measures are to be implemented (Muncie and Goldson, 2007).

Systematic assessment has suggested that 'flagship' structured group work programmes can have an important but modest effect, overall, in changing the future behaviour of young people. Some commentators argue that youth justice systems in the UK will not deliver even these modest benefits as the efficacy of specialist programmes on their own is a poor measure of the effectiveness of the system as a whole. The value of structured social education programmes in the 1970s era of intermediate treatment was similarly undermined. Only a small minority of young people processed by any system ever accessed such programmes, and then only after a long-term sequence of interactions with a range of different agencies (for example, the police, social work/probation, court or tribunal) which often were insufficiently coordinated to ensure action in one part of the system did not undermine action in another.

> Why is it unlikely that structured programmes, alone, will have the major impact on re-offending rates suggested by the 'what works?' literature?

Despite the recognised need for caution in applying this 'evidence', practitioners can be confident that some things do seem to work but not for all and not by applying the emerging principles in any mechanistic or overly correctional way. Practitioners are the crucial link between the application of scientific evidence and art of human service. From a social learning perspective the common findings add up to a kind of 'curriculum' for social education activities focusing on offending and other developmental aspects of young people's lives. The aim should be to build on young people's strengths and equip those who lack them with the kinds of knowledge, understanding, attitudes and skills required to begin to change their behaviour.

Existing evidence suggests that to be effective, intervention needs to be well focused, consistent, adapted both to the characteristics, positive and negative, of the young person and to the problem behaviours, particularly offending, and other relevant issues presented. The most successful approaches are likely to offer scope for the involvement of significant family members or positive social networks in planning and decision making in the supervision process. Effective intervention with young people is likely to combine methods ('multimodal') focusing on the individual, family and social networks, peer associations and schools and maintaining change over time through the medium of family or network conferences. Not all approaches will be solely offence-focused although this is likely to be an essential element in assisting young people to understand their behaviour and its consequences for victims, the community, their family and ultimately for themselves.

Programme-based intervention, that is, structured planned approaches, particularly those that focus on behaviour change and skill development, have been found to be, statistically, more effective than less structured approaches. This kind of programme-based intervention may involve the use of discrete 'pre-packaged' programmes, for example Ending Offending, Targets for Change, Reason and Rehabilitation, STOP, STAC or those devised by individual workers or agencies. However, it is important that each programme is delivered in ways that meet the needs of the individual concerned. Achievements from programmes should feed into work on other aspects of the young person's life through good case management and supervisory practice.

Evidence suggests that effectiveness is likely to be greatest where there is:

■ a focus on the nature and consequences of the offending behaviour;
■ an emphasis on problem solving and behaviour change, cognitive development, personal or social skills;
■ a diversity of methods of intervention;
■ use of positive authority;
■ an emphasis on community integration.

Models of change should recognise the different stages in the change process, each of which may require different methodologies, techniques and strategies to plan. Prochaska and Di Clemente's model of change (1982) (Table 3.2), although developed through work on addictions, can be a valuable practice aid to any process of social learning. It identifies a number of change stages, each one interrelated, with some stages more appropriate for social skills and cognitive methods and others for more reflective methods.

TABLE 3.2: Prochaska and Di Clemente's model of change

Pre-contemplation	Defensive, denial, projecting blame, depressed, unaware
Contemplation	Deciding to change, weighing up pros and cons, start of change process
Action	Rehearsing
Maintenance	Sustaining, internalising new behaviour
(Re)lapse	Return to some or all old behaviours, giving up or trying again

Directing principles of effective practice

Andrews et al (1990) incorporated findings from 150 research studies in their meta-analysis and concluded that reviews of recidivism rates revealed on average that appropriate intervention 'cut recidivism rates by about 50% (in fact, the mean reduction was 53.06%, SD=26.49)' (1990a, p 385). They, along with others, suggested that the most effective forms of intervention aimed specifically at offending behaviour are likely to conform to a series of broad practice principles. These directing principles can reasonably be applied to youth justice practice alongside childcare and development principles and provide evidence-based yardsticks for practitioners in designing 'customised' supervision programmes.

The first directing principle is that efforts should be made to match the level of service provided, as appropriate, to the assessed level of need and risk (the *risk principle*). This principle is consistent with the ethics of children's legislation (no order/minimal intervention principles of the UNCRC and ECHR); services should involve minimum intrusiveness with maximum levels of intervention reserved for the highest risk-offending behaviour. The priority group should be those assessed (either by criminal history or standardised measure) as being at medium to high risk of re-offending.

For more practical reasons intervention priorities should be those young people who are at sufficient risk of re-offending so that any reduction is meaningful. Programmes that provide intensive services for individuals at low risk of future re-offending are likely to use scarce resources on those unlikely to re-offend and may draw them into formal systems unnecessarily and to their detriment (net widening). Where the risk of re-offending is judged high, more intensive programmes are likely to be required; low risk-offending behaviour will require lower levels of intervention with graduated provision in between to avoid indiscriminate targeting which is often counter-productive.

A second directing principle is that a priority for intervention should be to alleviate those factors that are judged to sustain and support criminality (*criminogenic need principle*). In other words, intervention should be appropriately offence-focused. The causes of crime are complex, multifaceted and not easily within the power of practitioners to change or to assist young people to change. There is now little disagreement in criminological literature about predictors of offending such as age, gender, criminal history, early family factors, schooling and criminal associates. However, there has been much debate about which factors are more readily open to change (dynamic) and when changed in a positive direction are likely to be associated with a reduction in re-offending. In reality these will vary from young person to young person. Important crime-supporting factors may or may not be causal but they are often identifiable to practitioners as associations or 'intermediates' seen to contribute to the risk problem and offending.

The most promising changeable (dynamic) intermediate targets for intervention identified in research include anti-social attitudes, habitual criminal patterns of thoughts and feelings, personal control issues, criminal peer associations, criminality in the family, problematic parental style and familial affection, schooling and leisure activities. It is important to differentiate between 'criminogenic' needs and other personal and social needs that have no direct relationship with the propensity to offend. Although priority needs are likely to be those directly associated with criminality, in a child-focused approach many other needs, not associated with offending, will require priority attention.

A third directing principle relates to learning styles (*responsivity principle*). Young people change and learn in different ways and not surprisingly there is evidence to support the importance of matching the delivery of programmes and practitioner skills to the characteristics of the young person and their needs. A crucial element in responsivity is the nature of the working relationship between the young person and the practitioner and how it is utilised to model authority and positive social relations and to support motivation, participation and cooperation.

In general young people are likely to respond best to active rather than didactic learning approaches. The literature provides support for the constructive role that learning style frameworks can offer in shaping interventions to assist individual development and foster a sense of engagement within sessions (see Honey and Mumford, 2000). However, the notion of 'matching' intervention to learning styles, as promoted by 'what works?' advocates, is not straightforward in practice (Annison, 2006).

Education studies have found little evidence that matching an individual to a specific category of learning style in itself improves academic performance, that is, the acquisition of knowledge (Coffield et al, 2004). Learning style frameworks, however, can be seen to offer the potential to open up a genuine dialogue about how young people can learn best and how their own learning can be enhanced. In this respect Coffield et al (2004) suggest that all the advantages claimed for meta-cognition (that is, being aware of one's own thought and learning processes) can be gained by encouraging learners to become knowledgeable about their own learning as well as that of others as a crucial aspect of developing self-efficacy and a sense of control over their lives.

While the concepts of responsivity and learning style allow for a degree of generalisation about the matching of risk and need to key services and approaches, issues of diversity, particularly in terms of gender, ethnicity and age remain important (Shaw and Hannah-Moffat, 2004). Evidence of interventions with adult female offenders suggests that general responsivity factors seem to apply but there are likely to be specific responsivity factors that need to be recognised and addressed (Dowden and Andrews, 1999). There is little documented to assist practitioners in this regard with young females. However, as discussed earlier, the practitioner's expertise in narrative should be utilised to elicit 'voices' and 'scripts' that may be distinctive in females and in people with different cultural backgrounds to assist in understanding their needs/risks and how to adopt core methods to support effective change. So, while many social and situational aspects of female offending will seem similar to those of males, the narrative meaning, and consequently the style of response, may be different. The art of the practitioner is likely to operate to its greatest effect under the terms of responsivity.

The most successful structured programmes are, generally, but not exclusively, directed by behavioural or social learning principles and include a cognitive component which focuses on challenging attitudes, values and beliefs that support anti-social behaviour, provide pro-social modelling, rehearsal, role playing, resources and detailed guidance and explanation. Theories of change suggest that 'ultimately effectiveness depends upon the individual's active participation in the process of change' (Chapman and Hough, 1998, para 4.15).

A fourth directing principle is that programmes in the community seem to fare better than those in institutions (*community-based principle*). This does not imply that constructive or effective intervention cannot take place in institutions. However, the 'wash out' effect of returning to the community often results in poor outcomes from institutional intervention (Mendel, 2000), with some documented exceptions, such as therapeutic communities. Achievements gained in the community equally have to be maintained over time but are more likely to be sustainable.

A fifth principle stresses that effective interventions recognise the variety of problems experienced by young people who offend and tend to be those which employ a skills–oriented approach, using a range of methods (multimodal) drawing from behavioural, cognitive or cognitive behavioural sources (*modality principle*). The available practice evidence suggests that most effective programmes employ methods such as interpersonal skills training; behavioural interventions including social modelling, graduated practice, role playing and role reversal; cognitive skills training; structured individual counselling within a problem-solving framework; and mentoring linked to individual counselling which closely matches young people and mentors on key background variables.

A sixth principle suggests that effective interventions are strongly influenced by effective workers, who are warm, optimistic and enthusiastic, creative and imaginative and who use their personal influence through quality interaction with young people (*relational principle*). Key skills or 'core' practices include empathy, warmth, modelling, positive reinforcement and effective disapproval, providing structured learning in a suitable setting aimed at developing problem-solving skills and providing opportunities for restoration (Andrews et al, 2001).

A final principle is crucial but challenging to achieve. It relies on incorporating all of the other principles within a clear and explicit practice methodology, supported by effective agency strategic and operational systems. There is a strong relationship between clarity of objectives, theoretical base and methods employed within planned supervision and its overall effects. This is generally referred to as programme integrity (*programme integrity principle*).

Evidence suggests that the most effective interventions have clear and stated aims and objectives; connect the methods used to the objectives stated in a meaningful, transparent and measurable way; are carried out by staff who are trained and skilled in the particular method; are adequately resourced and managed; the programme initiators are involved in all the management phases of the programme; and the programme is subjected to monitoring and some form of evaluation from the outset. In short there is effective management and planning to ensure that what is intended to be done is actually carried out as planned. Problems with programme integrity can occur even for the best of motives, for example as practitioners try to adapt material – particularly for cultural contexts – to the learning style and to the pace of learning of individual young people. A shift in pace or adaptation of material to achieve the intended objective might be required to ensure responsivity but the aims, objectives and methods themselves should not be changed. Poorly implemented programmes, delivered by poorly trained personnel, where participants spend only a minimal amount of time in the programme, can hardly be expected to be successful in acquiring knowledge and skills or reducing re-offending.

> **What do you think are the key considerations in building a working alliance with Ali and her family?**
>
> **In what ways would these be different if she was under 13?**

Programme integrity can be undermined in a variety of ways through:

- programme drift – where aims and objectives of the programme are changed unsystematically over time;
- programme reversal – where the goals are directly undermined by professionals who, for example, fail to model positive behaviour, or who do not operate within the theoretical frame set, or who simply are not convinced that the programme is worthwhile;
- programme non-compliance – when changes are made to the content or targets of the programme without reference to theoretical principles or to the original objectives of the exercise (Hollins, 2001).

Applying all of these core principles to studies of interventions with young people and adults, Andrews et al (1990, p 384) concluded that the major source in variation on the effects of re-offending was the extent to which services were directed by three overarching principles of risk, need and responsivity (RNR). Almost all successful intervention programmes examined by Gendreau and Ross (1987) had a common feature that connected thinking, feeling and doing (a cognitive behavioural approach).

The RNR approach has become the centrepiece of the risk assessment and risk management paradigm dominating thinking on work with offenders in the Anglo-American world. Given the poor UK and US record on young people's rights and youth justice practice, this might seem reason enough for practitioners to reject them outright. Critiques of RNR are emerging which provide a better perspective on the strengths and limitations of these empirically based directing principles in guiding practitioners in their efforts to assist young people in developing a positive sense of self and in fulfilling their own ambitions for a 'good life' (Ward and Maruna, 2007). Too narrow a focus on risk and criminogenic need de-contextualises offending and is likely to underplay their developmental needs and neglect the young person as a whole.

Ultimately the value of effectiveness principles will be best measured in addressing the question 'Do they enhance approaches that support the social and welfare development of young people in ways that assist them towards desistance from crime and towards personal and social integration?'. Evidence suggests that they can or will only make an important contribution providing they are set within a framework of values that recognise the importance of social and cultural contexts in providing social education opportunities for young people. It is likely that utilising the effectiveness principles will be a necessary but not a sufficient requirement for practice aimed at reducing re-offending.

In addition to focusing on the environment, behaviour and skills, all effective approaches included some techniques which could be expected to have an impact on the person's thinking, to improve critical reasoning skills, problem-solving skills, to help develop alternative interpretations of social rules and obligations, and to comprehend the thoughts and feeling of other people. Ross, Fabiano and Ewles (1988) devised a cognitive model that provides a useful 'checklist' to help identify characteristics most likely to benefit as the focus of cognitive behavioural practice.

Characteristics likely to benefit from cognitive behavioural practice

- *Lack of self-control or impulsivity:* not stopping and thinking before acting.
- *Cognitive style:* feeling powerless to control what happens.
- *Concrete and abstract thinking:* having poor skills in abstract reasoning; major difficulties in understanding the reasons for rules or in understanding the thoughts and feelings of others.
- *Conceptual rigidity:* inflexible, dogmatic and unchanging attitudes and perceptions.
- *Interpersonal cognitive problem solving:* under-developed thinking skills required to solve problems; not good at considering alternatives or the consequences of behaviour.
- *Egocentricity:* the world seen mainly from self-perspective with little consideration or concern for others.
- *Values:* limited concern about what is right or acceptable and only about what affects self.
- *Critical reasoning:* thinking often irrational and illogical; lacking in constructive self-criticism.

In practice most young people involved in offending have a mixture of strengths and weaknesses and a variety of resilient qualities; many are survivors in many senses of the term. It is important that interventions operate in ways that help young people maximise their personal strengths and social resources, where they exist, as well as helping them acquire and/or utilise their cognitive capacities – their ability to connect their thinking, feeling and behaviour.

Evidence from reviews of programmes aimed at equipping young people with improved cognitive capacities (Ross et al, 1988) found that those based on theoretical principles were on average five times more effective than those that had no particular theoretical basis. Those that included a cognitive component were more than twice as effective as programmes that did not (1988, p 138). The evidence suggests that these kinds of structured programmes can provide a powerful means of assisting young people alongside other developmental (children and family) provisions, providing the relational and responsivity issues are addressed by skilled practitioners.

Language, however, is important and this author is concerned at the growing use of 'treatment' concepts for interventions that are clearly social education and developmental ones. In a small-scale evaluation Izzo and Ross stressed that many young people need to be:

> ... *taught* how to analyse interpersonal problems; understand other people's values, behaviour and feelings; recognise how their own behaviour affects other people and why others respond as they do; and develop alternative pro-social ways of reacting to interpersonal conflict. (Izzo and Ross, 1990, p 141)

> **What evidence is there that the attitudes, behaviours and circumstances of young people involved in offending, like Ali, can be changed for the better as a consequence of being subject to formal supervision?**

Conclusion

The search for meaningful and integrated practice for youth justice is given greater impetus by those effectiveness principles that are consistent with the social education approach promoted by the Beijing Rules and the UNCRC. Effective youth justice practitioners need a skill set for practice similar to that found in European ideas of *social pedagogy* or a social education approach discussed in Chapter One (Smith and Whyte, 2008). The social education ideal is to educate the whole young person through active involvement of the learner in the process. Three important elements – 'hands' (skills and action), 'heart' (emotional and psychological maturation) and 'head' (cognitive, intellectual and moral capacity) – capture traditional and holistic notions of social education (Silber, 1965). These are increasingly linked to ideas of social justice and improvement of social conditions (Petrie, 2004). In the

German tradition the concept of social education assumes more structural dimensions with distinct egalitarian and reformist underpinnings expressed in education action by which one aims to help the poor in society (infed. org, 2005). Social education in this sense is fundamentally linked with social and personal development (human capital) and with the generation of social capital and 'community' development.

While social pedagogy is generally concerned with direct practice with children and young people, its principles can be applied to wider questions of social integration in different phases of the life course, where the emphasis is as much on the 'social' as on the individual. The approach is based on the belief that you can influence social circumstances and social change through educative practices. It is grounded in opposition to individualistic approaches to education that fail to consider the social dimensions of human existence.

The approach broadens the focus of social help beyond the aims and objectives of individualised change and growth to one that includes the integration of the individual in society and the promotion of social functioning, inclusion, participation and identity as society members with shared responsibilities. The language, concepts and skills set hold out optimism for practitioners in the face of a decade of technocratic and managerial approaches to human services. The value base implicit in social education or pedagogic approaches is consistent with social workers' concerns over social justice and social change and with seeking solutions to social problems within normative conceptions of learning or 'upbringing', rather than a focus on deficits, pathology and criminalisation.

Social education/pedagogy has been defined as 'a perspective, including social action which aims to promote human welfare through child rearing and education practices; and to prevent or ease social problems by providing people with the means to manage their own lives, and make changes in their circumstances' (Cannan et al, 1992, p 73). It offers the potential of an integrating conceptual and practice framework from which to develop models of best practice across professional disciplines directed by research evidence to promote personal social well-being and community safety.

Key questions

(1) How could you explain Ali's persistent re-offending?
(2) What are the advantages, disadvantages, challenges and tensions for group or individual programmes guided by the directional principles of effective practice?
(3) How can holistic approaches to practice make use of the principles of effective practice?

Practice exercise

Use a case you are familiar with and complete the grid below to establish realistic goals for family and other relationships, peers, schools and the wider social community.

	Strengths	Limitations	Action objectives	Measure
Family				
School				
Peers				
Community				

Further reading and resources

- Cann, J., Falshaw, L. and Friendship, C. (2005) 'What works? Accredited cognitive skills programmes for young offenders', *Youth Justice*, vol 5, no 3, pp 165–79.
- McGuire, J. and Priestley, P. (1995) 'Reviewing "what works": past, present and future', in J. McGuire (ed) *What Works: Reducing Offending*, Chichester: Wiley.
- Harrington, R. and Bailey, S. (2005) *Mental Health Needs and Effectiveness in Provision for Young Offenders in Custody and in the Community*, London: YJB.
- Hackett, S. (2004) *What Works for Children and Young People with Harmful Sexual Behaviours?*, Ilford: Barnardo's.

Assessing needs and risks

4

Introduction

Nowhere is the conflict between justice and welfare approaches to youth crime clearer than in relation to the assessment of need and risk. The tensions are reflected in the different constructs of young people who offend. Sometimes they are viewed simultaneously as 'vulnerable children in need', as 'posers of risk to others', as 'objects of concern' and as 'sources of fear' (Cross et al, 2003). Despite policy emphasis on the welfare needs of the whole child as paramount, the needs of young people in trouble are often underplayed and undermined by concern over persistent offending.

Inevitably practice developments in youth justice reflect growing public and policy concerns with risk and danger (Kemshall, 2003; Webb, 2006). There are growing expectations for more intensive risk management of that relatively small group deemed 'serious' or 'dangerous'. It is only too easy to 'translate' need into risk and 'at-risk' children into 'risky' children and young offenders, without benefiting the young person or the community (Newburn, 2002). This chapter examines the nature of social work assessment and the place of standardised approaches to need and risk in formulating holistic action plans in which the objective of meeting the best interests of the young person and the community, in most instances, should not be incompatible.

Vignette: assessing needs and risks

James is a white 15½-year-old youth. You have to prepare an assessment report on James for offences of taking a car without consent, driving while disqualified and driving with no insurance. He has two similar previous referrals/convictions and is currently the subject of compulsory supervision. During interview James shows little remorse for his offending, does not seem to recognise the possible danger to others and is unconvincing about not driving illegally again. His offences have all been committed in the company of others. James has few friends and is currently excluded from school.

What is assessment?

There is a wide-ranging literature on assessment in social work in classic (Siporin, 1975) and more recent accounts (Parker and Bradley, 2003; Crisp et al, 2006) alongside specialist compilations focusing on assessing need and risk in specific contexts (Kemshall and Pritchard, 1997a, 1997b; Barry, 2007). Assessment has been characterised as:

> ... an ongoing process, in which the client participates, the purpose of which is to understand people in relation to their environment; it is a basis for planning what needs to be done to maintain, improve or bring about change in the person, the environment or both. (Coulshed and Orme, 1998, p 21)

Traditionally social work has conceived of assessment as involving a set of key stages including preparation, gathering information (the study), interpreting the data (differential analysis), establishing an overview or integrated view (formulation), leading to intervention (intervention plan) flexible enough to be adapted in an ongoing way (review). Most definitions revolve around key stages of beginning, middle and end, which form a relatively consistent conceptual framework.

Key stages of assessment

1. *Preparation:* clarifying sources and reasons for referral; deciding who to see, where and when; the purpose and scope of the task; the data likely to be relevant; and the limits of the task.
2. *Data collection:* key 'respondents' are met and engaged with; facts and feelings are explored; possible gaps addressed; participation and maximum choice are safeguarded as the task is approached with a critical mindset.
3. *Weighing the data* against current social and psychological theory, research findings and local empirical data to explore the questions 'Is this a problem?', 'How serious is it and for whom?', 'Is it likely to require external assistance and on what basis – voluntary or compulsory?'.
4. *Analysing the data:* generating an analytical framework to interpret the needs of the young person in their social context; assessing parenting capacity; understanding the meaning of the offence in its context; distinguishing the child and family's understanding and feelings from those of the professional in order to develop possible ideas as a basis for formulating a plan.

5.   *Utilising the analysis:* formulating a view on the best way(s) forward to inform decision making; reaching an understanding of what is happening, problems, strengths and difficulties, and the impact on the child, with the family wherever possible (Milner and O'Byrne, 2002, p 6).

Contemporary accounts recognise the importance of multidisciplinary and family/social network contributions to assessment and planning as well as issues of diversity. They warn against overly focusing on problems rather than building on strengths in taking account of needs and risks. Commentaries also portray assessment and intervention as primarily aimed at assisting change (Crisp et al, 2006). They deal less with more extreme circumstances in which monitoring or surveillance may also be legitimate objectives in their own right. However, it should only be in very extreme circumstances that 'social policing' objectives are detached from meaningful change objectives in youth justice practice.

In reality assessment is undertaken for a range of different reasons and it is important to be clear about its (often multiple) purpose, as this will influence the content, the emphasis given to the various factors, the subsequent analysis of the information gathered and the action planned and taken.

What is risk?

Risk is a widely used term in contemporary western society. A preoccupation with risk has seeped into the youth justice arena and in responses to youth in general, resulting in an increased 'problematisation of youth' (Kemshall, 2007). Although a complex and multifaceted concept, in its more traditional usage 'risk' is a neutral term with potentially positive and negative connotations, meaning the chance of gain or of loss (Parton, 1996). However, in 21st-century Britain, risk has become more associated with concepts of danger or harm.

A typical definition of risk is the probability that an adverse event or harmful behaviour will occur during a stated period of time (Warner, 1992; Kemshall, 1996, p v). This contains two key concepts relevant to any *risk assessment* of criminal behaviour: a calculation of the probability of an offence occurring and a calculation of the likely impact on potential victims, both set within an explicit time frame. Good risk assessment will consider the behaviour of concern (its meaning in time, space and social relations), the potential damage or harm likely from that behaviour and the probability that it will occur and under what circumstances.

Alternative definitions have cast risk as 'a situation or event in which something of human value (including humans themselves) is put at stake and where the outcome is uncertain' (Jaeger et al, 2001, p 17). This stresses the notion of an uncertain environment, both natural and personal, and the recognition of desirable and undesirable risks, which cannot be reduced to very accurate predictive measures. The challenge for practitioners working with young people involved in crime is to find the right mix and balance in assessment by framing the negative aspects of risk, alongside positive elements, including strengths, resilience and opportunity factors, which are likely to reduce harmful outcomes (Brearley et al, 1982, p 82). In the childcare field, professionals have tended to focus on the concept of 'significant harm' *to* the child rather than *by* the child, where what counts as 'significant' depends on the age and the situation of the individual as well as current social norms.

For children and young people who offend, risk is more often associated with the idea of dangerousness, despite the fact that traditional discourses on healthy adolescent development convey risk-taking activities and learning from mistakes as an essential characteristic of maturation. For young people, risk taking may be pleasurable or a response to boredom and, in reality, many young people face a range of social, cultural and economic 'risks' that make contemporary life particularly challenging, many of which are beyond their ability to influence and control (Furlong and Cartmel, 1997).

In the context of practice with young people who offend, risk has tended to be defined primarily as 'the risk of re-offending' and 'the risk of harm'. The former is located in governmental concerns with youth offending, particularly with rates of re-offending and the identification of a small core group of 'persistent' offenders responsible for a high proportion of all youth crime. In this sense, 'risk' and 'persistence' have been conflated and the distinction between persistence and seriousness not always well made.

Practitioners are constantly working with uncertainty in managing their workloads. However, there is a tendency to treat risk and uncertainty as conceptually synonymous. *Risk management* has been defined as 'the processes devised by organisations to minimise negative outcomes which can arise in the delivery of welfare or justice services' (Gurney, 2000, p 300). While it is generally acknowledged that assessing and managing risk can never be an exact science, the language tends to be used in criminal and youth justice policy as if somehow risk can be predicted accurately and 'managed' away – by implication that risk avoidance is of greater importance than meeting needs in ways that manage risk constructively. Risk management can be used to generate a comfortable illusion of objectivity altering relationships with practitioners and reducing the time spent directly with people (Webb, 2006).

How might James' needs and risks best be identified, met and reduced?

Gurney's (2000) definition suggests that the location of responsibility for managing risk within agencies often focuses on risk avoidance and places limited emphasis on helping young people take responsibility for managing the risks they face and pose to others. Risk avoidance practices carry the danger of creating further risks, both by heightening practitioner and decision maker anxiety and by prompting them to identify new areas of risk in young people's lives, resulting in a more controlling rather than facilitating approach. The language of risk can mask the social and personal problems facing young people and risk assessment may appear scientific, accurate and effective, but only really serve to give credence to an organisation in responding to crime (Horsefield, 2003, p 376).

The combination of increased emphasis on risk and the existence of a 'blame culture' in public services can focus concern on overt social regulation, placing an emphasis on risk avoidance rather than on social integration as an effective form of community well-being and safety. This is in contrast to organisations comfortable with risk who are open to change and learning – 'learning organisations are at the opposite end of the continuum from the "blame organisation" or low trust culture' (ADSW, 2005, p 12).

Young people should not be responded to as the passive recipients of interventions and controls based on practices with adult offenders. Risk management should be proportionate and fair in terms of intrusion and enforcement while being directed by well-assessed risk and needs factors, by the views and priorities of families and young people, having regard to the levels of maturity, learning capacity and social skills of the young person and the social supports available to them. Trying to manage risk of harm presents important issues that may require consideration of restrictive conditions that have to be fully explained while operating alongside meaningful help.

Assessing need and predicting re-offending

The purpose of need and risk assessment is to consider if there is evidence that a young person is likely to offend again and how this might be prevented or reduced, while considering what evidence there is of the degree of harm that might occur. All of this is in order to plan intervention that might best assist, prevent and reduce re-offending and its consequences and promote the well-being of the individual and the community. Matching service and other responses to needs and risks is an essential element in advice offered to decision makers, particularly on how best to shape compulsory measures and ensure that service providers as well as young people and their families are held to account for delivery of appropriate services.

There is a tendency to locate risk within young people themselves rather than in the relationships and context to which they belong or wish to belong. Professional assessment can, unintentionally, help to promote 'problem-saturated' identities for young people, a process which is counter-productive. Ungar (2004) argues that assessment should contribute to the construction of positive self-identity. He stresses that a young person with a positive sense of identity and competence is more likely to display resilience in difficult or daunting contexts.

In reality practitioners are often faced with young people seldom able, for a range of reasons, to exercise full adult responsibility or to have complete power or control over the many situational factors that influence their actions. While this does not excuse their behaviour, it sets the context for understanding it.

> What impacts are poverty, unemployment and neighbourhood likely to have on James' criminal behaviour?
>
> How might these be alleviated by the provision of local mainstream services for young people and changes in wider social policies?

Despite its frailties, need and risk assessment is an important aspect of practice. It can support constructive action built on realistic assumptions of the potential for positive change against available help and opportunities. Practitioners must maintain a critical disposition and view risk management primarily as change management within which risk features, neither as the only or always as the most important aspect of supervision and help (Franklin, 1998).

There are numerous typologies and approaches to predicting risk: technical, psychological, sociological, anthropological and geographical (Jaeger et al, 2001), all of them with major limitations. Despite this, when risk is conceived in terms of calculating probability, it tends to be conveyed as an objective fact and the basis for an 'expert' scientific and technical approach. This can be seen, for example, in the growing use of psychometric tests in community-based populations for whom they were often not designed or tested. From such a standpoint practitioners can present rather spuriously and misleadingly as 'experts', rather than as leaders and participants in an assessment process. This should take account of symbolic meanings and social indicators, without detaching the young person from their social world or separating particular 'risky' behaviour from the social context of associated risks and activities. Many commentators point out that clients' views are often, if not largely, missing from the risk literature when in reality they should be seen as a contributing 'expert' on issues affecting them (Stalker, 2003). It is a reasonable practice assumption that to be effective, clients should be closely involved in need and risk assessment even if, in principle, it is often others who make the decision about whether or not a certain risk is acceptable.

There is general agreement that there is no well-developed social model of risk that takes account of individual factors alongside environmental factors and social networks (Gurney, 2000). It is difficult to 'factor in' poverty and disadvantage, poor housing and ill health as equally harmful as unacceptable behaviour without being viewed as somehow excusing criminal behaviour by introducing these elements. The idea of trying to present better integrated need and risk formulations within formal assessments does not in itself negate the value of examining and highlighting those need and risk factors that are viewed as supporting and sustaining criminality (criminogenic factors). This is an important aspect of directing planning towards tackling priority social factors (dynamic need and risk), which, if changeable, may contribute to reducing offending. Those most commonly identified by research include:

- changing anti-social attitudes and feelings;
- reducing anti-social peer associations;
- promoting familial affection/communication;
- developing positive social role models;
- increasing self-control, self-management and problem-solving skills;
- replacing the skills of lying, stealing and aggression with more pro-social alternatives;
- reducing misuse of chemical substances;
- shifting the distribution of rewards and costs associated with offending behaviour so that non-criminal activity is favoured;
- ensuring that the offender is able to recognise risky situations and has concrete and well-rehearsed plans for dealing with those situations;
- confronting the personal and circumstantial barriers in the way of effective service outcomes (Andrews et al, 2001).

The likelihood of future violent offences tends to be associated with a history of violence, substance misuse and mental health problems (Limandri and Sheridan, 1996). However, on their own these characteristics are not good predictors. It is important to try and understand how they interplay with other personal characteristics and environmental factors such as leisure activities and peer associations where, for example, the situational 'hazards' of drinking with friends on a Saturday evening come into play. These have to be considered as part of an 'equation of crime' as a social phenomenon existing in time, physical space and within social relations (see Chapter Two).

Practitioners have to communicate to decision makers and others just how prone risk assessment is to error (Quinsey et al, 1998). In the context of youth crime, assessment is further complicated by the complexities of life transitions and the influence of neighbourhood, peer association, social networks, family and school experiences, all of which are important to the melting pot of normal adolescent transition. An over-emphasis on individualised 'risk' factors can obscure the fact that the subjects of assessment are young people first and foremost, both as social and legal entities. They often lack the power and self-efficacy to influence, at least on their own or without assistance, the environmental, social and family conditions that impinge on them and which constrain both their opportunities and choices.

Risk assessment methods

In order to assess and manage risk effectively, 'reliable' (in so far as they can be) methods for risk assessment are necessary. There are two basic approaches to risk assessment and prediction: *clinical* and *actuarial*.

Clinical assessment is essentially a diagnostic assessment derived in part from medical and mental health models (Monahan, 1981). It is an individual assessment based on detailed interviewing and observation by the practitioner in order to collect information on the personality, behavioural, social and environmental factors that have resulted in harmful behaviour(s) in the past. It is 'professional judgement' used in the day-to-day preparation of reports or supervision planning, well documented in social work literature on assessment (Higham, 2006). Predictions based on professional judgement are particularly plagued by unreliability partly because of the heavy reliance on self-report data and individual judgement (Quinsey et al, 1998). Understandably practitioners give great weight to case-based rather than statistical information, making judgements that are likely to be biased towards the frequency (rather than the probability) of individual events. Reliance on professional judgement alone in the production of a coherent narrative, while an essential part of any assessment, can literally impute causal connections between factors where none exist.

Actuarial risk assessment has its roots in insurance practice and is based on statistical calculations of probability. From studies of a large number of cases, key factors that statistically relate to risk are identified and then retrospectively validated in terms of statistical probabilities. These factors are often referred to as *static* risk factors as they are largely unchangeable and rooted in historical and demographic factors. Assessment is based on predicting an individual's likely behaviour from the behaviour of others in similar circumstances or with similar profiles (Farrington and Tarling, 1985). Issues of quality, consistency, reliability and accuracy remain major practice issues in risk assessment and are reflected in debates about the relative merits of 'clinical' and 'actuarial' approaches. Technologies for measuring and applying risk and needs assessment have developed in the past two decades, while youth justice practitioners often continue to rely on 'intuition' in making decisions that can have life-changing consequences for individuals (Sarri et al, 2001).

In their efforts to capture the steady progression of assessment technologies over the past several decades, commentators have come to describe assessment tools in generational terms (Bonta, 2002). The first generation of assessment instruments was based on 'clinical' approaches – professional knowledge, skills, judgement and the intuition of the individual practitioners conducting the assessment. Second generation tools involved more standardised assessments that made use of actuarial methods over subjective judgement. Typically, tools focused on static (unchangeable) risk factors, such as age at first arrest and age of first alcohol or drug misuse. These are statistically strong but offer no assistance in planning intervention and are virtually useless in making service referrals to address the problems and issues identified. Second generation tools tend to produce inconsistent decisions and so can contribute to inequalities, particularly in dealing with young people involved in crime.

Third generation instruments have tended to incorporate static and dynamic risk and need factors in a more comprehensive framework that can better guide decision making, including type and levels of services to assist with supervision and placement decisions (Bonta, 2002). Furthermore, needs and risk assessments can provide agencies with important aggregate information about the levels and types of service demand and usage, as well as information on service gaps and unmet need. A fourth generation of tools is emerging to compliment the others. These involve a series of more specialised instruments for particular or specific needs in such areas as education, family and peer relationships, substance misuse, sexually harmful behaviour and violence, in addition to psychometrics relating to mental health (Ferguson, 2002).

Use of dynamic need–risk factors

Dynamic risk factors have been described broadly as those factors which change over time, or which can be made to change through intervention (Quinsey et al, 1998). While it is generally agreed that dynamic risk factors do not out-perform static actuarial predictors, the role of dynamic factors in developing intervention plans is now well established. Giving weight to dynamic variables within need and risk assessments can present practice problems (Raynor, 1997). Criminal history remains the best statistical predictor of re-offending; those with multiple problems are more 'at risk'. Dynamic variables are more difficult to measure than criminal history and are often compiled from differing sources (including self-report data) and are open to wide interpretation by the assessor. Hagel (1998) notes that while there is 'an emerging consensus that multiple indicators are likely to be more successful than individual factors' (1998, p 56), which dynamic factors apply in individual cases and how factors overlap remains problematic. For many factors such as substance misuse or the use and availability of weapons, while consistently associated with re-offending, research evidence remains 'unclear' and 'insufficient' (1998, p 57).

Personal factors, such as general disposition or temperament, and cognitive factors such as lack of self-control, impulsivity, lack of victim empathy and high levels of hostility and aggressiveness have been raised as dynamic indicators of violent and more serious behaviour (Blackburn, 1994). While these are important in indicating *potential* focus for intervention, none of these factors can out-predict past history and convictions as predictors and so have to be used with caution. The challenge facing practitioners is how to distinguish between seriousness and persistence and how these relate to levels of need that are seen to sustain and support criminality alongside wider social needs.

Nonetheless, there is sufficient data and experience to support the practice of differentiating between young people who seem to present a 'high', 'medium' and 'low' risk of re-offending, no matter its limitations (see Webb, 2006). The majority of young people involved in crime fall broadly into one of three groups – those who commit trivial and minor offences, those who have multiple difficulties related to their offending behaviour, and serious and habitual offenders. The value of this classification is less the accuracy of predicting re-offending and much more in the profiling of needs and risks for the purpose of planning interventions. This can ensure that those considered 'high' and 'medium' risk are subject to the greatest intensity of effort and provided with the greatest assistance.

> What range of provision is likely to be required for those judged to present a low, medium and high risk of re-offending?

Combined need and risk assessments

Despite the growing body of evidence in support of third and fourth generation tools for both adult and youth populations, youth justice has found it difficult to keep up with the changes in assessment technologies. A key message is the need to replace 'old ways' of assessment with valid standardised tools (Dembo and Walters, 2003) without losing the value of traditional practice methods. The literature urges caution as political pressure to implement standardised tools has resulted in a rush to implement 'new methods' simply by taking tools 'off the shelf' and imposing them in jurisdictions without adequate preparation or attention to the need for acceptance and assimilation by staff, or dealing with potential problems related to transferability of results (Jones et al, 2001). Many challenges can result as a consequence, including the perceived loss of discretion and 'ownership' by practitioners, difficulty in obtaining quality information, resource limitations, time-consuming workloads and staff resistance to change and ultimately uncritical use of tools as risk predictors rather than as aids to planning (Ferguson, 2002).

The average practitioner is not required to be a statistical expert. However, it is important to have a basic understanding of the more obvious strengths and weaknesses of actuarial approaches. While these seem to have greater statistical accuracy than clinical assessment (Quinsey et al, 1998), they do have difficulties. These fall under three main headings:

- statistical fallacy
- low base rates
- limitations within meta-analysis.

An actuarial approach compares similarities of an individual's profile to the aggregated knowledge of past events and attempts to reduce the uncertainty of risk by 'attributing aggregate properties of a category to individuals within that category' (Heyman, 1997, p 8). This systemic flaw is commonly known as the 'statistical fallacy' (Dingwall, 1989). In practical terms, while the practitioner can locate the characteristics of an individual young person on a 'population map', this does not guarantee its application to the individual and, in any case, the characteristics of the population may vary not only from jurisdiction to jurisdiction but from town to town and neighbourhood to neighbourhood.

Reviews of a number of prediction studies suggest that most prediction scores cluster at around the 40% mark (Grubin and Wingate, 1996, p 353), with the best averaging around 75%. Even if this represents a significant improvement over chance, for those making decisions about individuals it merely states that 40-75 of 100 people falling within the classification are a potential risk. The method cannot identify with any reliability the risk in any individual case. Low baseline rates also present difficulties for accuracy. The 'base rate' is the known frequency of a behaviour occurring within the population as a whole, and provides the basis for an actuarial prediction of behaviour in similar cases. For behaviours with low base rates such as young people involved in serious or violent behaviour, prediction in ignorance of the relevant base rate can lead to error (Rice and Harris, 1995). These difficulties can be further exacerbated when meta-analysis is the preferred methodology for establishing actuarial predictors as the population is unlikely to be from the UK. The practice challenges are substantial and some commentators argue, for example, that three decades of 'vigorous research' have yet to produce the 'scientific knowledge needed to predict violent behaviour' (Pollock et al, 1989).

It is generally recognised that a combination of professional judgement alongside and guided by appropriate actuarial data present the best available option. Clinically based interviewing continues to have an important role in establishing the significant personality and situational factors which can trigger or exacerbate risky behaviour (Limandri and Sheridan, 1995). It helps identify individual and symbolic meaning important for explanations of behaviour and planning interventions. Practice based on data from evaluations of programmes and research findings on what is likely to be effective will continue to rely on structured clinical judgement, for example in the form of structured behavioural rating scales, as part of actuarially based tools. These, combined with narrative and descriptive data from key respondents, are most likely to enhance both the predictive accuracy and usefulness of assessments of those involved in more serious and violent offences.

It is clear that risk assessment is a highly fallible undertaking, and it is unlikely that any method can be found which will provide certainty or very high levels of accuracy for worker, agency and the public. At the same time practitioners are charged with minimising the risks young people present to others and to themselves and with identifying needs as the focus for purposeful intervention. Where accuracy cannot be guaranteed, the key to decisions withstanding subsequent public scrutiny is their 'defensibility' – how decisions are evaluated with hindsight after negative outcomes have occurred, and whether decisions can be considered to be 'reasonable'. A defensible assessment is one that is judged to be as accurate as possible and which would stand up to scrutiny if the handling of the case were to be investigated (Robinson, 2003).

Minimum standards for defensible need and risk assessment are likely to include:

- all reasonable steps have been taken;
- reliable assessment methods have been used;
- information is collected and thoroughly evaluated;
- decisions are recorded;
- staff work within agency policies and procedures; and
- they communicate with others and seek information they do not have (Kemshall, 1998).

Defensibility is likely to be subject to human rights legislation and principles and as such it is important that assessments are transparent, accountable, based on the most reliable tools available, grounded in empirical evidence, and that action plans are proportionate to the level of need and risk identified. At their best, actuarial tools provide a context and framework for more transparent professional judgements and decision making. They can assist 'defensibility' within UNCRC principles by making explicit evidence of what is likely to be effective against the needs and risk identified and not simply what is available, and equally identify unmet need or the absence of early diversionary and staged intervention.

Defensibility in itself is not evidence of ethical practice as defensibility can also be directed towards risk avoidance. Risk management, if over-rationalised, can result in blame avoidance practice, where risk minimisation and damage limitation replace concern with social justice and in effect involves an intensification of the governance of conduct for disadvantaged and difficult young people (Webb, 2006). Effective risk assessment requires intelligent and analytical deliberation markedly different from a sterile unreflective routinised 'tick box' approach.

Standardised assessment tools

Specialised and standardised need and risk assessment tools, such as ASSET (Baker et al, 2003), are widely used across UK jurisdictions to support evidence-based interventions in youth justice and to classify and focus resources at those priority issues that can be changed. Using dynamic and standardised tools is consistent with the 'risk principle' requirement of matching the intensity, duration and sequencing of interventions to need and risk levels and to allocating scarce resources in a rational and transparent way.

ASSET, for example, is intended for use with young people up to the age of 18 to facilitate systematic assessment of circumstances and key characteristics associated with offending. It consists of 12 research-based 'domains' associated with sustaining criminality, each of which is 'scored' 0-4, giving a total of 48.

The higher the rating the stronger the assumed association with offending; the higher the overall score, the higher the predicted risk of re-offending (Burnett and Appleton, 2004). The individual factor scores provide a helpful 'map' of priority needs and risks. An evaluation of ASSET involving over 3,000 cases showed that the overall rating score predicted reconviction with 67% accuracy; reliability levels were assessed as good (Baker et al, 2003). As yet there is no data on how effective the tool is in assisting measuring change over time.

TABLE 4.1: ASSET domains

Lifestyle
Family and personal relationships
Thinking and behaviour
Attitude to offending
Living arrangements
Education
Motivation to change
Emotional and mental health
Substance abuse
Perception of self
Neighbourhood
Physical health

ASSET does not attempt to provide a statistical prediction of risk of serious harm to others or a 'quasi-diagnosis'. Rather, the focus is on providing an inventory to assist practitioners in considering, for each individual case, a wide range of factors supporting offending. The core profile contains a section on indicators of serious harm to others intended to operate as a screening aid to highlight where more detailed enquiry and assessment may be needed. The issue of harm has to be addressed in its own right using additional aids. In a descriptive study examining the factors youth justice practitioners tend to consider in assessing possible harm, Baker (2007) found little evidence of theory-driven information gathering, although a mixture of theory and experience seemed to influence judgements.

The prediction rate for ASSET, statistically speaking, is good, but there remains a high margin of error in regard to individual cases. All standardised tools have strengths and disadvantages. Most standardised tools will produce on average 25% 'false positives' (finding risk when there is none) and 25% 'false negatives' (finding no risk when there is). While statistically 'strong', if you are one of the 25 out of 100, this is a large margin of error (see Grubin and Wingate, 1996).

The core tool is supplemented by a self-completed section for the young person ('What do you think?') to facilitate the young person's direct involvement in the assessment. It is equally important to involve the young person's family and to use approaches such as a network or family problem-solving conference to provide positive means of allowing the young person and their 'network' to influence, contribute to and, where possible, direct the assessment and planning. Some of the core domains such as education, substance misuse and mental health are likely to require specialist assessment and input from other disciplines to assist the practitioner in generating evidence for their rating of the respective section.

Concerns have been expressed about the ability of structured tools to accommodate and respect diversity and difference vis-à-vis gender and ethnicity in assessing risk (Robinson, 2003). Criticism can also be levelled at these tools as encouraging a 'tick box' mentality and an over-reliance on negative risk factors. While risk assessment tools attempt to reflect a broad range of 'criminogenic' needs including social factors such as neighbourhood, education and employment, the balance of 'needs' is still located *within* the personal and family domain. In addition, social factors tend to be re-framed as individual needs, as if disadvantage and exclusion are somehow matters of choice and not of structure. The accurate weighting of dynamic factors is also problematic. Which criminogenic need is the most significant and why? This difficulty tends to be exacerbated by subjective bias where the assessment process is heavily dependent on key information being available and being sound, for example school reports or details of previous convictions (Raynor, 1997). Even when available, the temptation to miss out or skirt over evidence requirements has been noted (Baker, 2007). Risk assessment tools can also struggle to demonstrate 'multivariant effects', that is, they cannot identify how dynamic factors may be interacting and how risk factors are 'intercorrelated' (Jones, 1996, p 67).

> Why is respecting diversity important in assessing risk and needs?
>
> What would differ in James' case if he were female, a Muslim or a recent Polish immigrant?

These are genuine concerns that practitioners need to take account of in the use of standardised measures as part of assessment. With these kinds of 'challenges', one could be forgiven for asking if using standardised tools is worth the effort. Their limitations, however, do not provide an excuse for avoiding their use; indeed the opposite is the case. They provide all the reasons why they must be used critically, rigorously and transparently. The case for using them critically is compelling to add to professional competence and innovation but not to detract from or replace practitioner judgement.

The designers have always emphasised that such tools can only ever be aids to practice and, in effect, are only as good as the practitioner completing them. The real strength of standardised approaches is less their predictive validity and reliability and more their transparency in identifying which individual domains practitioners associate strongly with criminality, evidence that can be accepted or challenged, and the degree to which those identified 'needs and risks' can then be incorporated meaningfully into an action plan which is dynamic, open to revision and for which service providers as well as service 'users' are accountable.

Emerging research evidence on what sustains change and desistance, and what supports better personal and social integration continues to underline the importance of the positive qualities of the individual, the quality of available resources for supporting change within their social networks and the qualities and skills of the worker in developing working relationships within which information is gathered and analysed.

Holistic and integrated assessment

UNCRC commitments and UK children's legislation should ensure that a range of universal 'checks' and assessments are in place. However, evidence suggests that the most vulnerable and difficult children are seldom subject to meaningful holistic and integrated planning. Turf issues and professional differences often result in the same vulnerable young people being made subject to multiple assessments and separate planning. The most challenging tend to be 'passed on' to specialist agencies rather than specialist agencies contributing to coordinated and progressive mainstream provision.

> What role would other key agencies have to play – the police, prosecutor or reporter, child protection, education, community and leisure, drug and mental health provision – in helping to reduce James' offending?

A major contributing element to the future delivery of better holistic and integrated services is the development of shared assessment protocols in all UK countries such as the common assessment framework for children and young people (CAF) in England, Wales and Northern Ireland or the single assessment plan (SAP) in Scotland. These require local authorities to provide a shared assessment framework and single plan for all young people 'with additional needs' up to the age of 18 including those who offend. These are for use across all children's services and disciplines including health, education, social work, youth work, leisure and community provision, to help early identification of needs and promote coordinated service provision. They emphasise the importance of generating a purposeful sense of corporate responsibility across local authority provision and partners to meet the needs of children in adversity, including those involved in offending.

These integrated frameworks should support earlier assessment of needs and early intervention including early years intervention. While this strategy is not without its risks of amplifying difficulties, if successful it would be difficult to imagine a young person with multiple difficulties and chronic or serious offending facing compulsory state intervention who had not had a major investment of help before coming to the attention of youth justice – a scenario that is still a long way away. In principle a common framework should address wider social needs alongside those seen to sustain and support criminality, particularly in relation to education and employment, leisure activity, peer association, mental health and drug misuse.

The ambition of generating a single or linked plan is to ensure cooperation and avoid unnecessary duplication. The focus on shared information, in turn, will require a clear understanding of who will have the power and authority to lead and hold all the relevant partners to account for their contribution and to ensure the sequencing, duration and intensity is well coordinated. Terms like 'additional' rather than 'targeted' needs recognise that universal services should respond to meeting needs in general and integrated assessment should provide a gateway to progressive, graduated and multidisciplinary provision capable of positive impact on a young person's life.

The concept of a lead professional is not a new one, nor is the idea of a single point of contact for children with additional needs supported by more than one practitioner. The so-called Kilbrandon 'one door' approach was incorporated into law in Scotland in the 1960s (Whyte, 2004). The lack of success in achieving the intended 'leadership' and coordination reflects the enormity of the challenge. Lack of strategic mechanisms to deliver planned service pathways and professional 'turf' issues have combined to undermine the role of a lead professional or case manager, stripping them of meaningful coordinating authority. Success will require protocols to allow 'complex mixes' of provision and ultimately a way of identifying shortfall and 'blowing the whistle' on unmet need.

Many young people who offend will present a wide range of problems including difficulties as a result of trauma, attachment problems, loss and separation, risk of self-harm, vulnerability to bullying or abuse, as well as presenting behaviour that puts others at risk. One absence or shortage of provision consistently reported in the literature is a lack of effective education provision. For example, one study (YJB, 2005a) found 48% of young people involved in offending had unmet education needs. Substance misuse has emerged *as a key predictor* of serious or persistent offending among 12- to 17-year-old boys (Flood-Page et al, 2000). Despite the longstanding evidence and well-established practice experience that young people who are 'heavy' or 'binge' drinkers are more likely to be involved in violent offences (Honess et al, 2000), only limited drug or alcohol-related provision is routinely available to young people involved in youth justice.

Specialist assessment

For a very small group of young people involved in serious offending judgements on the level of harm they may present to themselves or others will inevitably determine the balance of activity within an action plan; who should be involved; and in what ways. A detailed examination of risk of serious harm needs to be undertaken where there are any significant indications of risks to self or others. The definitions of serious harm tend to include death or injury (either physical or psychological) which is life threatening and/or traumatic, physical or psychological, and from which recovery is expected to be difficult, incomplete or impossible. In practical terms practitioners will be alerted by a preoccupation with knives or weapons, or disturbing behaviour such as cruelty to animals or revengeful desires towards individuals.

Young people involved in serious sexual and violent offences are thankfully very rare in the UK but nonetheless present particular challenges. Currently there are no validated actuarial tools for assessing risk in young people involved in sexually harmful behaviour. Risk assessment tools for these young people, where they exist, are particularly problematic, not least because of the very low base rates (that is, the frequency of the behaviour in the population at large) and the difficulty in rooting these sufficiently in actuarial factors. However, it is these kinds of offences and the assessment of 'risk of serious harm' that tend to attract most public attention and media coverage.

Many assessment tools take into account only static risk factors (for example, early life experiences, permanent disabilities, etc) while stable (for example, temperament, intellect, etc) and dynamic risk factors are also equally important (Longo, 2003). Development work on tools such as J-SOAP (juvenile sex offender assessment protocol) (Righthand et al, 2005) and ERASOR (estimate of risk of adolescent sexual offence recidivism) (Worling, 2004) is progressing. The early assessment risk list for boys (EARL-B) or girls (EARL-G) for under-12s and Structured Assessment of Violence Risk in Youth (SAVRY) for both between 12 and 18 are well established in US practice. Probably the most useful aid used currently in the UK is the assessment, intervention and moving-on project (AIM) framework (Griffin and Beech, 2004), which is a clinically adjusted actuarial tool. It allows a young person to be assessed across the four domains of offence-specific factors, developmental issues, family and environment. The assessment is intended to give an indication of the needs of the young person as well as the level and type of intervention that may be useful in their particular case. It is important to remember young people non-sexually offending are more similar than dissimilar to young people involved in sexual harmful behaviour.

Commentaries providing guidance for assessors from all disciplines tend to identify core concepts that are transferable to work with dangerous young people. These include examining:

- the nature of the harm involved
- its magnitude
- its imminence
- its frequency
- the likelihood or unlikelihood that harm will occur
- the situational circumstances and conditions where harm is likely to occur

- the balance between the alleged harm on the one hand and the nature and consequence of state intervention on the other.

The most serious cases may cross into the realm of multi-agency public protection arrangements (MAPPAs) and their three-tiered approach to risk management broadly reflecting high, medium and low risk. MAPPA coordinators are expected to assist the multi-agency risk management process in focusing on the right people in a timely and efficient manner with the aim of delivering robust and defensible risk management plans. The principles of this approach are considered best practice even for young people without convictions. Although they cannot be managed through formal MAPPA arrangements, where a young person has been assessed as posing a high risk, good practice would dictate that the MAPPA and child protection coordinator for the area in which the young person is resident (and/or currently residing) should be informed and advised of the supervisory arrangements.

Fulfilling protocols will not in itself achieve effectiveness as decades of research from multiagency child protection arrangements have shown. No situation is risk-free and risks cannot be eliminated, but they can be reduced. When the risks identified cannot be managed by a single agency and where the needs and risks are sufficiently complex or significant to require a coordination of effort, a multi-agency assessment and plan will be required aimed at risk reduction. Even in serious cases, promoting activities to help young people and their families or 'mentors' to contribute to managing their own change and risk as part of a range of meaningful service provision to prevent family breakdown should remain central to any plan. The key aims of risk management in this context can be summarised as:

- harm reduction – of both likelihood and impact;
- protection and warning of victims (including potential victims);
- limiting opportunities for risky behaviour and access to victims;
- reduction of trigger factors and individual stressors;
- changing risky behaviours wherever possible;
- enhancing self-risk management skills and coping strategies;
- monitoring, surveillance, enforcement and control (Kemshall, 2002).

There is growing evidence that children and young people who commit 'serious crimes' have themselves experienced sexual or physical abuse, significant family stressors such as witnessing family violence, or traumatic life experiences such as the loss of a parent. It is important to stress that not all children who experience abuse and loss will become violent offenders, and young people who commit a serious or grave crime as a first offence do not necessarily go on to commit further offences of this type (Boswell, 1997, 1999).

Research on the prevalence of mental health problems or mental disorders and youth crime remains limited compared with similar research among adults. Some estimates have suggested that at least one out of every five youths in the justice system has some notable if not serious mental health problem (Burns, 1999). Studies have highlighted a wide range of mental health issues facing young people involved in offending. In one study, 31% had mental health problems, 18% suffered from depression, 10% from anxiety, 9% had a history of self-harm in the preceding month, 9% were suffering from post-traumatic stress disorder, 7% had problems with hyperactivity and 5% reported psychotic-like symptoms (YJB, 2005b). The evidence of social factors that are seen to be associated with sustaining criminality in young people is similarly associated with mental health difficulties (Mental Health Foundation, 2002).

One difficulty is the varying uses and definitions of the terms 'mental health problem' and 'mental illness'. The use of language and stigmatisation are important to social workers and to families who are concerned about further labelling a young person as mentally ill, adding to the stigma of being seen as 'an offender' and 'looked after'. The use of the term 'mental health problem' does not necessarily mean that young people have a diagnosable major illness, but does assume that they are affected enough by the poor status of their mental health for it to be causing problems for them (Mental Health Foundation, 1999, p 6).

There are numerous reasons why high rates of mental health problems are apparent in populations of young people involved in offending. Some are coincidental overlaps in conditions, some because anti-social behaviour is often diagnosed as 'conduct disorder', but also because of a tendency to medicalise young people's social problems. Provision is characterised by gaps and overlaps – Child and Adolescent Mental Health Services (CAMHS), social and education services – with little cohesion and coordination across agencies and disciplines (Audit Commission, 1999). Despite the paucity of adequate practice research there are also some encouraging signs of investment in community-based CAMHS to work alongside other provision in dealing with very vulnerable young people (Harrington and Bailey, 2004).

CAMHS standards (DH, 2004) set out a vision of a comprehensive service in which a young person in contact with the criminal or youth justice system whether in detention or in the community should have the same access to health services as any other child or young person. Standardised assessment can provide an important point to document mental health concerns and/or trigger referral to more specialist provision, but the tools were not designed to constitute a proper screen for signs of mental health problems. Screening assessment using SQIFA – a mental health screening questionnaire – and SIFA – a mental health interview schedule for adolescents – are available for use alongside other assessment tools (Grisso et al, 2005; Bailey and Tarbuck, 2006). These will have limited impact if there are no shared protocols for assisting social workers or other professionals in deciding when specialist assessment or intervention may be required, or if specialist staff are not available to respond in time as part of integrated planning.

Developing an action plan: managing change and risk

Different styles of change and risk management are located along a continuum ranging from empowerment at one end to control at the other. The emphasis within a plan on specific need and risk factors is inevitably intended to minimise negative outcomes and maximise potential benefits. The intention, nonetheless, is to meet need and to manage or deal with risk, not simply to avoid it by trying to calculate the incalculable. Practitioners need to have the support of their agency and decision makers to operate as 'experts in uncertainty' if they are to develop mutually trusting relationships and respectful working alliances with their clients, make fine judgements about need and risk, and work creatively, innovatively and effectively.

Standardised tools encourage practitioners to make assessments that are clear and defensible. However, so much emphasis can be placed on the completion of the inventory and establishing and scoring individual risk factors associated with re-offending that the more crucial part of the process, namely making explicit the evidence to support the assessment and translating this into a practical action plan, is neglected. Implementing complex plans with young people who are often reluctant, sometimes damaged and occasionally dangerous, in order to achieve multiple objectives, some of which are in tension with one another, will always present a major practice challenge. Effective multidisciplinary case management (see Chapter Nine) cannot be made into a simple process and requires good strategic planning systems to support and guide practitioners.

Effective change management requires a staged and graduated approach to supervision and service provision to ensure the most relevant approaches are delivered to those in greatest need, and effective review mechanisms are required to ensure that motivation, engagement, resource availability, compliance, monitoring and evaluation are addressed. In the most serious cases monitoring elements may involve electronic surveillance.

There are no ideal or perfect planning frameworks and life planning can operate on the dual purposes of empowerment and self-efficacy on the one hand and regulation within prescribed frameworks on the other (Webb, 2006). Nonetheless, any plan has to make explicit and address key issues identified in the literature. The action plan framework (see Table 4.2) is not intended to be a template for an action plan but simply a summary framework of key elements that should be included in a plan for it to be meaningful.

The intention of a good action plan should be to ensure that practice is evidence-led in terms of prioritising needs and risks to be addressed. Change management should be based on specific descriptions of needs and risk in terms of behaviour and circumstances rather than generalised labels, and linked to the kinds of provision likely to achieve the change identified. Short- and long-term objectives are important in order to recognise the crucial issues of sequencing, intensity and duration of interventions to ensure that key steps are in place to support short-term changes and longer-term desistance. Positive changes in key domains do not guarantee reduction in offending but are likely to accompany, and in some instances precede, it.

The timescales for intended change have to be realistic and objectives relevant. Acquisition of knowledge, understanding, changes in attitudes and the acquisition of skills may be relatively short-term achievements in building individual 'human capital'. Opportunities to apply these acquisitions with the support of positive social associations to help sustain them over time may well take much longer to achieve. Achieving 'reduction' in offending is unlikely to mean suddenly 'stopping' offending in the short or medium term and so evidence of short-term change should be provided to decision makers to avoid forms of intervention likely to undermine the change process which may ultimately confirm failure, particularly use of detention. For young people with longstanding multiple difficulties, it is unlikely that they will turn their lives around and achieve desistance through better personal and social integration in a matter of months or even years.

Why might a compulsory order in the community achieve the objectives set in James' action plan?

TABLE 4.2: Summary action plan framework

Standard tools domains and other issues	SMART* and SMARTER** objective	Services and sequence	Implementation and intensity	Limits	Measures	Duration	Evidence
What are the (scored) needs and risks?	What are you trying to achieve?	What work will be undertaken to achieve each objective and in what order?	Who will do what and how often?	What are the service gaps or unmet needs?	How will change or progress be measured for each objective?	What is the level of input and timescale for the work and review?	What evidence will be required for the next review?

Notes: *SMART = specific, measurable, achievable, relevant, time-limited (Talbot, 1996).
**SMARTER = specific, measurable, achievable, relevant, time-limited, evaluated, resourced.

Conclusion

For generations the importance of multidisciplinary and whole agency responsibility has been emphasised by policy in relation to youth crime. This has proved difficult to achieve and will not be possible without an accountability framework built into the action planning process through regular and structured reviews. These should 'harvest' evidence of progress, hold providers to account for delivery and be able to blow the whistle on service failure, unmet need and shortfall as well as holding young people and families accountable. Interventions should be integrated into broader change and risk management strategies to ensure monitoring, surveillance and appropriate action to enforce conditions and to sanction inappropriate behaviours.

There is little documented practice information about positive risk taking, and more needs to be known about protective factors, for example what protects most people from potentially dangerous situations (Parsloe, 1999). In public organisations as large and dispersed as those delivering youth justice provision, there are often significant discrepancies between directions and policies promulgated by agencies and the reality of practice in the field. An effective strategic approach should support greater synergy between professionals but also between practitioners and service planners working directly in partnership. Risk is an ever-present phenomenon and social work needs to look for better models of practice that are ethically valid and functionally accountable to avoid sinking into managerialism (Webb, 2006). Practitioners need to exercise caution as the risk factor prevention paradigm is 'easy to understand and to communicate, and is readily accepted by policy makers, practitioners and the general public'. However, it conveniently individualises offending, suggesting that risk factors are 'modifiable' by the individual alone rather than alongside societal efforts. In reality, the vast majority of 'risk factors' appear to be beyond the individual's control. While practice aimed at prevention and desistance will require changes within individuals, the focus of effective practice is likely to be on building capacity and resilience to assist young people in responding to and managing their life circumstances, rather than on the life circumstances themselves. These should not be presented solely as a matter of individual responsibility, but rather as a shared responsibility in the context of social justice (Brown, 2005, p 101).

Key questions

(1) What are the roles and responsibilities of the supervising youth justice social worker?
(2) What levels of need and risk are unlikely to be a priority for specialist youth justice agencies but may indicate the need for help from other children and family services?
(3) What, if any, role and purpose do Multi-Agency Public Protection Arrangements (MAPPAs) have in youth justice practice?
(4) In what ways, if any, should child protection structures and MAPPAs overlap?
(5) What impact does poverty and neighbourhood have on assessing needs and risks?

Practice exercise

Complete the summary action plan framework (see Table 4.2 above) using a case you know or for James.

Risk assessment practice ABC (adapted from Kemshall, 2002)

What risk assessment tools are used in your team?

What are the advantages and disadvantages of formal risk assessment and what are the mechanisms for this?

Taking the case of James at the beginning of this chapter or another you know, use the ABC risk assessment model below to identify the possible level and nature or risk(s) in the case.

Try to answer the questions in the risk assessment schedule below.

What other information would you need to carry out a thorough risk assessment? Do you have enough information on antecedents, behaviours and conditions?

Formulate a risk assessment paragraph for your report including any suggested intervention to reduce risk.

ABC

1. Antecedents (patterns)

Collect information on previous convictions and history of behaviours.

This information can address the question 'Is re-offending likely?'.

The indicators used are usually *actuarial*.

2. Behaviours

Collect information on behaviour traits and learned responses.

This information can address the questions 'Is re-offending likely?' and 'Why is it likely?'.

The indicators used are usually *actuarial* and *clinical*.

3. Conditions

Collect information on situational triggers, stressors, conditions and circumstances of behaviour. This information can address the questions 'Is re-offending likely?' and 'When, and under what conditions?'.

The indicators used are usually *clinical*.

Risk assessment schedule (adapted from Kemshall, 1996)

Generally predictive indicators? For example, gender, age at first referral or conviction; number of previous offences; serious offences.

Specific risk indicators? Risk of what? To whom?

Consequences of the risk? To whom?

Other social needs?

Strengths in the situation (of the individual, others or environment)

Rate the level of risk present   1   2   3   4   5 (1 = low)

Dangers present?

Action to minimise hazards?

Action to enhance strengths?

Recommendations? (Include an initial case plan reflecting work on proposed risks, needs, strengths; include evidence of levels of risk determined.)

Further reading and resources

- Kemshall, H. (2008) 'Risks, rights and justice: understanding and responding to youth risk', *Youth Justice*, vol 8, pp 21–37.
- Haines, K. and Case, S. (2008) 'The rhetoric and reality of the "risk factor prevention paradigm" approach to preventing and reducing youth offending', *Youth Justice*, vol 8, no 1, pp 5-20.
- Howell, J. and Hawkins, J. (1998) 'Prevention of youth violence', in M. Tonry and M. Moore (eds) *Youth Violence*, Chicago, IL: University of Chicago Press.
- Guerra, N. and Slaby, R. (1990) 'Cognitive mediators of aggression in adolescent offenders: 2 intervention', *Developmental Psychology*, vol 26, no 2, pp 269-77.

Early intervention and restorative practice

Introduction

Most UK jurisdictions would claim, in principle, even if the empirical evidence does not always support it in practice, that they are seeking a better balance in youth justice that incorporates the concept of child welfare outlined in ECM (HM Treasury, 2003) and GIRFEC (Scottish Executive, 2004). These aim explicitly to raise all children to be confident, effective, successful and responsible and for children to be safe, nurtured, healthy, achieving, active, respected, responsible and included – which is much easier to list than to deliver. This political emphasis on promoting prevention, care and protection is intended to be part of a more holistic, better integrated and coordinated approach to provision, which, alongside offence-related work, addresses the child's capacities and potential, their social environment and, crucially, the interaction between the two.

Youth justice provision has the potential to be a bridge between preventive child and family services, consistent with the requirements of UNCRC, and crime-focused interventions in later years. Youth justice practitioners are challenged to ensure that every child really does matter even if they offend and that their views are heard in decision making directed by their best interests. The practice challenge is to find the right balance between universal services, targeted provision to vulnerable groups within universal provision and specialist offence-focused interventions so that early intervention does not have a net-widening effect on vulnerable young people. This chapter explores practice issues in relation to early intervention and restorative practices.

Vignette: young person involved in first-time offending

Sarah, aged 10, is caught shoplifting in Boots. This is the first time she has come to the attention of the police. She is taken to the police station. Sarah lives with her mother and younger brother aged 7 in social housing. She never sees her father, who left 6 months ago to form a new relationship. She knows he has a new baby. Sarah has been unsettled and withdrawn at school. She appears unpopular, doesn't mix well and has been subject to bullying.

Think about what kind of action can be taken to deal with Sarah's shoplifting in your jurisdiction.

Early onset

Of all the proposed approaches to young people who offend, it is the promotion of effective early intervention that presents the greatest opportunities, challenges and risks for youth justice practitioners. Early assistance has to be set alongside the very real risk of inappropriate early intervention that can confirm and amplify difficulties. Some commentators have suggested that the practice model on offer in UK jurisdictions for many years has been dominated by diversion without appropriate service – an inadequate version of radical non-intervention (Prior and Paris, 2006). There is and always should be an important place for 'radical non-intervention' (Schur, 1973), particularly for minor offences, allowing families to resolve their own problems and to avoid greater harm by inappropriate intervention.

However, there is a tendency in an increasingly risk-averse climate for the police and other public services to impose formal sanctions for petty misdemeanours. Minor skirmishes among or between children can be formative childhood experiences. They do not predict a life of crime or anti-social behaviour and can help children understand the norms and conventions that shape much of social activity. Non-intervention should operate on the empirically justifiable premise that family resolution is more likely to be lasting and that many young people will 'grow out' of crime with minimal assistance following detection. However, some simply will not and doing 'nothing' may prove to be a missed opportunity to provide constructive and positive help at an early stage, particularly for those with complex needs.

Where and how difficulties are 'picked up' and responded to will impact on outcomes. There are some striking 'markers' within the literature to assist decision making on when and when not to offer professional assistance. For some young people early problem behaviour, including anti-social and criminal activity, combined with multiple disadvantages, can provide a warning sign for later difficulties (Rutter et al, 1998). Early involvement in offending or anti-social behaviour may be a stepping stone on a pathway to more serious, violent and persistent offending (Loeber and Farrington,

2000). One US youth survey suggested that the risk of becoming involved in persistent offending is two to three times higher for a child who has offended or been involved in anti-social activity under the age of 12 than for a young person whose onset of delinquency is later (McGarrell, 2001). However, because children tend not to commit particularly serious or violent offences and because they usually have not acquired an extended pattern of criminal behaviour, they often receive limited help or attention when they need it.

Lipsey and Derzon's review (1998) identified the predictive characteristics of violent or serious delinquency at ages 6–11 and at ages 12–14 in their order of statistical significance based on estimated aggregated effect size (see Table 5.1). Early offending is presented as the strongest predictor in the under-12 group of subsequent violence or serious delinquency even if the early offence did not involve violence. Statistically speaking, the more previous charges, referrals or convictions they have, the higher the risk that they will offend again. For the over-12s, previous offending is the second most powerful predictor of subsequent offending. Substance misuse is one of the best predictors in the under-12s, but one of the poorest predictors for over-12s, where the two strongest predictors of subsequent violence are the 'lack of social ties' and 'involvement with anti-social peers'. The same predictors, however, are somewhat weaker for the under-12 group.

The consistency of the evidence that violence and other chronic forms of anti-social behaviour and persistence of criminal activity tend to be strongly associated with early age of onset underlines the potential value of timely family, school and leisure-based provision (Sampson and Laub, 1993; Farrington, 1996). Table 5.1 lists the predictive characteristics of violent or serious delinquency at ages 6–11 and at ages 12–14 in their order of statistical significance based on estimated aggregated effect size (Lipsey and Derzon, 1998).

However, it is not possible to predict which children displaying these recognisable characteristics will go on to adult offending and so each factor should be considered in detail and in context to avoid confirmatory responses. Youth justice practitioners should examine the efforts made to assist these young people before they came to their attention, and pass on lessons to planners and early years providers. It is seldom clear if young people involved persistently in offending have themselves 'failed' despite effective provision or whether the help they received early, if any, was ineffective or counter-productive.

Many studies have noted that problem behaviour often starts very early in childhood with the combination of temperamentally difficult toddlers and inexperienced or vulnerable parents. This can lead to a downward spiral towards early onset where ineffective parental supervision and discipline inadvertently reinforces pre-school childhood difficulties. It has been argued

TABLE 5.1: Ranking of predictors at ages 6–11 and ages 12–14 of violent or serious delinquency at ages 15–25

Predictors at ages 6–11	Predictors at ages 12–14
Rank 1 Group	
General offences (0.38) Substance use (0.30)	Social ties (0.39) Anti-social peers (0.37)
Rank 2 Group	
Gender (male) (0.26) Family socioeconomic status (0.24) Anti-social parents (0.23)	General offences (0.26)
Rank 3 Group	
Aggression (0.21) Ethnicity (0.20)	Aggression (0.19) School attitude/performance (0.19) Psychological condition (0.19) Parent–child relations (0.19) Gender (male) (0.19) Physical violence (0.18)
Rank 4 Group	
Psychological condition (0.15) Parent–child relations (0.15) Social ties (0.15) Problem behaviour (0.13) School attitude/performance (0.13) Medical/physical characteristics (0.13) IQ (0.12) Other family characteristics (0.12)	Anti-social parents (0.16) Person crimes (0.14) Problem behaviour (0.12) IQ (0.11)
Rank 5 Group	
Broken home (0.9) Abusive parents (0.7) Anti-social peers (0.04)	Broken home (0.10) Family socioeconomic status (0.10) Abusive parents (0.09) Other family characteristics (0.08) Substance abuse (0.06) Ethnicity (0.04)

Note: The value in parentheses is the mean correlation between the predictor and the outcome, adjusted to equate the source studies on relevant methodological features.
Source: Lipsey and Derzon (1998)

that the early onset group are not only different but more 'predictable' and their needs identifiable early compared to the adolescent onset group (Patterson and Yoerger, 1997). Patterson (1996) concluded that this is often reflected in a mix of temperamental risk and coercive parenting. The longitudinal Dunedin study found that poor parenting in early life was associated with a two-fold increase in delinquent behaviour and was an especially important predictor of delinquent behaviour among children judged to have an irritable temperament (Henry et al, 1996).

Patterson's 'coercion model' (Patterson and Yoerger, 1997) traces a developmental course that begins during the toddler stage and is transformed during pre-school and primary (elementary) school. For example, it describes persistent attention-seeking behaviours during infancy that, in turn, lead to non-compliance and aggression by age 24 months, with the consequence that overt anti-social behaviours are often well established by the time the child begins school. At primary school these 'successful' strategies for gaining attention tend to expand to include lying, stealing, cheating and truancy. Lack of appropriate social skills to engage teachers or peers positively can mean these children become isolated, unpopular, do not mix well and are rejected by other children, which in turn results in their gravitation towards the company of similarly isolated peers.

Many children arrive at school already educationally disadvantaged and three major risk factors associated with anti-social behaviour are reported as becoming observable in primary school years. These include persistent physically aggressive behaviour, fighting and bullying (Farrington, 1996); poor academic attainment and failure (Maguin and Loeber, 1996); and low commitment to school (Dreyfoos, 1990).

Anti-social behaviour and protecting communities

Labour-led administrations across the UK expressed a commitment to tackling child poverty 'within a generation', and substantial investment has been made on child poverty measures in what is essentially a long-term strategy. The impact to date remains limited, however. The emphasis on enforcement of early interventions relating to anti-social behaviour has reflected a shift in the political discourse away from the language of children in need and from welfare-oriented strategies towards a language of correctionalism, personal responsibility and punishment.

In some areas anti-social behaviour practices seem to have fallen into the trap of operating outwith any framework of children's needs or rights, and risk making matters worse rather than better (Wain, 2007). Early intervention measures, unless routed through the existing childcare system, are likely to reinforce criminalising pathways for children and young people. Local authorities have duties under children's legislation to deliver well-coordinated provision that should incorporate dealing with anti-social behaviour effectively within an integrated framework for vulnerable children and families. The challenge is to make early intervention relevant and effective by ensuring agreements that are binding on young people and families are equally binding on all parties including service providers.

A cautionary tale was presented by Nacro (2003), suggesting that enforcement approaches to anti-social behaviour may have been associated with the rise in detention rates for young people in England and Wales. The report argued that the apparent determination to be seen as tough on youth crime has been counter-productive and 'an increasingly punitive environment for all those who offend has been combined with a particularly reduced tolerance for children who break the law' (Nacro, 2003, p 11).

Studies have shown that early childhood difficulties predominate in prison populations. In one study, compared with the general population, prisoners were 13 times more likely to have been in care as a child; 10 times more likely to have been a regular truant from school; 13 times more likely to be unemployed; 2.5 times more likely to have a family member who has been convicted of a criminal offence; 6 times more likely to had been a young father; and 15 times more likely to be HIV positive (Social Exclusion Unit, 2002). In respect of basic skills, 80% had the writing skills, 65% the numeracy skills and 50% the reading skills of an 11-year-old; 70% had used drugs before coming to prison; 70% suffered from at least two mental disorders; 20% of male prisoners had previously attempted suicide; and 37% of women prisoners had attempted suicide. Clear links have been established between alcohol/drug misuse and offending. Houchin (2005) found that half of the population of prisoners in Barlinnie prison on the night of 30 June 2003 came from home addresses in just 155 of the 1,222 local government wards.

It is important to understand the nature of crime as a social phenomenon as well as understanding the developmental needs and social characteristics of those who commit it. For many young people offending is exciting and enjoyable. It occurs in a social context that provides peer approval and leads to enhanced self-esteem, albeit of a negative nature. Research suggests that many of these young people have conventional aspirations, and intervention must offer opportunities for equally rewarding behaviour that provides opportunities to realise their aspirations in the community (Loucks et al, 2000). The most effective forms of early intervention will focus on the wider and related social and welfare needs of children, young people and their families. Models of practice equally must adopt an offence and restorative focus when appropriate.

Early years preventive practice

Critical transitional points have been identified as important where children may be more susceptible to movement into 'harmful' paths or equally open to preventive interventions (Prior and Paris, 2006). These key transitional points have the potential to operate as universal 'pick-up' points. This may be through health visiting of (all) very young children (under-5s), and throughout the life course, through education at the transitions to primary school (between 5 and 8) and to secondary school (11-13), preparation for leaving school (over 15) and entering the world of work. At these points children and young people are often subject to some form of universal professional assessment which could mobilise positive help early before they are viewed as 'risky'. Universal provision at the lower end of the risk spectrum, such as simple and short-term interventions offering advice and information, has been shown to boost parent knowledge and change behaviour. At the higher end of the spectrum, longer social education or cognitive and behavioural interventions combined with follow-up and booster sessions have shown encouraging results (Moran et al, 2004; DfES, 2007).

Six broad categories of crime prevention programmes emerge as promising from research (Farrington and Welsh, 2003). These include home visitation services working directly with parents and young children using social modelling techniques; day care and pre-school provision for children under five; direct child development work, parent training and school-based provision for the primary-aged child; home/community programmes and structured family work for older children and adolescents; and multisystemic interventions incorporating and integrating many of the other programmes for those aged 15 and over. Skills-based behavioural parent training seems most effective and school-based programmes seem least effective.

Using progressive universal provision should minimise the risk of stigma before anti-social behaviour consolidates through peer association and further school failure in later adolescence. Universal 'pick-up' points provide a positive context for helping children early, which is quite distinct from the 'catch them and sort them' early rhetoric that anti-social and youth crime-focused strategies tend to convey. Evidence from early years intervention provides lessons to service planners and practitioners about the importance of programme integrity. Programme drift is easily understandable when practitioners are under pressure and without good supportive supervision. However, agency drift can also occur even when substantial resources are spent but the methods evidenced as effective, intentional or unintentional, disappear in the new 'mix' of provision at roll-out.

The Perry Pre-school Programme is heralded as an exemplary programme showing exceptionally positive long-term effects on crime and crime risk factors (Schweinhart and Weikart, 1997). Targeting both high- and low-risk parents and children, it combined early childhood instruction with weekly home visits, providing parenting assistance and modelling. Central to the success of the approach was home visitation work based on social modelling provided by trained and committed volunteers or skilled professionals such as health visitors and social workers. They demonstrated and sometimes trained parents of young children in basic child management skills. Its political appeal was that it was estimated that every dollar spent on the programme resulted in savings of $7 of public money in the long term – a punch line every applied researcher or practitioner would love to achieve. These encouraging findings gave rise to a range of service developments in the UK including Sure Start, Home Start and Health Start-style projects.

The key ingredients to success, namely the intensive home visiting and the in-home social modelling methods adopted, have proved to be the elements most likely to be 'watered down' following roll-out and often replaced by centre-based provision. Two separate and recent studies conducted in the US on the long-term effects of early and pre-school centre-based childcare (Belsky et al, 2007; Loeb et al, 2007) reported that early experience of centre-based childcare was significantly associated with an increase in problem behaviour in later childhood and not a reduction. Loeb et al (2007) claim that the younger the child on commencing centre-based childcare, the greater the negative behaviour effect. Many factors may be at play here other than the setting and methods; nonetheless, the outcomes suggest low-level negative behaviour may be 'fuelled' by young children, particularly vulnerable ones, competing for attention in a context of inappropriate responses.

Such findings are important to bear in mind given the vast investment in children and family centres in the UK for disadvantaged families. It is clear that centre-based childcare, while offering a number of potential benefits in terms of cognitive outcomes, is not necessarily a desirable response for this vulnerable age group unless the methods adopted meet the specific needs of individual parents and children. The evidence re-enforces the message that intervention is no guarantee of good outcome unless it is an appropriate method of intervention for the objectives set.

Efforts to overcome these unintended negative consequences are evident in approaches such as the multilevel, preventive Triple-P Positive Parenting programme. Triple-P provides five levels of intervention for parents of children from birth to age 16, ranging from universal distribution of parenting information to intensive behavioural family intervention. The various levels of Triple-P have been subject to rigorous evaluation and been found to be successful in reducing child behaviour problems, although its effectiveness as a population-level strategy has yet to be determined (Bunting, 2004, pp 338-9).

Tunstill et al (2007), in an evaluation of community-based projects, reported that parents found the Webster-Stratton parent and child programmes similarly helpful and challenging and would have liked more help with the literacy element. Parents enjoyed meeting other parents using the same services to socialise, and the opportunity to share their experiences and difficulties with those in similar situations, and appreciated the informal parent-led sessions wherein they could 'chat' with other parents. The effectiveness of family and parenting interventions seems to increase exponentially when children are very young, before anti-social, aggressive or criminal behaviours are fully developed (Webster-Stratton and Hancock, 1998). The findings highlight the need for suitable assessment of parents in order to target appropriate support and attention for those who may struggle with programme demands.

School-based programmes such as Roots of Empathy (Gordon, 2005) aim to develop empathy as a way of strengthening skills in communication and emotional literacy, and reducing stress and anxiety associated with social exclusion in primary-aged children. The programme brings mothers and young babies into a classroom setting and children are coached over time by an instructor to observe parent–child interactions. The baby is intended to be a 'laboratory for human development' (2005, p 14) through which children can learn and reflect on behaviour and development in ways that may have an impact on their own behaviour. The programme catchphrase 'empathy is caught and not taught' reflects the strong emphasis on the importance of experiential learning (p 42).

The evidence has to be considered with some critical caution as it does not provide a clear formula for the best 'mix' of universal, targeted and special services required at each age and stage or how to avoid the unintended consequences of labelling, stigma, net widening and deviancy amplification. The issue of the importance of a 'gendered approach' to the development and implementation of interventions remains under-developed.

> **What responses are likely to be effective in helping Sarah stop offending?**

While most youth justice specialists are not likely to be involved as lead professionals in early years intervention provided by child, health and education professionals, it is important to understand the kinds of experience of children and young people when they 'emerge' into the youth justice system, often well known to other services providers at a much earlier age.

Effective engagement of parents is a key factor in success at resolving the problems of children and young people, and it is in this context that the value of the use of compulsion on parents and Parenting Orders has emerged. It has been argued that attempts to achieve compliance with the terms of attendance at a programme without the client's cooperation, collaboration and readiness to change are likely to result in the client merely 'going through the motions' (Yatchmenoff, 2005, p 84). However, much of the existing literature on engagement relies on professional commentary rather than on empirical evidence for its claims.

> What barriers might mean that Sarah's parents do not participate in the services and interventions that you decide will help Sarah? How might these barriers be overcome?

There are different levels of parental compliance, including legal or technical compliance, that may or may not involve meaningful and purposeful engagement and finally compliance required to sustain change in the long term. There is little published data to profile the characteristics of those who are less likely to engage with services and little or no exploration of the perspectives of this group on the barriers and attitudes towards participation in services and interventions. At one end of the spectrum studies on engagement highlight a number of barriers to families that could be relatively easily overcome. These include the approach and timing of an individual worker, for example an overzealous worker who attempts to tackle too much too soon with a family can run the risk of overwhelming family members (Pearson and Thurston, 2006). Other barriers to engagement include the ethnic background of parents, single parenthood and lack of family support networks, age of parents, the age of the child and the severity and history of anti-social behaviour.

Studies of social work practice have also found a tendency for systematic exclusion of fathers and that assessments can be 'riddled with gendered assumptions' about male and female roles (Taylor and Daniel, 2000, p 15). Practical barriers such as the timing of parenting classes or a lack of transport for accessing services can create barriers to family involvement. Parenting programmes are often geared towards parents who do not have paid employment and as a consequence those who are employed are effectively excluded from participation. Gordon (2002) argues that the responsibility for engagement lies with the agency and the practitioner and not with the client. Barriers to effective communication between client and worker can be imposed by the structure of the system of statutory involvement. Compulsion may not readily be conducive to effective engagement by vulnerable and mistrusting parents and can generate communication barriers that impede the development of an effective action plan to address client-defined problems (Petras et al, 2002).

An imbalance of power relations can affect parents' attitudes towards practitioners and participation. For vulnerable families experiencing multiple difficulties the power of the local authority can appear 'indomitable'

(Dumbrill, 2006, p 31). Spratt and Callan (2004) found families reporting their inability to question or challenge the view of social workers despite dissatisfaction with what they perceived as unnecessary or inappropriate intervention. They had fears of workers being judgemental and heavy-handed in their approach, and fears of intervention being forced on them. Where family members perceive fewer practical barriers, even where a high number of barriers may actually be present, their 'optimism' can support increased participation (Morawska and Sanders, 2006). Parents in these situations can react in one of two ways: they can 'fight' and openly challenge the worker (sometimes in formal proceedings) or learn to 'play the game' and feign cooperation or disengage ('flight'). Collaboration between parents and the worker, where they have an active role in defining goals and planning the support they receive, seems a crucial element of client engagement.

> What rights do Sarah and her family have?

Victimisation, resilience and protection

The characterisation of 'victims' and 'villains' is difficult to maintain empirically for many if not for most young people involved in anti-social or criminal activity. Young people might easily change places as victim and offender and do not neatly correspond to this artificial dichotomy. Much child development literature identifies that risk and protective factors for potential neglect are similar to the known risk and protective factors for potential disruptive or criminal behaviour. Neglected children often display a variety of emotional, psychosocial and behavioural problems at various stages in their developmental life cycle, including failing to cope intellectually and socially at school (DePanfilis, 2006). Examples of this include an inability to control emotions or impulses; having difficulty getting along with siblings or classmates; acting socially or emotionally inappropriately for their age; displaying apathy and poor coping skills; misusing alcohol or drugs. The evidence on the precise mechanisms of the interrelationship between anti-social behaviour, neglect and abuse remains limited.

> In what ways would your approach to working with Sarah be different if she was well known for anti-social and offending behaviour *or* if she was known to Child Protection?

While abuse is not necessarily a predictor of offending behaviour and neither fully explains nor excuses it, a high proportion of young people involved in offending, particularly those who have committed violent offences, appear to have suffered severe neglect, abuse and trauma during childhood. Problems of early attachment and loss are frequently present in later years. The victim child and the offending young person are often the same, at different stages of their life cycle.

Studies have concluded that up to a third of young people who offend have been maltreated as children (Weatherburn and Lind, 1997). In one study of 465 young people, the average age of first referral for offending was 10; over 30% had already been referred as at risk of being victims of crime, in particular, abuse (Whyte, 2004, p 404). Another longitudinal study found that being a victim of crime by age 12 was strongly associated with subsequent delinquency and that victimisation predicted delinquency three years later (Smith, 2004). Follow-up sweeps of 14- and 15-year-olds found delinquency 'seven times as high' among those who had been victims of five types of crime (2004, p 3). Being a victim of assault with a weapon and of robbery was most associated with later delinquency. The most important factors explaining the link between victimisation and offending included getting involved in risky activities/situations and social associations. The study concluded that victimisation and offending are 'twin aspects of the same social settings, social interactions, behaviour patterns and personal characteristics' (Smith, 2004, p 18).

There has been growing interest within social work in the concept of resilience. Not all children and young people exposed to multiple risk factors become offenders or are involved in anti-social behaviour, nor do all children and young people who offend or who are involved in anti-social behaviour grow up in socioeconomic difficulty. Research has highlighted that there are important aspects of the lives of young people that can protect them against risk in the same way that some personal and social factors are strongly associated with the likelihood of offending (Kirby and Fraser, 1998; Newman and Blackburn, 2002). Many young people, despite their circumstances and experience, have 'potential' and abilities that are often under-developed.

Childhood resilience is generally defined as resulting from an individual constellation of characteristics and capacities, or as the result of interpersonal processes that mitigate the impact of biological, psychological and social factors that threaten a child's health and well-being. Fraser and Galinsky define resilience as:

> ... an interaction between risk and protective factors within a person's background, which can interrupt and reverse what might otherwise be damaging processes. (1997, pp 265-75)

Resilience can take the form of individual characteristics, family factors or extra-familial circumstances which can be enhanced by social workers building on existing strengths and reducing risk factors (Jackson, 2000). Just as risks can have a cumulative effect, so cumulative protection is thought to reduce and act as a buffer against risk in relation to many social and health problems. Individual characteristics, such as having a resilient temperament or a positive social orientation, positive and warm relationships that promote close bonds with family members, teachers and other adults who encourage and recognise a young person's competence, as well as close friendships with peers, can operate as protective factors that can reduce the impact of risks or change the way a child responds to them.

Research on resilience in children has documented a lengthy list of characteristics associated with positive outcomes and shown that a number of protective mechanisms operate in children's lives. Protective mechanisms are processes and factors that promote favoured outcomes. According to Rutter et al (1998) these include the eight mechanisms listed below.

Protective mechanisms are those that:

- reduce the child's sensitivity to risk, usually through experiences of successful coping;
- reduce the potential for risk factors to impact on a child, as when a parent in a high-crime neighbourhood adequately monitors their adolescents' social activities;
- reduce negative chain reactions so that a problem like family strife does not lead to family breakdown;
- increase positive chain reactions as when that same family in crisis finds the supports it needs to stay together;
- promote self-esteem and self-efficacy through experiences of coping successfully with stress;
- neutralise or compensate for the risks the child faces, as when an abused child is placed in a secure and loving foster home;
- open up positive opportunities for change and growth, as when access is gained to good schools and recreation facilities, coaches and equipment; and finally,
- encourage the positive cognitive processing of negative life events in order that hopefulness may replace feelings of helplessness.

Combined, these eight mechanisms provide a matrix of ways children and young people can successfully overcome adversities.

The literature on resilience, while empirically based, still includes relatively few accounts of specific strategies for achieving positive outcomes. Some resilience characteristics may be relatively fixed while others are variable but may be difficult to influence, especially for children and families facing multiple and complex difficulties. Nonetheless, the evidence counter-balances the tendency of over-focusing on deficits. Positive self-identity constructed by a young person or co-constructed with responsive adults is crucial to positive mental health (Ungar, 2004).

> **In what ways could your practice with Sarah strengthen her resilience?**

Understanding a young person's criminal behaviour can highlight the strengths in their social and mental functioning that may have successfully gained them status, power and acceptance in a world that is meaningful to them even if unacceptable to society. A young person can only navigate towards what is available and easily accessed. Making the most out of whatever is available to him or her should be considered as resilience and an effort made to harness these strengths in a positive context (Ungar, 2006). When children are helped to succeed, the most important influences are often members of extended families, informal networks and positive peer association, particularly associated with family conferencing and restorative practices.

Restorative practice

The emphasis on involving those most affected by crime has resulted in an increased use of restorative practices in youth and adult justice systems in different jurisdictions. Restorative practices operate on the premise that crime and conflict creates harm for individuals and communities and that they can heal fractured social relationships. Effective responses should seek to balance the concerns of the victim and 'communities of interest' with the need to better integrate the individual within a community or society. Restorative practices are often linked with traditional or indigenous practices. However, these are generally concerned less with individual restoration and more with social and community cohesion (Whyte, 2007).

If conflict is viewed as an opportunity for individuals and communities to take individual or shared responsibility for the harm done, then an important outcome for any effective approach should be to assist those involved to learn and to have their needs addressed. From this perspective it can be argued that it is in the best interests of young people to understand the harm done and its consequences on themselves and others as an important element in their social and moral development. It is equally valuable to have a positive opportunity to share in the resolution of the harm with the support of family or significant others as a way of promoting their sense of personal control and self-efficacy as well as building social capital by strengthening the positive aspects of their social support networks. In this sense restorative practices are intended to be holistic and integrative. Implicitly or explicitly, the state has a major role in creating conditions for promoting individual and social well-being and community safety, in which 'communities of interest' can be co-producers in decision making (Whyte, 2007).

Many of the aspirations of restorative practice articulate well with the requirements for desistance and better personal and social integration of young people involved in offending. There is no universally accepted or concise definition of restorative practice in justice and practices vary greatly in their apparent intention. Marshall's definition appears to encompass the generally accepted principles:

> Restorative justice is a process whereby all the parties with a stake in a particular offence come together to resolve collectively how to deal with the aftermath of the offence and its implications for the future. (cited in Braithwaite, 1999, p 5)

The UN Declaration on Basic Principles on the Use of Restorative Justice Programmes in Criminal Matters (2000) defines restorative justice as a process in which the victim, offender and/or any other individuals or community members affected by a crime participate actively together in the resolution of matters arising from the crime, often with the help of a fair and impartial third party. While active participation is a central concept, there is no stress on better social integration or community cohesion as an essential characteristic of restorative practice, and the UN definition places little emphasis on mutually beneficial outcomes. Nonetheless, for many advocates, restorative practice must evidence the consistent involvement of all parties affected by the crime, and focus on the development, implementation and maintenance of mutual healing, reparation and satisfaction, rather than retribution and punishment (Schiff, 1998). Bazemore and Umbreit (1994) argue the involvement of the person who causes harm and the person who experiences it is essential and that both (victims and offenders) need to benefit in any balanced system of restorative justice.

Braithwaite's (1989) theory of 're-integrative shaming' suggests that people are generally not deterred from committing crime by the threat of official punishment but by two informal processes of social control: fear of social disapproval and social conscience. Through restorative practice the offender can be made powerfully aware of the disapproval of their actions by significant others in their lives. The potentially alienating and stigmatising effects of shaming are overcome by re-acceptance and affirmation of the person's value in the social community. As a consequence agreements reached by family members, friends or other individuals important to a young person are likely to be more effective and lasting in their impact than those imposed by an impersonal legal institution. From this point of view, not only does restorative practice provide an opportunity for young people to accept their share of responsibility for their actions, it also affords them the opportunity, where possible, to repair the harm they have caused with the support of their families while involving victims in the process, strengthening their sense of social cohesion, self-efficacy and responsibility.

In practice the term 'restorative' is used for a plethora of activities within adult and youth justice including mediation and reparation, family group conferencing, restorative and community conferencing, restorative cautions, sentencing and healing circles, community panels or courts and other communitarian associations (Braithwaite, 1999). While restorative practices often provide alternatives to formal justice processes, in some jurisdictions, they are police-led and in others are incorporated within the formal justice process with explicit criminal justice objectives including punishment and retribution as part of formal judicial disposals (Daly and Hayes, 2001). Developments in restorative practices for some reflect attempts at a new paradigm; for others simply attempts to salvage the existing criminal justice paradigm by providing more meaningful and 'humane' practices alongside punishment and retribution. Daly (2003) argues that restorative practice within state mechanisms is intended to be a punishment, albeit an alternative punishment, that is not humiliating, harming or degrading and that it should combine retribution and rehabilitation.

Family group conferences

Family group conferences are generally modelled on an approach developed in New Zealand and bring together family members of both the offender and victim, friends, people from the local community and professional social workers or justice personnel to look at:

- the facts – what happened and why;
- the consequences – how the victim and others were affected; and
- the future – how the person can make amends

in an effort to produce a mutually satisfactory resolution. They, and associated variations, aim to enable victims, the offender and their respective families or support people to participate actively in the process of addressing the harm caused by the offence, to talk about why an event occurred and how it affected them and to decide on a plan of action, which may specify what needs to be done to put right the harm and to prevent it happening in the future.

The agreed plan should, as far as possible, be based on a consensus of views of those at the meeting and will usually outline what is to happen, and who is to oversee or support those taking action to ensure that the plan is carried out. The plan may include compensating the victim, family and/or friends, changing their routines to provide support and encouragement to both victim and offender, the provision of practical and financial assistance or other services by statutory authorities or other agencies and involvement in local programmes. In some jurisdictions the plan is presented to professionals or to a court who will normally accept it as part of the final disposal.

These types of restorative practices place a very clear focus on the co-production of mutually beneficial outcomes through direct participation of the people most affected by the event and on personal 'uplift' achieved in taking responsibility for problem resolution while supported and affirmed by families or other positive social supports. It is not always possible to involve victims or other supporters directly in restorative practices. In the case of damage to community property, for example, a representative such as a teacher from a school or from the retail community may attend and represent the victim(s) or community perspective.

Some practices such as restorative police cautioning have no explicit aim of repairing family or social bonds, and victims are seldom involved directly. Some would argue equally that reparative activities are not of themselves restorative and that it is only in the addressing of harm that the term 'restorative' has meaning.

The most frequently asked question by politicians, professionals and the public alike is: do restorative practices work and do they help stop re-offending? Studies have used indicators such as re-offending rates, costs, participant (including offender and victim) satisfaction, restitution, compliance and public perceptions, but the fundamental principles and values of restorative practices are somewhat incompatible with traditional methods of measuring success in criminal justice. Many studies do indicate with varying degrees of caution that people diverted to restorative practices in justice do reduce re-offending, and that all who are involved in the process generally feel more satisfaction when compared to traditional methods. However, restorative practice proponents would argue that reducing the concept of restorative practice to these types of goals is a misunderstanding of the vision it attempts to accomplish.

Braithwaite's review (1999) of the evidence reached encouraging, although cautious, conclusions about the efficacy of restorative practice. Only one of more than 30 studies examined could be interpreted as showing an increase in re-offending for any type of offender and many showed reduced offending. Properly implemented programmes using specialist mediators and pre-conference preparation seemed to result in agreements between parties in upwards of 90% of cases and similar rates for fulfilment of agreements. The majority of victims and offenders typically express strong satisfaction with the process and outcome. While restitution appears an important motivator for victim participation, data suggest it is less important to victims than the opportunity to talk about the offence and its impact (Bazemore and Umbreit, 2001). Studies of family group conferences have shown that reconviction rates were no worse and probably better than for court-based samples (Morris and Maxwell, 1998).

The Canberra Re-integrative Shaming Experiments (RISE) produced results from their first year follow-up period measuring repeat offending from official criminal history data and self-report criminal history data. This well-designed study reported across all four offence categories involved that both offenders and victims found conferences to be procedurally fairer and more satisfactory than a court process (Sherman et al, 2000). The study reported a substantial drop in offending rates by violent offenders (by 38 crimes per 100 offenders per year) relative to the effect of being sent to court. A small increase in re-offending was reported by drink drivers (by 6 crimes per 100 offenders per year). For juvenile property offences (shoplifting apprehended by store security officers) and for juvenile property offences (personal victims) the experiment showed no differences in offending rates according to whether offenders were assigned to court or conference.

The Indianapolis Restorative Justice Conferencing Experiment (McGarrell et al, 2000) involved first-time offenders up to the age of 14 who committed a non-serious, non-violent offence. Findings showed 30.1% of the conferencing group were re-arrested within 12 months, compared with 42.3% of the control group, a statistically significant difference. Re-arrest rates at 12 months for only those young people who had successfully completed a programme did not achieve statistically significant results. In a similar study in Glasgow (Dutton and Whyte, 2006), young people aged 15 and under involved in first or minor offending were diverted to restorative caution. Outcomes were equivocal, with 73% not re-referred for offending in the subsequent 12-month period compared with 68% of the comparison group. Consistently high levels of satisfaction with the restorative processes were recorded from the police, young people and victims.

> What benefits and disadvantages can you see in incorporating a restorative approach into work with Sarah?

Meta-analysis provides the most promising approach to establishing outcomes and controlling for key variables in restorative practices. A review of six studies with young people (Rowe, W., 2002) concluded that the young people acquired a greater understanding of the harm they had done, feelings of empathy towards the people or organisations they harmed and were less likely to engage in future delinquent and criminal behaviour. A more substantial meta-analysis of 22 studies (Latimer et al, 2005) reported moderate increases in satisfaction and a slight decrease in re-offending compared with offenders in the traditional justice system. Methodological limitations and the low number of effect sizes did not allow for firm conclusions to be drawn. Another meta-analytic review that included mediation and conferences found re-offending rates to be no higher for restorative practice than for the court process (McCold, 2003).

Despite some encouraging findings, restorative practices are not without their critics, who point to a variety of dangers and possible unintended outcomes both for people who offend and for their victims. There is the potential for victims to be 're-victimised' during conferences and emerge more traumatised or fearful than before, especially if they are faced by an unrepentant and belligerent respondent. Concerns have also been raised about legal rights under conferencing models and that young people, in particular, may end up receiving 'excessive punishment' at the hands of vengeful victims.

A warning for those embarking on establishing restorative practices, uncritically, is contained in an early evaluation (Morris and Maxwell, 1993), which identified a number of risks associated with the approach. It pointed out that active participation of victims in the conferences could be low – only about half of conferences included victims or their representatives. Furthermore, the process could be dominated by professionals, resulting in questionable pressure, intentional or unintentional, placed on people to accept guilt for the offence.

Crawford and Newburn (2003) caution that restorative practices may result in net widening when they represent simply an adaptation to existing justice practice rather that an alternative to prosecution. Some restorative practices are similarly criticised for their narrow focus on the resolution of the offence and because they fail to take account of the wider context, economic, personal and social, especially police-led practice contrasted with more holistic approaches supporting access to necessary resources. For vulnerable young people and families, a lack of available welfare and family support services could result in more shaming and restitution than assistance and social integration.

Restorative practice can mean different things to different people but in most of its guises it presents challenges to establishment thinking on justice, particularly for young people, on how to achieve a constructive shift from sterile punishment to better forms of problem resolution and social integration. Methodological limitations make firm conclusions impossible. The most recently published review (Sherman and Strang, 2007) concluded in regard to re-offending that restorative practice 'works differently on different kinds of people' (p 8). Rigorous tests in diverse samples have found substantial reductions in repeat offending for both violence and property crime; other tests have failed to find such effects. The evidence points to greater effectiveness with crimes involving personal victims than for crimes without them, with violent crimes more consistently than with property crimes, and with more, rather than less, serious crimes.

The evidence does not readily allow accurate predictions of the kinds of offences or offenders for whom restorative practice may be more likely to be effective (Sherman and Strang, 2007, p 70), and the evidence in regard to young people who offend seems even more equivocal. Its greatest impact on young people is in supporting their removal from criminal processes. Nonetheless, studies produce consistently encouraging results against the four major objectives of victim satisfaction, offender satisfaction, restitution compliance and reduced re-offending.

Restorative practices are developing as an alternative to formal processing of young people involved in bullying or other anti-social behaviour in schools. It is important that anti-bullying initiatives do not show signs of excessive risk aversion in the way that they define the problem. It can be difficult for adults to judge whether or not a particular incident is bullying, and how best to intervene. There is a constant danger that adults will overreact and suppress all conflict behaviour that, unlike serious bullying, has a key role in helping children learn for themselves how to deal with difficult social situations. Anything short of a whole-school restorative approach appears to be difficult to manage and difficult to assess in terms of impact.

Evaluation has been patchy and usually not rigorous. Kane et al (2006) found evidence of a change in culture towards disciplinary practices in primary schools but less in high schools, where considerable staff resistance was encountered towards restorative alternatives to punishment. A national evaluation of a whole-school approach (YJB, 2004), examining the impact of restorative practices for incidents of bullying, name calling, gossiping, family feuds, conflict with teachers and minor property and violent crime, found no statistically significant effects on student attitudes. It concluded that if a conference was held, it was usually successful in resolving the dispute and 'may be a useful resource that improves the school environment and enhances the learning and development of young people' (YJB, 2004, p 65).

Conclusion

Child-centred services and institutions have much to do to move from a 'philosophy of protection' to a 'philosophy of resilience' in which early intervention within mainstream provision bolsters social and personal integration rather than excludes identified offenders. There is sufficient evidence to suggest that if intervention is necessary to address harm caused by the behaviour of another, then restorative approaches may provide a meaningful context for dealing with it constructively. However, because intervention is restorative, this does not mean that it is required. Early assistance is best provided through mainstream channels where possible.

Key questions

(1) Have you ever been the victim of an offence? What did it feel like? What were your concerns, fears and expectations?

(2) What challenges might face a supervising social worker in working directly or on behalf of victims? What factors would you need to take into account?

(3) What critical transitional points in a young person's life can be identified to assist preventive intervention?

(4) What contribution, if any, should youth justice practitioners make to early years intervention?

(5) What is your understanding of net widening? How might it apply to early intervention?

(6) What traps can anti-social behaviour practices fall into? How can these be avoided?

Practice exercise

Using Newman and Blackburn's classification of resilience-promoting interventions (2002, p 10) identify benefits to children and young people.

All developmental stages: key resilience-promoting interventions	Identify kinds of activity	What are the possible benefits for Sarah?
Opportunities to take part in demanding and challenging activities		
Where children are in situations of conflict at home, contact with a reliable and supportive other		
Facilitating contacts with helpful others or networks that can provide activities or opportunities for work		
Opportunities to succeed in valued tasks		
Compensatory experiences – exposure to people or events that contradict risk effects		
Opportunities for careers or further education		
Teaching coping strategies and skills and being helped to view negative experience positively		

Further reading and resources

⮕   Laub, J. and Sampson, R. (2003) 'Turning points in the life course: Why change matters to the study of crime', *Criminology*, vol 31, no 3, pp 301-25.

⮕   Marshall, T. (1999) *Restorative Justice: An Overview*, London: Home Office.

⮕   Schoon, I. and Bynner, H. (2003) 'Risk and resilience in the life course: implications for interventions and social policies', *Journal of Youth Studies*, vol 6, no 1, pp 21-31.

⮕   Ungar, M., Dumond, C. and McDonald, W. (2005) 'Risk, resilience and outdoor programmes for at-risk children', *Journal of Social Work*, vol 5, no 3, pp 319-38.

Effective responses to reducing youth crime

Introduction

Most practitioners will be familiar with the discourses on evidence-based practice and effective practice ('what works?') in reducing re-offending (see Chapter Three). Much of the literature on effectiveness is, implicitly at least, about how best to equip people for change through the development of their personal resources (human capital). Indeed, some of the literature has been criticised for being preoccupied with human capital to the neglect of social context and in particular with regard to the role of social resources in change (Farrall, 2002). This chapter explores how supervision can help young people develop their skills, personal resources and the qualities that are required for maturation, personal change and social integration. All of these are crucial to the process of desistance from criminal behaviour.

Vignette: unhappy and rebellious teenager

Roberta (aged 15) was involved in an assault on another girl at school. Her mother was telephoned and asked to take her home. Roberta ran away and the police were contacted. She returned later that evening. The following day she again disappeared from school and stayed out overnight.

Roberta has been found using cocaine on numerous occasions by the police and her mother thinks she is drinking regularly. She and her friends were caught stealing wine from an off-licence.

Roberta lives with her mum and two elder brothers. Her parents divorced when she was 10. Her father remarried and lives 200 miles away. Her mum is finding Roberta 'difficult to control' and they have become very frustrated with each other. She feels that if she doesn't 'give in' to Roberta she would 'crack up'.

Roberta's way of coping seems to be to storm off with her friends, returning very late or after a weekend. Roberta's attendance at school is poor. She shows little interest in her work and receives learning support. She seems unhappy.

What approaches might be useful to help Roberta reduce her offending?

What kinds of support would you need to carry them out?

Human capital

Social learning theorists argue that change requires a 'productive investment' in young people as a form of 'human capital' to make 'possible the achievement of certain ends that would not be attainable in its absence' (Coleman, 1994, p 302). At the heart of an effective programme of supervision will be methods aimed at equipping young people with knowledge and understanding, skills and opportunities to develop new ways of thinking, feeling and behaving. Not all young people in trouble with the law will have the same requirements. Some will have capacities that can be strengthened in the context of their family or wider social network; others will have very limited personal and social resources other than those provided by the state and public care. Many will have experienced attachment problems, loss and trauma that will require focused and possibly specialist help alongside provision aimed at impacting on their offending.

Human capital broadly relates to personal resources – skills, capacities and knowledge – that individuals require to facilitate access to positive social associations, education and employment and to other important social resources. It has been argued that just as physical capital is created by changes in materials to form the tools that facilitate 'production', human capital is the result of changes in individuals which create the skills and capabilities to make them able to act in new ways and to do new things (Coleman, 1994). Personal resources are important for the development of a strong sense of self and for the promotion of self-efficacy that is generally recognised as an important aspect of healthy adolescent development and a key quality in successful personal change, maturation and individuation.

If physical capital is very tangible, human capital is much less so. Well-structured social interventions including group work or individual social education programmes can help young people enhance their cognitive and social skills. The concept of building personal resources captures the ambition of many social work practitioners in trying to ensure that supervision is both productive and invests meaningfully in the individual for their benefit and for the benefit of the community at large. The concept stresses the importance of the 'mutuality' of that investment, or 'co-production'. Co-production takes place when some of the investment is contributed by the individuals who are the 'clients' or 'users' of a service. The distinction between professional and client is not rigid and success is associated with a sustained relationship between the practitioner, young person and their family or social network, where both make substantial contributions to the change effort. Attempts to share power, authority and responsibility between the supervisor and young people and their families (although not necessarily equally) are, consequently, an important means of achieving a dynamic and effective process and mutually beneficial outcomes for participants.

Social capital

The concept of social capital is increasingly used to refer to the resources that people derive from their relationships with others. Social capital has been defined as consisting of 'social networks, the reciprocities that arise from them, and the value of these for achieving mutual goals' (Baron et al, 2000, p 1). The concept is a contentious one and some would argue that people now say 'social capital' where once they might have said 'community' or more simply 'neighbourhood'. What is important about the concept of social capital in youth justice is that it asks practitioners to view a whole range of social connections and networks as a resource, which may help young people advance their interests by cooperating with others. It equally recognises that a lack of social capital can undermine efforts at positive individual change and reducing or ending offending.

> In what areas might Roberta lack social capital?

Little is known about the way social networks help create human capital and assist the acquisition and exchange of skills, knowledge and attitudes that in turn allow access to other social benefits. The theoretical assumption is that the more social capital an individual has, the stronger and more extensive network ties including strong ties within families, reinforced by close bonds among the main social, ethnic or religious groupings, then the more they can acquire and learn new things than those with less social capital.

Commentators have argued that developing social capital is central to the process of desistance and social integration (Farrall, 2004). The term 'capital' tends to refer to the resources and assets that individuals struggle to acquire and on which they 'trade' in pursuit of power and influence. Bourdieu, the French sociologist, distinguished three forms of capital: economic, cultural and social capital, emphasising the interplay between them. Where economic capital refers to money and material resources, cultural capital refers to resources acquired through education and socialisation. Social capital is defined as the aggregate of the actual or potential resources that are linked to possession of a durable network of social relationships of mutual acquaintance and recognition (Bourdieu and Wacquant, 1992, p 119). The analogy with capital can be misleading to the extent that, unlike traditional forms of capital, social capital is not depleted by use, but is in fact depleted by non-use. People use their social capital to gain access to skills and knowledge in a variety of ways; it is important, however, to note that this need not always be a pro-social process. Negative or pro-criminal social capital can sustain and support criminality.

Probably the two most influential figures in developing the concept of social capital are from the US: James Coleman and Robert Putnam. Coleman defined social capital as anything that facilitates individual or collective action, generated by networks of relationships, reciprocity, trust and social norms. To some degree Coleman treats social capital as a *neutral* resource that facilitates any manner of action and therefore depends on the individual uses to which it is put. He defined social capital as:

> ... the set of resources that inhere in family relations and in community social organisation and that are useful for the cognitive or social development of a child or young person. These resources differ for different persons and can constitute an important advantage for children and adolescents in their development of human capital. (Coleman, 1994, p 300)

Coleman's research (which relates primarily to education) argued that social capital was critical to enabling the development of individual human capital and provides a bridge between the interests of an individual and collective interests. He claimed to find that, even when social class, ethnicity and other factors were taken into account, education outcomes were better for young people whose families had access to greater social capital. Although Bourdieu might agree with Coleman that social capital in the abstract is a neutral resource, his work tries to show how it can be used practically to produce or reproduce benefits and, equally, how the uneven distribution of social capital can maintain hierarchies and inequalities. Social capital is not equally available to all and the value of a specific source of social capital depends in no small part on the socioeconomic position of the individual within society. As a consequence, while the goal of building social capital is to assist reintegration of those marginalised from the rewards of the economic system into the community, its effects can be exclusionary.

Putnam presents social capital less as a resource possessed by individuals and more as an attribute of collectives. He refers to the collective value of all *social networks* and the inclinations that arise from these networks to do things for each other. Social resources are built particularly effectively through *civic engagement* and active citizenship, creating a web of social networks underpinned by shared values and producing high levels of social trust, which in turn foster further cooperation between people, making it harder to defect or opt out of social responsibilities (Putnam, 2000). Civil society refers to voluntary associations and organisations outside the market and state that connect people with each other. For Putnam the 'presence of social capital has been linked to various positive outcomes, particularly in education'; 'child development is powerfully shaped by social capital' and is often the result of parents' social capital in a community (Putnam, 2000, p 300).

Putnam identified two main components: bonding social capital and bridging social capital. Bonding capital refers to the value assigned to social networks between similar groups of people (for example, families, friends, neighbours or even criminal gangs). Bridging capital refers to social networks of socially different groups, for example social associations through leisure from joining sports ('bowling' in Putnam's example) or youth clubs. Horizontal networks of individuals and groups that enhance community productivity and cohesion are said to be positive social capital assets whereas self-serving exclusive gangs or hierarchical patronage systems that operate at cross-purposes to societal interests can be thought of as negative social capital.

The theoretical concept of social capital is a rich one and can bring an important dimension to practice planning. The concept of social capital encourages practitioners to ask whether or not certain social arrangements are better than others at promoting positive learning or providing access to benefits including positive social relationships and greater social cohesion. However, there is no practical consensus on how to establish or measure social capital, which is one of its major weaknesses. The practitioner is left to develop an intuitive sense of the level or amount of social capital present in a given relationship or available to a specific young person. Quantifying and giving 'value' to this is not straightforward.

Nonetheless, Putnam and Coleman point more practically to education, family and community practices, arguing that where there are high social resources there is high education performance. When parents participate in their children's education and schooling, teachers report lower levels of misbehaviour such as bringing weapons to school, engaging in physical violence, truanting and being generally apathetic about education – all of which can be seen as 'interim' measures for successful intervention. Putnam drew on Coleman's work to argue 'the importance of the embeddedness of young persons in the enclaves of adults most proximate to them, first and most prominent the family and second, a surrounding community of adults' (Putnam, 2000, p 301). This reflects the intention of wraparound approaches to practice (see Chapter Seven) in which many of the components come from the 'natural' social world of the young person.

Inevitably the limiting factors to such an approach are the structural barriers created by poorly resourced social networks and fragmented neighbourhoods. A further practice difficulty has been the limited success of local authorities to express their corporate responsibility through the provision of effective multiagency services.

Strong networks both empower people in exercising informal social control over young people and assist young people in their integration into their wider communities (Halpern, 2001). Barry's empirical study of young men and women's criminal careers (2006) argues that the status of young people often results in the denial of access to means of accumulating legitimate capital (economic, social, cultural and symbolic). They are therefore vulnerable to being drawn into further offending in order to acquire social status and respect within their peer or social grouping. This is a reminder, if needed, that adolescent transitions are not simply biological but occur in a rapidly changing social context (Bottoms et al, 2004).

From action plan to intervention

The relationship between the practitioner and their agency on the one hand and the young person and their family on the other are critical factors in planning and implementing effective interventions. A practitioner's working alliance with a young person and their family is the basis for learning about and gaining the cooperation of the young person, and for matching and modifying interventions to suit individual characteristics and circumstances. Building effective relationships is, in turn, underpinned by the practitioner's ability to develop and use strong authoritative communication, reflective person–centred approaches and interpersonal skills.

Ultimately no one can be coerced to think deeply about their behaviour and its consequences for themselves or for others, or to undertake the difficult and time-consuming work necessary for controlling and changing behaviour. Positive motivation, commitment and readiness to change are important but not necessarily a prerequisite to change. There is a difference between coercion and informed decision making in constrained circumstances (Barber, 1991). If compulsory intervention is to be meaningful it must be understood by the young person and, as far as is possible, be directed by their priorities as well as the system's, and based on a clear understanding of what is a 'must' and what is negotiable.

One study (Jamieson et al, 1999) found that young people aged 14–15 related positive behaviour change and ending offending to increased maturity, which was seen to be linked to a growing recognition that offending was pointless or wrong; understanding the real or potential consequences of their offending; and related transitional events like securing a job or a place at college. Graham and Bowling (1995) found two factors to be positively associated with desistance for males in the 16–25 age range: firstly, their perception that their school work was above average, and, secondly, continuing to live at home; the latter, of course, may have been associated with relatively positive relationships with parents operating as a protective factor.

Although age and, in particular, the transitions associated with it, seemed to be a more important determinant of desistance than gender, Jamieson et al (1999) found notable gender differences. Failure to desist in young men seemed to be best explained by three sets of risk factors: a high frequency of offending, continued contact with criminal peers, and alcohol and drug misuse. Some young women linked their decisions to stopping offending to the assumption of future parental responsibilities, while young men focused more on personal choice and personal agency. More recent studies, however, suggest that young men do experience processes of change that are similar to those for young women, developing responsibilities in and through personal relationships and employment, but these seem to take longer to emerge (Farrall and Bowling, 1999; Flood-Page et al, 2000).

Qualitative data has suggested that young people's decisions about offending and desisting are often related to their need to feel included in their social world, through friendships and through wider commitments in moving towards adulthood (Barry, 2006). Most of the young people studied had limited access to mainstream opportunities (education, employment, housing and social status) because of their age and because of their social circumstances. Despite their disadvantaged backgrounds many showed resolve in their efforts to stop offending but lacked opportunities for social recognition necessary to sustain positive changes. Access to opportunities to exercise responsibility is often absent for young people from disadvantaged backgrounds.

One of the most consistent findings related to ending offending is that those who do so have somehow to develop the ability to resolve and overcome problems and obstacles to change as part of taking responsibility for their life. Adults trying to make the transition from a criminal to a non-criminal lifestyle often comment on the impact of the stigma of the past on future possibilities (Farrall, 2004). Obstacles experienced on the way include problems with alcohol and drugs, and with getting work, financial difficulties, other social problems and personal issues including changing associations, relationships with families and friends, and education difficulties. Many of these, of course, are developmental issues for all vulnerable and disadvantaged adolescents, not simply those in trouble with the law.

Farrall (2004) described differences between those who saw themselves as confident, optimistic or pessimistic about their future prospects, with the 'confidents' having the shortest criminal careers (around five years), compared to 'optimists' and 'pessimists' who had longer criminal careers (six plus years). It is worth noting that fewer of the 'confidents' faced major obstacles in their lives, while half of the 'optimists' and most of the 'pessimists' did. The ability to overcome obstacles requires personal abilities and human skills. Social and personal circumstances including positive life chances were strongly associated with positive outcomes, emphasising the interplay between motivation, skills in identifying and overcoming obstacles and social circumstances and resources.

Motivational interviewing

Positive motivation to avoid further offending is an important factor in contributing to change for people facing obstacles and difficulties. Factors that seem to influence positive motivation and orientation include the desire to avoid negative consequences, realising that legitimate gains (financial or social) outweigh criminal gains, wanting to lead a 'quieter' life, or embarking on a committed personal relationship.

Motivational interviewing (MI) is recognised as having an important part to play in work with people who offend (Miller and Rollnick, 2002). However, models of MI have been developed from clinical practice in the mental health field and need to be adapted to community settings and used flexibly with young people, where adult–adult transactions through reflective conversations will often be difficult to achieve without the use of active methods. A practical guide is in the exchange itself – if the practitioner is doing most of the talking, the young person is not doing any work.

MI has been defined as a directive, client-centred counselling style for eliciting behaviour change by helping to explore and resolve ambivalence (Rollnick and Miller, 1995). 'Directive' in this context refers to the focus being rigorously on a problem, goal-directed and participative approach rather than on an authoritarian or overtly 'expert' one. The approach actively discourages direct persuasion, suggesting that the person needs to be involved in active change and as a consequence an overly didactic or expert stance or behaving in a punitive or coercive manner which leaves the young person in a passive role is likely to be counter-productive.

The rationale for an MI approach is based on a recognition that ambivalence and limited motivation to change (often common features in adolescence towards any kind of authority) are commonly at the root of intervention failure and have to be overcome. Maturational issues will determine the extent to which such an approach can be used. Every effort should be made to use a negotiation style where the young person is encouraged to identify their hopes and priorities, to analyse the pros and cons of their behaviour through the use of self-motivational statements, and to provide choice with a variety of alternative change strategies through goal setting, role playing and modelling.

Motivation and readiness to change are multifaceted concepts, and in making decisions about community supervision interventions, an apparent lack of motivation is not in itself a reason for excluding young people from supervision but, rather, can be a reason for good preparation before embarking on a planned programme of supervision. Studies have reported that those initially most motivated are often less entrenched in criminality and criminal associations (Burnett, 2004). Those most at need and presenting greatest risk are often more entrenched in their behaviour and attitudes and less motivated to change.

The benefits of a motivational approach are often described in terms of a model of change recognising that there are different stages of change from early stages of 'pre-contemplation' and 'contemplation' to the more advanced active stages of 'preparation', 'action' and 'maintenance' (Prochaska and Di Clemente, 1982). When presented diagrammatically Prochaska and Di Clemente's model of change is often pictured as a 'wheel' in recognition that change is not necessarily linear and will not always start at the 'beginning' with 'reflection' and work its way to the end in 'action'. For young people in particular, action and active methods are more likely to support reflection than reflection lead to action.

> What might the implications of Prochaska and Di Clemente's model of change be for different stages of intervention with Roberta?

FIGURE 6.1: **A model of change**

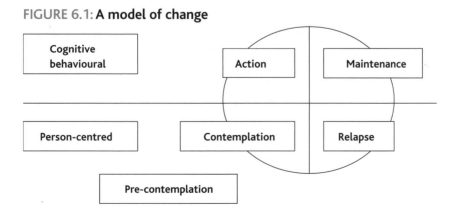

A key to making progress is for the practitioner to make use of the young person's view of their social world and how they see change as possible. Aids such as the ASSET 'What do you think?' form can provide a basis for this type of negotiated exploration alongside contributions from family, possibly through family conferences, to plan action and maintain engagement throughout supervision. Many young people's families may have a realistic understanding of what needs to be done, have a contribution to make to practical supervision and a need to be recognised as partners in the process of change. Many will also need assistance.

Two elements in the model of change discussed above are crucial to practice. One is conceived of as '(re)lapse', which in this context is likely to mean getting into further trouble or drifting back into risky behaviour or associations. This will often re-appear despite evidence of positive change. It is unlikely that offending and other challenging behaviour will suddenly stop and decision makers may require other evidence of positive change to convince them to maintain young people in the community. A further challenge is the maintenance of change over the longer term, which for adolescents could be a number of years and not simply months. This is likely to require follow-up or 'call-back' work to reinforce existing social resources and social supports provided by family members, buddies or mentors, to help young people use newly acquired skills and attitudes in a meaningful and enduring way.

An important role for practitioners is to attempt to operate as a positive model of authority and helper by conveying a response to or understanding of criminal behaviour where this may often differ from the young person's view. Person-centred and solution-focused approaches by definition are built on the young person's own perspectives and concerns, building a trusting relationship as an essential basis for assisting and influencing change. This is not incompatible with a victim-focused, offence-focused perspective or restorative approach negotiated within a plan.

Person-centred approaches can be either directive or non-directive. Classically person-centred approaches are non-directive and intended to engage the person as a 'fellow traveller' on a journey of change albeit focused and goal-oriented. Where a non-directive approach can be achieved, it is likely to be more effective with involuntary and vulnerable clients, particularly reluctant young people who can be difficult to work with when they are 'defensive and oppositional' (Marshall and Serran, 2004, p 315). Young people are likely to have ambivalent feelings about change and whether they are able to achieve their objectives and, as such, may be less cooperative and less responsive to directive approaches. Practitioners have to find a balance between being 'beside' the young person and simply being 'on their side' (Mearns, 2003), particularly for vulnerable young people who may 'dissociate' or separate themselves from others, perhaps following abuse in childhood or traumatic experiences.

It is important for practitioners to make positive use of the 'leverage' that is placed on young people by courts or panels, by the police and schools, as well as help them deal with pressures from peers and parents to enhance positive motivation and action. Desistance is an active process in which the young person's ability to exercise choice and manage their own life within a family or similar context is 'discovered'. While change-based strategies can be somewhat uncertain in their effects, control-based strategies are only as effective as the technical methods on which they rely. The slower process of winning young people over by example, by persistence and by persuasion is, in the longer term, more effective than mere threats.

Pro-social modelling

The 'core' conditions for effective social interventions relate to the ability of practitioners to convey accurate empathy, respect, warmth and genuineness; to establish a working alliance based on mutual understanding and explicit (written) agreement about the nature and purpose of the intervention; and to develop an approach that, as far as possible, is person-centred or collaborative.

Core practices identified in the effectiveness literature with adult offenders (Dowden and Andrews, 2004) suggest that the qualities of practitioners are associated with positive outcomes in reducing re-offending. These include the quality of the interpersonal relationship, the effective use of authority, anti-criminal (or pro-social) modelling and reinforcement, problem solving and accessing community resources. Empirical studies of supervision have found that the use of pro-social modelling consistently correlated with lower re-offending and tends to be most effective with young, high-risk, violent and drug-using offenders.

Central principles of pro-social modelling

- *Role clarification:* involving frequent and open discussions about roles, purposes, expectations, the use of authority, negotiable and non-negotiable aspects of intervention, and confidentiality.
- *Pro-social modelling and reinforcement:* involving the identification, reward and modelling of behaviours to be promoted and the identification, discouragement and confrontation of behaviours to be changed.

■   *Problem solving:* involving the survey, ranking and exploration of problems, goal setting and contracting, the development of strategies and ongoing monitoring.
■   *Relationship:* involving the worker being open and honest, empathic, able to challenge and not minimise rationalisations, non-blaming, optimistic, able to articulate the client's and family members' feelings and problems, using appropriate self-disclosure and humour (Trotter, 2006).

These findings stress that practitioner style and skills as well as the content and methods adopted can have an important impact on outcomes. Rex's study (1999) of probationers found that those who attributed changes in their behaviour to supervision described it as active and participatory. Commitment to desist appeared to be strongly reinforced by the personal and professional commitment shown by supervisors, whose reasonableness, fairness and encouragement seemed to engender a sense of personal loyalty and accountability. They interpreted advice about their behaviours and underlying problems as evidence of concern for them as people, and 'were motivated by what they saw as a display of interest in their well-being' (Rex, 1999, p 375).

The practitioner–client relationship, however, is neither the only nor the most important resource in promoting reduced re-offending and desistance. Related studies of young people in trouble suggest that their own resources and social networks, where they exist, are likely to be better at resolving their difficulties than professional staff (Hill, 1999). The potential of family and social networks is highlighted by 'resilience perspectives' that, in contrast to approaches that overly dwell on risks and/or needs, consider the 'protective factors and processes' involved in positive adaptation despite adversity. The stress on the interplay between personal agency, self-efficacy and social structure gives more meaningful expression to a 'responsibility model' than overly correctional or punitive methods. This is premised on the view that offending can be discouraged through interventions that promote individual responsibility for behaviour together with social responsibility for alleviating adverse circumstances.

Planning effective supervision should follow from thorough assessment. The plan should articulate the rationale for the interventions: why will doing what is proposed bring about the results that are sought? Arguably, this is the logical step that is most commonly neglected in practice (Bonta et al, 2004). Whatever the nature of the intervention, at a practical level supervision planning is likely to require cooperation and partnership with young people and families to set realistic targets that can be measured or identified as delivering the intended outcomes.

Structured programme approaches

Effective supervision involves using interpersonal processes to assist young people plan for change. Much of the evidence influencing the revival of structured group work programmes has come from meta-analyses undertaken mainly in North America (Andrews et al, 1990a) alongside a growing number of studies in the UK (Hollins et al, 2004).

> **What might be the pros and cons of working with Roberta in group work programmes?**

Intervention approaches showing greatest promise and consistency of positive effects and outcomes tend to draw on social learning theory and to adopt cognitive behavioural and social education methods alongside others, to improve problem identification and problem resolution skills associated with offending, which are then applied to the identification and establishment of alternative positive solutions. The effectiveness principles discussed in Chapter Three should direct the design and delivery of structured programmes. While they have strong empirical foundations, the provision of group work programmes does not represent a panacea and they do not automatically produce successful and lasting outcomes (Hollins et al, 2004). The underlying assumption is that structured approaches may accelerate the learning and maturing process and assist the abandonment of criminal activities, an assumption that fits, in some respects, with findings from criminal career research on impulsivity and poor abstract reasoning among persistent offenders (Farrington, 1996).

Published outcomes in the use of structured group work programmes in probation have proved disappointing in their early findings (Hollins et al, 2004). The evidence suggests that, on their own, structured programmes are unlikely to result in a major impact on re-offending rates, until and unless they are part of integrated provision, in this case relating to families, schooling and community associations. Structured programmes need not be group work programmes. However, effective one-to-one work should attempt to meet the same demanding standards set by effectiveness principles and provide a clear and staged 'curriculum' for acquiring social learning.

Youth crime tends to be a group activity so it is hardly surprising that social group work should be a key methodology for youth justice practice. This is first and foremost a social education method for acquiring knowledge, skills and experience. There are many 'off the shelf' programmes that provide specific aims, measurable objectives and a sequenced social learning 'curriculum'. However, group work as a method also creates a group dynamic that allows for modelling, rehearsal and reinforcement necessary for integrated learning. Andrews et al (1990) warn against the use of 'milieu' groups unless practitioners can be sure they can control the negative modelling and anti-social reinforcement that is likely to be generated between a group of adolescents with multiple difficulties and a long history of crime. Group work can make young people worse by 'contamination' if there is no rigorous planning on how group workers intend to achieve the stated outcomes, particularly anti-social and offence-related ones. Staff training and ongoing supervision on roles and practice is essential to good group work.

Social education group work was a core method used across the UK in the 1970s and early 1980s, particularly in 'intermediate treatment' (IT). The emphasis on outward-bound and activity-based group work that was a characteristic of practice still has an important role to play in youth justice (see 'Community-based approaches' below). However, the lack of well-structured offence-focused 'content' alongside or as part of leisure or outdoor activity rather earned life skill group work and IT the reputation of being intermediate 'treats' rather than serious change- and desistance-oriented group work.

One of the most influential group work frameworks is Tuckman's four-stage model (1965), *forming*, *storming*, *norming* and *performing*; a fifth stage, *adjourning*, was added subsequently (Tuckman and Jensen, 1977). Based on observations of group behaviour in a variety of settings, Tuckman suggested groups are likely to go through distinct stages, whether or not these are recognised by participants. By implication a better appreciation of the processes surrounding group development may enhance group effectiveness and functioning.

Tuckman's model of group work

Forming: group orientation accomplished primarily through testing boundaries of both interpersonal and task behaviours; the establishment of dependency relationships with leaders, other group members or pre-existing standards.

Storming: conflict and polarisation around interpersonal issues; resistance to group influence and task requirements.

Norming: overcoming resistance; establishing cohesiveness; new standards evolve, new roles are adopted; intimate, personal opinions expressed.

Performing: interpersonal structure becomes the tool of task activities; roles become flexible and functional, group energy is channelled to the task. (Tuckman, 1965, p 78)

Adjourning involves dissolution; termination of roles, completion of tasks and reduction of dependency; it raises the issue of loss and maintenance.

Group processes are seldom linear and are more likely to reflect circular models of change where group members seek a balance between accomplishing the task and building interpersonal relationships in the group. Not all stages will occur and the model should not be adopted uncritically as other ways of understanding a phase may be more appropriate. Nonetheless, the framework can be a helpful starting point in understanding individuals in a group context and offering insights into group behaviour to be reinforced or challenged.

Recent published data from probation group work programme evaluations highlight a number of important issues for practice in youth justice. A major issue, for example, with the *Think First* cognitive behavioural programme (Roberts, 2004) was the lack of effective implementation and sufficient compliance for the programme to have an impact of some sort. The findings reinforce longstanding non-intervention principles that suggest that inadequate amounts of poor quality intervention may be more harmful than none. They underline the message of the preceding chapters that good engagement and the development of effective working relationships are a necessary prerequisite to programme work. Completion rates were very low but reconviction rates for completers were significantly better than for non-completers.

Practical steps often need to be taken to assist young people to attend and complete programmes. Non-attendance needs to be acknowledged swiftly and every possible step taken to re-engage people and to re-run missed sessions to emphasise their value and importance to the programme as a whole. Failure to do this gives a clear message that the missed session was not very important. If the wider safety needs of the community are to be met, good assessment and planning work is required to address a wide range of issues that might undermine programme attendance and completion.

Family-based approaches

Family experiences play a critical role in promoting or reinforcing criminal behaviour by young people. The idea that practice can hope to assist in reducing and in ending offending without involving families directly, no matter their shortcomings, is not credible. Families are often part of the problem and have to be part of the solution for most young people, even for those in residential or institutional care. As a consequence it is important to develop interventions targeted towards parents, siblings or the entire family unit. Effective interventions that involve the family often complement group work programmes and work carried out simultaneously in schools or other parts of the community.

> **What impacts might Roberta's relationship with her mother and her mother's actions have on Roberta's behaviour?**

Families vary widely in their structure – two-parent nuclear, extended, lone parent, reconstituted, same-sex partnerships. Research indicates that structure seems less important than how members view it and the parenting style adopted within it. Biological relatedness, however, should be ignored, particularly in regard to 'missing' family members. Some parents and families will be so overwhelmed by difficulties that they find it a challenge to be positive about any aspect of their functioning. Nonetheless, most will have positive aspirations for their child's future – not to be in trouble, to get a good education, a good job, to grow up well and meet someone nice, have children and so on. It is important to learn to speak the language of the family and to focus on it as a whole. The concept of the young person's life space stresses the importance of understanding the rhythms and routines of family life to improve relationships and to assist new ways of interaction as situations present (Garfat, 2003).

Family work can be difficult to define and can range from general family and youth approaches through to specialist structured family work. Four broad categories of family-based interventions are associated with effective outcomes with children and young people: pre-school education programmes, home visitation provision, parent training and structured family work. Early years intervention is discussed in Chapter Five. Reviews of direct family work and parent training with adolescents show promising outcomes.

Parent training courses aim to help parents respond more constructively to young people, to use discipline less harshly and more consistently and to manage conflict situations better than with control groups. By the time a child reaches adolescence, both the child and the parents are following well-established patterns and are more resistant to long-term change (Patterson et al, 1992). The most promising parent and family-based interventions combine training in parenting skills and education about adolescent development and the factors that predispose young people to criminal behaviour with other approaches such as social and problem-solving skills for young people, proactive classroom management and peer-related programmes (O'Donnell et al, 1995). Effective programmes typically include exercises to help parents develop skills for communicating with their children and for resolving conflict in non-violent ways.

The Adolescent Transition Programme (Irvine et al, 1999), for example, aimed to improve seven classic parenting skills: making neutral requests, using rewards, monitoring and supervision, making rules, providing reasonable consequences for rule violations, problem solving and active listening. Sessions, conducted weekly for 12 weeks in groups of 8-16 parents, follow a skills-based curriculum. In a randomised controlled trial involving 303 families over a four-year period, parents in the programme reported a lower tendency to over-react to their child's behaviour, greater diligence in dealing with problem behaviour, less depression and lower levels of daily anti-social behaviour than the control group. The more sessions a parent attended (many did not complete the 12-week programme), the greater the reported improvements in behaviour. In a rural context, Parenting Adolescents Wisely, a self-directed intervention CD-ROM-based programme, similarly reported positive outcomes.

Solution-focused work is strengths-based and explores knowledge and resources within the family and young person. Practice focuses on the present and future to explore what the individual wants to achieve rather than simply on problems. The intention is to help construct a concrete vision of a 'preferred future', identifying aspects of current life that are closer to this future, bringing small successes to awareness in order to reinforce them. The approach requires regular commitment of time by all family members and attempts to achieve change by opening lines of communication, challenging scapegoating, reducing blame and guilt, increasing empathy and acceptance of differences and making new agreements for being together and resolving problems.

Well-structured family work has shown a positive impact in reversing negative behaviours among troubled youth, particularly those with substance abuse problems (Schmidt et al, 1996). Functional family work or therapy (FFT) focuses on the multiple domains and systems within which young people and their families live. It attempts to target both the family and the individual behaviour of the young people by employing intensive and research-driven techniques aimed at identifying and reversing negative family dynamics that produce problem behaviours. FFT has been shown to reduce the re-offending rates of youth by 25% to 80% in repeated trials, carried out mainly in the US. In one trial FFT with serious and persistent offenders showed that participants were almost six times as likely to avoid arrest (40% versus 7%) than the control group (Barton et al, 1985).

Multi-systemic family work or 'therapy' (MST) can assist families to identify the factors in the young person's social 'ecology', including peers, school and community, that contribute to the identified problems and to design interventions to address these factors. The practitioner is responsible for removing barriers to service access and for drawing on youth and family strengths to achieve sustainable outcomes. Evaluations have shown reductions in re-offending rates of young people persistent in their offending by 25% to 70% in a series of rigorous trials. Eight studies showed very positive results when compared with individual counselling (Borduin et al, 1995). All forms of structured family work approaches, although costly, are likely to cost less than a quarter of the expense of institutional care.

Foster care for young people aged 12-18 involved in serious and persistent offending is likely to provide a more effective alternative to secure or institutional care. Evaluations have shown fewer arrests, less time spent in custody and more time at home over the subsequent two years than controls (Chamberlain, 1998). Evidence from UK schemes suggests that foster families looking after 'high-risk' children experience significant relationship difficulties (Chamberlain et al, 2007). Nonetheless, a high proportion of young people involved in serious or repeat offending placed with foster parents succeed in staying out of trouble during their placement (Utting and Vennard, 2000).

School-based approaches

Few school-based programmes aimed at reducing offending, violent behaviour or substance misuse have been subject to meaningful outcome evaluation. The evidence available indicates that most programmes offered by schools, particularly quick, one-dimensional programmes implemented without strong planning or special staff training, make little or no long-term difference on youth behaviour including offending. This lack of impact by school-based programmes is not due to a shortage of effective models. Research consistently finds that school-based programmes can produce sustained behaviour changes when they are carefully implemented, developmentally appropriate, sustained over time and focused, at least in part, on building social competence (Mendel, 2000).

School programmes can be divided into those that attempt to influence the organisation and ethos of a school such as anti-bullying initiatives, family–school partnerships and restorative practices. The PATHE Project (Gottfredson and Gottfredson, 1986) combined organisational changes in a high school with initiatives aimed at improving education attainment and reducing offending. The organisational changes seemed to have only marginal effects on offending after one year. The most dramatic improvement occurred in official recording of suspensions, which dropped by 14% in one year compared with a 10% increase in a control school. The individual-focused initiatives seemed to have limited effect on offending but did improve commitment of 'at-risk' pupils to education, resulting in improved attendance and attainment.

School bullies are at significant risk of becoming serious violent offenders. A bullying prevention project pioneered in Norway in 42 schools found that by engaging the entire school community (students, teachers and parents), setting and enforcing clear rules about bullying behaviour, and supporting and protecting the victims of bullying, the incidence of bullying was cut in half. Rates of vandalism, truancy and theft in participating schools also declined over a 20-month period (Olweus, 1997). A similar initiative in 23 schools in Sheffield was successful in reducing bullying in primary schools but had only small effects in secondary schools.

On the whole research studies show that schools which are characterised by high-quality classroom management, good leadership and organisation and where young people feel emotionally and educationally supported are best placed to impact on offending and anti-social behaviour. One family school initiative (CPPRG, 1992) aimed at reducing anti-social behaviour, provided promising outcomes including increased academic achievement and social/cognitive development by improving parent–child and family–school relationships. The approach involved a combination of methods including parent training, bi-weekly home visits, social skills training, academic tutoring and teacher-based academic interventions to improve behavioural management. Findings after one year suggested that the programme group were showing signs of better parental involvement in school, increased cognitive skills and reduced problem behaviour compared with controls (Dodge, 1993).

A multi-component social development programme offered schoolchildren six years (grades 1–6) of social training, parenting skills training and training for teachers in classroom management and interactive instructional techniques. Researchers followed the students to age 18 and found that compared with a control group, they committed fewer offences or violent acts, did less heavy drinking, misbehaved less in school and were more committed and attached to school (Catalano et al, 1998).

Community-based approaches

Reducing offending has not been a primary goal of after-school activities and other youth development programmes in the UK. Consequently few studies have measured the direct impact of this work on crime compared with other jurisdictions. Yet logic suggests their potential to curb criminal activity. In Ottawa an after-school recreation programme targeting all children in a local state housing project led to a 75% drop in the number of arrests for youth residing in the targeted project, compared with a 67% rise for a comparison group. A Columbia University study compared public housing complexes with and without an on-site club for boys and girls.

Complexes with a club that also delivered a social skills training curriculum for youth suffered significantly less vandalism, drug trafficking and juvenile crime (Schinke et al, 1992).

Commentators suggest that when community members are asked to help plan and become involved in a programme with young people in trouble, they develop a sense of ownership (Graham, 1998). Involving the community can also make it easier to obtain resources and volunteers to carry out interventions.

Mentoring programmes provide a promising approach to reducing youth offending and to involving community members. However, there are limited data to demonstrate whether, and under what circumstances, mentoring is effective in reducing offending. More rigorous and systematic evaluations are still needed. A study of a Big Brothers/Big Sisters mentoring project revealed that youth assigned a mentor were 46% less likely to take drugs, 27% less likely to drink alcohol and almost one third less likely to strike another person than a control group (Tierney et al, 1995). Mentoring programmes are increasingly popular in the UK as a way of offering maintenance support through frequent contact with a socially positive adult or older peer (Utting and Vennard, 2000). Like restorative practice approaches with young people, positive mentoring can provide a vehicle or a 'lever' for change as part of a wider programme. Mentoring on its own is unlikely to be enough to impact significantly on the offending behaviour of a young person with multiple difficulties persistent in their offending.

Association with criminal peers in the community is a well-established factor in subsequent criminality. Influencing this is difficult and there are few good examples of effective interventions, particularly with gangs. One promising model was based on building a contracted social network between young people and workers who acted as mentors and advocates. Peer pressure was used to exercise discipline and control. Participants were taught to manage anger and to develop personal skills. Serious delinquent behaviour decreased by a third for the programme group compared with a slight increase for the control group over a 19-month period (Baker et al, 1995). Group work and peer work can have unintended consequences and some commentators warn that bringing together young people involved in persistent offending can make them worse without skilled workers and the appropriate models of practice to challenge their criminal attitudes and to assist them to change positively.

A community approach to risk and protection-focused prevention is at the heart of the Communities that Care and other 'whole community' approaches. Developed in the US and Europe, Communities that Care projects are now established across UK jurisdictions. Using a public health model they operate on the assumption that action to tackle priority risk factors for children across a whole neighbourhood will in due course reduce the levels of youth crime (Utting and Venard, 2000).

Although there is an apparent fit between the stated goals of outdoor-based experiential programming and effective interventions that seek to mitigate the effect of risk on vulnerable populations, this link has been neither well conceptualised nor well researched. Intuitively, sport, leisure and outdoor challenge pursuits seem both an obvious and attractive means of diverting young people from crime and a means of preventing crime. Large investments have been made in projects aimed at providing positive leisure experience for vulnerable young people. There is evidence that participation in outdoor recreation programmes can contribute to increased self-esteem, perceptions of mastery and control as well as increased social skills. However, there is no guaranteed linear relationship between participation and outcome. Many programmes have low completion rates, raising the possibility of 'self-selection', with those most positively affected being those least likely to re-offend. Further, returning participants to their original peer environment after short periods of time inevitably means that, for some, there will be a return to criminal or anti-social associations and behaviour (Taylor et al, 1999).

The debate about the relationship between sports participation and crime divides broadly into theories of prevention (or diversion) and theories about the re-integration of offenders. The former tends to express itself in relatively large-scale sports programmes targeted at specific areas, or during specific time periods (for example, summer sports programmes and police-led 'midnight football'). The re-integrative approach is often based on intensive counselling alongside sport or leisure programmes, in which the needs of the young people are identified and programmes adapted to suit their needs that it is hoped will transfer to the wider social context and reduce offending behaviour (Coalter et al, 2000).

Coalter et al's review suggests that location and personnel are important factors in successful outcomes. Traditional facility-based programmes provided by professional recreation and sports staff seem unlikely to have the desired impact. The evidence suggests that people with excellent coaching skills are not necessarily good with difficult young people and those who are skilled in working with difficult young people not necessarily good sports instructors. Effective approaches may require partnership working.

Organisations like the Venture Trust provide adventure and wilderness programmes for male and female offenders aged 16-21, all of which attempt to provide compensatory experiences to help young people avoid crime and maintain desistance. However, there is a shortage of independent evaluations providing dependable evidence on the effectiveness of such programmes. Outdoor wilderness, or adventure, programming seeks to challenge participants in ways that make them rely on or develop personal and social resources. The focus is primarily on personal growth and recreation, with nature providing a setting or context. In contrast, environmental education and other forms of outdoor programmes that sensitise participants to nature and stress the interdependence of humans with the natural world emphasise the engagement of participants intimately with the natural environment (Ungar, 2006). Although professionals endorse programmes at both ends of the continuum between adventure and education, the evidence remains weak that exposure to the environment, in itself, changes behaviour. Few studies have managed to show definitive results linking outdoor programming to the cessation of problematic internalising and externalising behaviours among children (Berman and Davis-Berman, 1999).

Utting and Vennard (2000) report a few examples of sports and adventure programmes that achieve at least short-term reductions in re-offending. Lipsey and Wilson's (1998) meta-analysis identified wilderness and outdoor challenge programmes as among the least effective types of intervention for serious and violent young offenders whether in institutional or community settings, while Barret's review (1996) of programmes cites some reduction in the frequency and severity of offending. Little research has been concerned with longer-term outcomes. The limited evidence suggests that merely introducing young people who offend to sport, leisure or adventure activities is unlikely on its own to reduce criminality, unless it is combined or integrated with other measures associated with effective outcomes. A more recent review (Wilson et al, 2000) specifically of wilderness challenge programmes found moderately positive overall results which suggests, on balance, that these kinds of programmes can be effective for young people involved in crime up to age 21. A social intervention component is recommended to enhance the 'offending' effects of challenge programmes.

Burns (1999) found that as long as supports were provided after the programme ended, recidivism was reduced temporarily. However, when supports were withdrawn recidivism rates rose after two years to levels similar to those expected for the equivalent populations who did not receive outdoor programming. The findings suggest that the mechanism of growth was not the outdoor programme, as such, but the integrated level of support provided during and afterwards.

One important area of uncertainty raised by reviews is an apparent counter-intuitive relationship between outdoor programme duration and outcome. The analysis shows that programme length was not related to the size of the effect on re-offending for programmes up to six weeks long. Programmes beyond this length, however, showed a marked decrease in effectiveness. The information reported in the available studies, unfortunately, is not sufficient to identify which characteristics are most influential. This topic warrants further investigation and provides a warning to practitioners to monitor the impact of these approaches carefully. Proponents of wilderness programmes suggest the importance of having certain 'defining' experiences that result from the challenges a participant must meet and that these experiences are presumed to trigger changes in self-esteem and anti-social behaviour. Lipsey poses the question as to whether these 'defining' moments are influenced negatively by the other components of a youth's overall intervention programme and social circumstances in longer programmes.

The commonly argued rationale for including sport and outdoor activities is as a catalyst within a multimodal programme with young people who offend. A Home Office study (Taylor et al, 1999) highlighted the problem of finding qualitative evaluation techniques that adequately monitor the complex outcomes which most of the programmes aspire to. It concluded that:

> ... all programmes agree that physical activities do not by themselves reduce offending.... All agree that there are personal and social development objectives which form part of a matrix of outcomes. These developments may, sooner or later, improve offending behaviour, but their impact is unpredictable in scale and timing. To expect anything more tangible is unrealistic. (p 50)

It remains unclear which aspects of leisure, sport and outdoor adventure programmes are most valuable. There is limited information on whether certain activities and ways of organising them are more effective than others and whether they work better with certain types of young offenders than others. This lack of a direct relationship between intervention and outcome is not surprising given what is known about complex associations between risk, protective mechanisms and health outcomes, or resilience, in populations facing adversity. A better understanding of the risk and resilience literature can provide a conceptual frame to study the effect of these programmes on participants. However, a conceptual frame sufficiently robust to explain what happens during these programmes and research to demonstrate the successful fit between interventions and populations is lacking. Without this evidence there are serious risks of these kinds of programmes attracting inappropriate referrals.

Residential and institutional approaches

There are young people who present such risks to others and to themselves that containment is required or demanded. Containment will prevent crimes that these young people would otherwise commit on the street and give communities or individual victims respite. While there is evidence to suggest that 'effective methodologies' applied in some institutional settings can result in positive outcomes with serious offenders (Lipsey and Derzon, 1998), existing studies on large residential training schools have consistently failed to show effective outcomes in re-integrating young people who offend or steering them from crime.

A follow-up study on youth released from two training schools in Minnesota found that 91% were arrested within five years of release. In Maryland a study of 947 youths found that 82% were referred to juvenile or criminal courts within two-and-a-half years after release (MDJJ, 1997). In fact, virtually every study examining re-offending among young people sent to training schools in the past three decades has found that at least 50% to 70% of offenders are arrested within one or two years after release. Some reviews conclude that training schools actually increase re-offending in comparison with community-based provision (Mendel, 2000).

Missouri in the US closed all its residential training schools in the early 1980s and replaced them with unlocked residential centres and with a comprehensive series of non-residential programmes including day centres providing intensive education, life skills training, structured family work and intensive mentoring supervision. This matrix of programmes and services produced relatively positive long-term results. A follow-up study in Missouri of nearly 5,000 young people released from residential schools as part of the closure programme in the 1980s found that only 15% went on to collect adult criminal records (Gorsuch et al, 1992).

Despite the substantial investment in the UK in these facilities for young people who offend, only limited outcome data is available in the public domain from institutional or residential school-based programmes. More specialist secure detention facilities, even when aimed at training such as 'boot camps' in the US, show consistently poor outcomes. Recidivism rates range from 64% to 75% in reviews. Despite the overwhelming direction of the evidence, most continue to operate as usual – a clear indication that policy and planning of expenditure and provision can ignore even good evidence.

Conclusion

Programmes for young people who offend make little coherent sense unless they are embedded within locally defined responses to individual need. The division between offence-focused, person-focused and community-focused priorities is often artificial and not necessarily helpful to practitioners. There are risks in focusing exclusively on developing individual resources (human capital) when working with young people who have experienced multiple social disadvantage and exclusion or who have perpetrated serious and violent offences. However, social resources can be most effectively utilised only when the individual also has positive personal resources that can support or resist criminality.

To ensure ongoing reinforcement of learning from programmes and more integrated objectives for supervision, it is essential to generate effective arrangements for ensuring active collaboration with other community agencies and protocols for liaison. It is almost impossible for individual supervisors to achieve such a comprehensive approach to supervision without the existence of good strategic planning and of suitable service pathways to respond to the range of needs and risks presented by this client group.

Adopting social education methods that help young people acquire personal capital or resources while providing assistance in applying them to real social situations looks the most promising approach to developing a strong sense of self-efficacy and supporting human agency and personal responsibility. Normative processes play an important part in people's movement away from crime and a common theme is of getting out of crime because they acquire 'something to lose' through the investment they have made and the relationships they have established (Devlin and Turney, 1999). The challenge facing supervisors is how to help young people move from one social world (pro-criminal) to a social world that is pro-social as they move from childhood to adulthood.

Key questions

(1) Think of a situation in which you planned and made a change in your life. What made you change? What methods did you adopt? What were your reasons for choosing those methods? How well did it (they) work? (Score 1-10.)
(2) Draw an eco-map of your own family, including:
- people (parents, relatives, friends, siblings, social worker)
- feelings or thoughts (dreams, fears, hopes, worries)
- other parts of the network (school, religion, clubs, hobbies, achievements).

Use the same approach for a case with which you are familiar or for Roberta.

Practice exercise

Role rotation: group, family or simulation exercise
Allocate the role of youth justice social worker to act in an advisory capacity, and two roles – a parent and a young person.

Help the young person get into someone else's shoes – their parent, teacher, victim of crime, friend etc – with a view to changing attitudes in a pro-social direction.

Parent: your teenage son/daughter has agreed to be home by 10.30pm at the latest on a school day. S/He arrives home at 11.30pm for the second time this week. You are angry and worried about him/her getting into trouble. 'What time is this to get back?' you ask.

Teenager: you know you are supposed to be in by 10.30pm. But you were hanging out with your friends talking outside the local shops and just forgot about the time. Everyone else seems to be allowed to stay out as long as they like and you don't think there is much chance of getting into trouble – except with your parents. You defend yourself but don't want to make your parent too angry.

Swap roles after a few minutes. Feed back when you have played all three roles at least once. Share the experience from the different ends of the encounter. Draw out the learning points. Encourage participants to elicit self-motivating statements.

A similar exercise can be used with a young person. Using two chairs, get them to sit in one and be themselves. Ask them to describe the day of their offence, morning, afternoon, evening including the offence itself in some detail. At each stage explore what they were doing, thinking and feeling. Ask them to swap chairs and do the same exercise for the victim of their offence.

Further reading and resources

- Harper, R. and Hardy, S. (2000) 'An evaluation of interviewing as a method of intervention with clients in a probation setting', *British Journal of Social Work*, vol 30, no 3, pp 393-400.
- McMurran, M. (ed) (2004) *Motivating Offenders to Change*, Chichester: Wiley.
- Lin, N. (2001) *Social Capital: A Theory of Social Structure and Action*, Cambridge: Cambridge University Press.
- Myers, S. (2007) *Solution Focused Approaches*, London: Russell House.
- Yates, J. (2004) 'Evidence, Effectiveness and Groupwork Developments in Youth Justice', *Groupwork*, vol 14, no 3, pp 112-32.

Intensive intervention

Introduction

Youth crime is multi-determined and its contributing factors relate to the individual, family, peers, school and the neighbourhood. Evidence supports the view that effective intervention must attempt to tackle these multiple determinants of criminal behaviour, as far as possible, in their 'naturally occurring contexts' (Henggeler et al, 1993, p 286) and provide broad-level as well as complex focused interventions, which are community-based, 'multimodal' and holistic.

Re-emergence of intensive supervision for young people in the UK seems to have developed more on the back of growing numbers of young people in detention, secure and residential facilities and associated costs rather than on a conscious evidence-led re-think of philosophy and practice. Nonetheless the political imperative to establish 'tougher', more accountable types of community provision has generated a practice debate on how to ensure that the most challenging young people are made 'secure' in every sense of the word, not simply in their physical location but through the provision of graduated and appropriately intensive supervision aimed at long-term reduction and ending of their offending (Armstrong, 2003). This chapter examines the practice evidence on intensive community supervision and on secure accommodation.

Vignette: serious offender leaving secure accommodation

Beni is nearly 16. He is currently in a secure facility and will soon be leaving. He first came to the attention of social work services at the age of six because his parents were having difficulty controlling him. He has a history of truancy and exclusion from mainstream schooling and has been receiving specialist education. Records show evidence of early physical and emotional abuse and neglect, domestic violence, parental rejection and peer difficulties.

Beni has a prior history of interpersonal violence with previous convictions or accepted grounds for vandalism, assault and numerous petty offences. His most recent offence involved a 16-year-old female unknown to Beni. He approached her in an alley way and used violent threats, exposed himself and touched her breasts and genitals. He has subsequently disclosed numerous unreported incidents of exposure and touching females aged between 11 and 17 over the last three years. This sexually problematic behaviour began around the age of 12. Beni has few social supports but his parents are able to offer him accommodation when he leaves the secure facility.

Definition of 'intensive'

Matching the intensity of supervision to levels of need and risk is a well-established practice principle. However, there is limited research on effective models of practice, their design, delivery and expected outcomes. In some jurisdictions intensive supervision amounts to little more than increased surveillance and monitoring, electronic or otherwise. In most, the practice challenge relates to finding the right blend of intervention, supervision and surveillance along a continuum of provision ranging from high levels of surveillance (an enforcement approach) to achieving long-term social, behavioural and personal change and desistance (a social integration approach).

The sizeable amount of research reported in recent decades on intervention effectiveness has highlighted intensity, duration and sequencing as important features in effective practice. The over-arching principle of reserving the highest intensity for those at high need or risk reflects both the practical concern of using scarce resources efficiently but also heeding research findings that inappropriately intensive intervention can be counter-productive. Findings from meta-analysis have indicated that a median duration of 23 weeks for a structured programme is positively associated with reduction while the number of hours per week below the median of 5-10 hours is negatively associated with reducing re-offending (Lipsey, 1999). Other commentators suggest that intensive programmes should 'occupy 40%-70% of the offender's time over a period of 3-9 months, (Gendreau et al, 1994, p 75) if they are to be effective. These conclusions are drawn from aggregate findings and caution is needed in applying them in any routine way. Nonetheless, they stress that interventions have to be long enough to achieve the intended outcomes, which may be related to acquisition of knowledge, skills, attitude changes and their application to real world situations.

No educationalist would expect young people to acquire knowledge from minimal contact used to reflect on life in general. It is not unreasonable to assume that the acquisition of individual resources will demand substantial time, even if methods of achievement may be different from traditional teaching methods. Different domains of need and risk that are the focus of change will have different 'duration' and 'sequencing' demands depending on the outcome expected. Some will require a relatively short input; others may be very long term.

The notion of intensive involvement for those in difficulty has a common-sense value. Families who have reasons to be concerned about their children, intuitively or consciously, will increase their vigilance and supervision during the day – getting to and from school, closely monitoring and structuring after-school contacts – and attempt to direct evening and weekend activity through safe structured channels such as youth or sports clubs, positive peers and so on. Daytime and evening 'planning' takes a different shape at weekends and holidays when the structure of a young person's day changes, with greater scope for unsupervised time. In situations of concern this will be accompanied by parental 'checks'. Depending on age, night-time 'planning' may be necessary where young people are out unsupervised after 10pm or when they leave the family home after dark. With modern technology many young people will be subject to a form of 'electronic' monitoring through the use of mobile phones: 'Where are you? Shouldn't you be on your way home by now? Shall I come and pick you up?'.

It seems rather paradoxical that a 'wraparound' model of 'security' and 'intensive supervision' operated naturally by families seems not to have been incorporated into constructive models of community-based supervision in the UK until relatively recently. The reasons may be related to an over-professionalisation of intervention that fails to maximise the use of 'natural' family and community practices and resources (see Chapter Five). It may reflect bureaucratisation resulting in multidisciplinary community provision operating within the confines of a 'Monday to Friday 9 'til 5' structure unsuited to the needs and requirements of young people. The absence, until recently, of appropriate 24-hour supervisory provision has been a reflection of a lack of effective strategic planning for the most troubled and troublesome young people.

Families involved in formal state systems who have social network resources can be assisted to provide greater security and intensive support for their young people by structuring daytime, evening and night time supervision, mobilising anyone in the family or network who can make a positive contribution to the plan. Family problem-solving conferences can mobilise family or wider neighbourhood resources to identify strengths and weaknesses in the situation and any need for assistance and to offer plans for action, including restorative activities (see pages 154 and 157). In a graduated system of service provision, family and other community resources can be supplemented by volunteer, professional and/or specialist help as required along a continuum until state help, voluntary or compulsory, may be the dominant input because of the level of need or risk presented.

> Who should take the lead responsibility for supervising Beni in the community during weekdays, at weekends, in the evenings and during the night?

Secure accommodation

UK jurisdictions lock up a greater number of children and young people under 21 than any other country in Europe and imprison them younger than most (Neustatter, 2002). As a consequence, expenditure on young people in institutional provision is high and suggests an over-reliance on creating 'security' for young people and communities through the use of 'buildings' rather than people and social networks. Locking up children in their 'best interests', whether reflecting individual 'pathology' or systemic failure, seems difficult to justify, given its great expense, without prior efforts to provide meaningful and intense security in the community. Nonetheless, there will always be a relatively small group of young people who present such serious risks to themselves or to others that a period of physical security may be required, whatever the consequences for them and the likely outcomes.

The UNCRC 'mandate' to keep young people out of prison emphasises it should be a last resort for those presenting risk of significant harm and for most only after appropriate forms of intensive community-based intervention have been implemented. The reality of UK practice seems very different and the number of young people in detention in UK jurisdictions is little short of a scandal but one that is often not within the power of individual practitioners directly. Nonetheless it is important that practitioners convey to decision makers the existing evidence on the likely outcomes from institutional provision for young people, where re-offending is often between 70%-80% on return to the community from detention (Scottish Executive, 2006). It is equally important for practitioners to raise the issue of the interests of the community versus the interests of the young person to ensure informed decisions operate on the basis of existing evidence.

Research on secure accommodation carried out between 2002 and 2005 (Walker et al, 2006) tracked a sample of young people for approximately two years from admission. Practitioners interviewed were in broad agreement that the main functions of secure accommodation were to:

- protect the young person and the public;
- assess needs and allow young people to take stock of their situation;
- engage with young people and effect change;
- equip young people to move back into the community.

The 53 young people who formed the secure sample, 28 girls and 25 boys, ranged in age from 12 to 16, and all had the complex characteristics generally associated with very troubled and troublesome young people. Most had known significant trauma, loss and disruption in their family life, 10 having experienced the death of a parent; over half were known to social work services before the age of 10; all the young people had been looked after and accommodated at some point prior to admission; and only 17% were admitted from a home base in the community, the remainder from a residential unit (58%) or a residential school (25%). In most cases their difficulties had continued to escalate after admission to residential care, raising as many questions about the effectiveness of the facilities as of the young people. Most (57%) were described as reluctant to 'engage' with service providers. Unsurprisingly, most young people had had a disrupted education and were viewed as putting themselves or others at risk because of their behaviour. In addition to their offending, additional triggers signalling the need for greater 'security' were the likelihood of absconding (a legal criterion in Scotland), spending time with people and in circumstances considered dangerous, excessive drug and/or alcohol use, risk of sexual exploitation and self-harming behaviour.

Not surprisingly secure placements were viewed by practitioners as generally effective in keeping young people physically safe, although many recognised the potential 'contamination' effect of the mixed group of residents and the implicit message to the young person that he or she could only be 'secure' when controlled and/or kept safe in a locked setting. This value of physical safety is reflected in earlier studies (Goldson, 2002b) where young people felt that had they not been admitted to secure accommodation, they may have died or certainly would not have stopped offending.

Admission can provide a practical opportunity to contain young people for the purpose of assessment and planning on how best to address education, health or psychological needs, in particular opportunities to complete structured programmes, to develop life skills and to build self-confidence through physical exercise. However, these potential benefits were offset by the fact that many of the young people had longstanding difficulties, for example in relation to attachment or unresolved trauma and loss, which could not be addressed in a short-term secure placement. Other studies (Neustatter, 2002) have suggested that bullying is endemic in locked institutions as a way of gaining status and a sense of power and control by intimidating others.

The experience can often serve only to reinforce a view of the world as a place where the toughest and hardest win and are respected.

While it is important to make the experience of a locked institution as positive and constructive as possible, being released can be a very frightening experience for young people, especially for those who have little in the way of social resources. The early days of release can be crucial, as those who feel scared and lost will often fall back on what they know – old haunts, contacts and practices. It is important that practitioners help them negotiate the transition to the outside world. At the point of discharge social workers claimed there were benefits for all of the young people in being kept safe with good personal care and regular attendance at school. These benefits, however, were undermined by the disadvantages of distance from home, further disrupted family relations and the associated difficulties of involving practitioners from their home area, making it difficult to begin meaningful family work and structured throughcare. Institutional placements were considered particularly ineffectual in addressing drug misuse.

Approximately two years after admission to secure accommodation, practitioners described the longer-term outcomes for the young people as 'good' (26%), 'medium' (45%) and 'poor' (28%). A further two years on, over 45% of this sample of young people were still in some form of institutional setting including detention or secure accommodation, residential and close support unit, homeless/hostel or residential school. The remainder were living in the community mainly with a parent or other relative or in foster care. Of the small number in independent living (11%), two thirds were considered to be in a 'stable' family situation.

Practitioners attributed outcomes, positive and negative, to the nature and quality of service provision following return to the community rather than to 'gains' made during the secure placement, although better outcomes were noted in cases where there were good transitional practices that gradually reduced the level of structure and supervision over time. A small comparison sample ($n=23$), where secure provision was requested but not achieved, were all living 'reasonably stable' lives in the community a year later.

While the scale of the study demands caution in interpreting the findings, two broad messages emerged; firstly, if young people can be made 'secure' in the community, equally good outcomes are likely to be achieved and sustained at no greater cost (although not necessarily more cheaply); and secondly, for those who are admitted to institutional provision, careful graduated transitional work is likely to be essential to achieving positive outcomes in the long term and to avoid a 'wash-out effect' of any benefits acquired in institutions (community-based principle). These findings are consistent with major international reviews that have concluded:

> A century of experience with training schools and youth prisons demonstrates that they are the one extensively evaluated and clearly ineffective method to 'treat' delinquents…. (Feld, 1998, p 280)

Despite the consistency of findings, political leaders and decision makers rely on institutional controls and penal confinement 'with ever greater vengeance' (p 280).

> If there is one clear finding to be gleaned from the research on youth justice programming in recent decades, it is that removing youthful offenders from their homes is often not a winning strategy for reducing long-term delinquency. Most … facilities … suffer very high recidivism rates. Intensive community-based supervision programs typically produce recidivism rates as low or lower than out-of-home placement … while intensive family-focused or multi-dimensional intervention programs have produced the lowest recidivism rates of all. (Mendel, 2000, p 16)

Removing young people from the community and placing them in locked facilities serves to 'reassure' the public but does not appear more effective than community-based intervention (Mendel, 2000). One YOI governor is quoted as saying 'if I were running a business that had the success rate I and other youth prisons have, then I'd be forced to resign' (cited in Neustatter, 2002, p 28).

Ultimately it is decision makers who remove young people from the community. It is essential that practitioners in weighing up the evidence and formulating a view highlight the substantial evidence indicating institutional provision may well prove unsuccessful. It is important to stress the weight of evidence indicating that a young person's difficulties are often only compounded when they return to the very environment that afforded the initial opportunities for criminal behaviour. This is particularly crucial if no intensive intervention at the family or community level or well-structured maintenance work has been provided prior to admission or if admission is because of the lack of availability of appropriate intensive provision.

It is equally important that those young people who find themselves in detention, secure accommodation or residential provision because of their offending are provided positive opportunities to build their personal resources during their stay and that effective preparatory and transitional work is undertaken to safeguard their return to the community. Family involvement is likely to be critical to sustaining the young person's return to the community and to building on any gains made while in a residential or institutional facility. Families do not choose institutional provision. It is forced on them. As a result they can feel that they are on unequal terms in regard to power and influence.

Effective strategies for engaging families in planning and supervision are likely to include:

- putting families at ease and taking care not to overwhelm them;
- making sure they get all the information they need to be informed partners with a meaningful role;
- taking time to explain technical data, complicated situations, or the political environment in which a decision has to be made;
- orienting family members to their roles and responsibilities;
- presenting written materials to family members in advance (when possible), in their primary language, without jargon;
- identifying shared goals and focusing on these while recognising that agreement on everything is not likely or even desirable;
- evaluating progress together;
- keeping communication open, honest and consistent;
- sharing decision making and working to find win-win resolutions to problems encountered during the process;
- recruiting a diverse team of family members, training and supporting those who are willing to become engaged (Osher and Huff, 2006).

Service standards in UK jurisdictions stress the importance of meaningful action plans (including after- and throughcare plans) to ensure opportunities for developing specific aspects of a young person's life, in particular their health, education and social skills as a way of addressing social and crime-related need. While the living environment is 'artificial', it can provide a platform for developing skills in personal management, in social relationships with peers and with adults in authority, and in understanding the consequences of criminal behaviour for victims, their family and themselves.

All staff, whatever their function or status, have the opportunity to provide adult social models for young people, good or bad. Learning from a structured programme should be directed towards application or 'practice' opportunities within the facility and ultimately towards meaningful opportunities in the community through preparation for transition and return to the community. Too often young people return to the community for short periods on leave with no weekend planning in place to direct their daytime, evening or night-time arrangements; and with no handover work between those responsible in the institution and practitioners or family within community with supervisory responsibility. Without good planning and the positive contribution of family or equivalent, the transition back to the community for young people is a risky one for them and for the community.

Models of positive residential practice are available and community-based practitioners who are responsible for planning have an important role in ensuring that agreed work is carried out and that practical weekend and transitional plans are in place. UK practice is littered with inquiries highlighting the lack of collaboration and integrated planning between institutional and community supervision, particularly with very serious offenders, which in some cases may have contributed to murderous outcomes (SWIA, 2005). There is consensus that even young people involved in sexually harmful behaviour can be satisfactorily supervised and treated in the community, avoiding issues such as family separation and possible exposure to a deviant environment. There is no convincing evidence (Becker and Hicks, 2003, p 405) to suggest that an emphasis on public safety and punishment, that is, removing sexually offending young people from the community, is any more effective than community-based reintegrative supervision and treatment. While there may be other public considerations, in fact, detention or secure accommodation may do more harm than good.

The dilemma facing practitioners is that the practicalities of placing a young person in institutional provision are often much more straightforward, despite cost and poor outcomes, than providing a meaningful intensive supervision service in the community if no formal project is available in the area. Simply making a strong case to decision makers of the value of keeping young people in the community does not provide a solution, without the guarantee that graduated and intensive supervision is available and can be delivered to 'wrap around' a young person and provide help and 'security' within the community.

Secure in the community: 'wraparound' provision

A community-based wraparound approach is intended to provide a comprehensive model, which replaces bricks and mortar by joining, in the first instance, the efforts of significant individuals in the young person's life in the community, where they exist, to provide a comprehensive plan for supervision. In a graduated system 'natural' resources may be supplemented by trained volunteers and as required by trained and specialist professionals. The approach aims to identify and build on the strengths of the young person and their family and to encourage behaviours that will reduce the likelihood of any further involvement with the youth justice system. Drawing from various other service models, the wraparound services approach has been developed more in the US than in the UK. At its foundation are two major beliefs: (a) that families need to be and often want to be involved in helping their family member and (b) that maintaining community living is paramount to sustaining positive change (Bruns et al, 1995).

Wraparound Milwaukee (The Community Resources Cooperative, 1993) was developed as a coordinated system of community-based care and resources, initially, for families and children with severe emotional, behavioural and mental health problems. The features of this care management model are the establishment of a 'provider network' that delivers a wide range of services and supervision. This model includes: an individualised plan of care; a management system to ensure that services are coordinated, monitored and evaluated; a mobile urgent response team to provide crisis intervention services; and a managed care approach including pre-authorisation of services based on contingency planning and service monitoring. Since its inception in 1994, outcomes for youth participating in Wraparound Milwaukee have been encouraging: the use of residential provision decreased by 60% over a five-year period and inpatient psychiatric hospitalisation dropped by 80%. The average overall cost of care per child dropped from more than $5,000 per month to less than $3,300 per month.

Outcomes for young people involved in criminal activity improved significantly, measured by changes in the young person's functioning at home, at school and in the community by the Child and Adolescent Functional Assessment Scale (Hodges, 1994). Rates in reduction in re-offending were also encouraging. Data on offending from the year prior to involvement with wraparound and one year after found reductions in re-offending patterns that were statistically significant (Carney and Buttell, 2003). While the evaluation demonstrated positive findings, it did not uncover a specific relationship between wraparound and re-offending and much more research is needed to define better the elements of these multisystemic or ecological approaches that are critical to achieving the desired outcome of reduced re-offending.

The research findings suggest that young people involved in youth justice with complex difficulties, and in particular mental health problems, who experience integrated and individualised wraparound planning within a system of care are less likely to re-offend and are likely to serve less time in detention or other institutional provision. The model is based on the evidence that young people who are supported to stay in school, who do not run away from home assault other people, or are not picked up by the police are likely to fare better in the long run than those for whom this is not true. It attempts to address the multiple determinants of offending in a comprehensive and holistic way often lacking in traditional supervision practice.

The Wraparound Milwaukee model relies on 'core tasks' that provide a useful directing framework for all intensive supervision in the community:

1. Identify key 'players' in the lives of the young person and family.
2. Adopt a strong non-judgmental family-centred approach.
3. Organise a wraparound 'team' or 'network group' and facilitate a meeting (group or family conference) to produce a creative service plan and meaningful action plan.
4. Identify existing multidisciplinary services, assessing their usefulness to the needs of the young person and family.
5. Prepare a services plan with outcome indicators and resource cost as appropriate.
6. Assess the training needs and arrange for training of key individuals.
7. Prepare a crisis plan and set expectations for unconditional care.
8. Identify gaps and arrange to implement needed services that do not presently exist or deal with contingencies.
9. Manage funds flexibly and work with staff responsible for finance.
10. Deliver direct services as needed.
11. Evaluate the progress of services, holding quarterly reviews, modifying service plans as needed.
12. Prepare transition plans and long-term follow-up.
13. Summarise outcome data for use in programme improvement.

The key social factors or 'domains' for action adopted in the US model include:

- Home/living arrangement
- Family/surrogate family
- Psychological/emotional
- Educational/vocational
- Legal
- Social
- Safety
- Medical (The Community Resources Cooperative, 1993).

These have similarities to the domains included in the CAF and in Onset or ASSET that could equally be substituted as the basis for a wraparound or intensive supervision plan.

As for any form of intensive supervision, the wraparound model necessarily involves the cooperation of a range of individuals in planning, delivering and monitoring intervention. Pulling them together to address the behaviour also serves to focus on that behaviour. The scrutiny provided by family and others in the community places the actions of the young person under intensive but constructive and meaningful observation that has parallels with integrative and restorative practice philosophies (Braithwaite, 1998) and with 'circles of support'.

> **What do you see as the advantages and disadvantages in Beni's case of graduated or wraparound provision?**

The Wraparound Milwaukee model included the young person and their family operating as part of the 'team' or 'action network', which may include a guardian or significant other(s) in the young person's life, community resource people (church members, neighbours, mentors and others as identified by the family), as well as agency staff cooperating to serve the identified needs of the young person and their family. The frequency of meetings of wraparound teams varied with the needs and risks presented by the young person, but all members of the 'team' normally met at least once a month to review progress, goals achieved, to troubleshoot, clarify roles and establish new goals or objectives. Ideally the wraparound team is intended to remain in place until the problems are resolved and the young person exits the programme, turns 18 or moves away.

Findings from evaluation support the hypothesis that young people who received community-based wraparound services are less likely to engage in subsequent risky behaviour. Those who received wraparound services were less likely to miss school unexcused, get expelled or suspended from school, run away from home or get picked up by the police as frequently as the young people who received conventional court services. Parents and guardians of young people involved in wraparound services also reported fewer instances of assault against another people compared with their conventional services counterparts. There remain limitations, however, in generalisability of current findings that are of importance to practitioners.

While the findings suggest important 'intermediate' gains from the approach, the Milwaukee evaluation failed to find strong empirical support that informal networks and wraparound support on their own are sufficient to result in fewer criminal offences compared with those provided by conventional youth court services. The initial wraparound services model relied on informal resources – family, neighbours and the community. These individuals, in many cases, were not accustomed to being involved in addressing the service needs of young people, particularly focused on criminogenic need. The initial model relied almost exclusively on non-professionals with no training provided. In this sense the initial model fits with a family problem-solving, conferencing or other restorative practice approaches which model and reinforce the response of 'healthy' families to adversity. However, the characteristics and circumstances of young people with multiple difficulties regularly involved in crime do not suggest that this wraparound or intensive supervision can be applied in a simplistic or straightforward way without the combination of 'natural' and 'professional' resources. A subsequent study (Pullmann et al, 2006) showed more positive results when wraparound teams were composed of trained individuals who were supervised in their activities.

Intensive support services

The wraparound findings point to the value of maximising natural community resources within a framework of professional direction and support. The aim should be to allow for graduated intensity along a continuum from maximum network support and minimum professional supervision through to maximum professional supervision.

Formal schemes of intensive supervision such as the Intensive Supervision and Surveillance Programme (ISSP) and the Intensive Supervision and Monitoring Scheme (ISMS) are intended to be rigorous community-based interventions provided as an alternative to secure accommodation or to detention for the most active repeat offenders, and for those who commit the most serious crimes. These approaches combine intense levels of community-based professional supervision and surveillance with a sustained focus on personal change, tackling the factors that contribute to the young person's offending behaviour, family work and bringing these together with education and training for employment, drug and accommodation services, mental health provision, life skills, leisure and voluntary sector services. Most schemes include electronic monitoring as part of the programme to provide reassurance to communities through close surveillance backed up by rigorous enforcement.

Responsibility for delivering intensive supervision tends to lie with dedicated teams that work closely with local youth justice and child services staff and other professionals. The amount of time spent on an intensive programme of supervision varies across UK jurisdictions. In ISSP schemes most young people will spend six months on ISSP, with the most intensive supervision (a minimum of 25 hours a week) lasting for the first three months of the programme. Following this, the supervision is likely to continue at a reduced intensity (a minimum of five hours a week and weekend support) for a further three months. On completion of ISSP the young person will continue to be supervised for the remaining period of their order. In Glasgow ISMS orders last about 20 weeks. Movement restriction conditions (MRCs) and types of curfews enforced by electronic tagging can be in place for up to 70 hours per week, for a maximum of 12 hours per day, for around 12 weeks. The average timetabled interventions cover around 28 hours per week.

Evaluation data (YJB, 2007) on young people on ISSP programmes found that most had led chaotic lives, had faced multiple problems, and many were seen as damaged by their early life experiences. The ISSP teams were faced with a major challenge in addressing these young people's complex underlying needs and their related offending behaviour. The comparative data from six-month orders and 12-month orders showed 12-month ISSP completion rates were lower than for the six-month programme, with 32% completing successfully compared with 42% of those on a six-month ISSP. An analysis of those who completed showed that 'serious only' were most likely to complete but that their completions rate was only 42%. Not surprisingly young people were reported to find the length of the 12-month programme a challenge although they reported enjoying the levels of attention.

Although the study had limitations – it was retrospective and had a modest sample size – findings from both the six- and 12-month ISSP programmes showed reductions in the risks associated with re-offending. Analysis of final ASSET assessments found that problem area scores decreased overall, suggesting an impact on underlying personal difficulties and problems. Whether this was as a consequence of the intervention or chance is not possible to establish. For the very intensive and intrusive 12-month programme, levels of non-compliance before breach proceedings were activated were higher than for the six-month group. The findings suggest that long-term programmes may be less suitable for 'serious only' offences. Qualitative feedback from staff suggested that this group presented with fewer underlying problems than the chronic and persistent group and that the main value of the 12-month ISSP was in diverting them from custody. Staff and decision makers were broadly satisfied with outcomes.

The Ohio Intensive Probation Supervision (IPS) programme was developed to provide intensive supervision and treatment services for serious offences by the 14-18 age group. The programme used a team structure approach for supervision, while the basic service model was through service brokerage. The supervisor and the young person together developed a behavioural contract that stipulated the objectives to be accomplished during the period of supervision, covering anywhere from 8 to 14½ months. Outcome data were tracked for 18 months and showed that the IPS programme produced a large reduction in re-offending over the comparison group, resulting in a reduction of 28.7% after the implementation of the IPS programme.

The results seemed to be attributable to four key factors:

1. A graduated sanctions system driven by an empirically validated risk assessment instrument to ensure that only those rated as 'high risk' were admitted to the IPS programme.
2. Intensive services delivered along with intensive supervision.
3. A needs assessment instrument to identify priority needs and to develop and implement plans.

4. The senior colleague in each unit team ensuring that supervisors abided by the classification system in making placement decisions and practised in a manner consistent with the programme guidelines.

Electronic monitoring

It is difficult to be precise about the effectiveness of component parts of any supervision that utilises combinations of offending behaviour programmes, one-to-one supervision, family work, education, leisure activities, etc. The contribution of electronic tagging to the supervision of young people, therefore, is not easy to determine. Tagging of young people remains controversial and the use of an electronic tag has obvious limitations. In itself it is not an active change agent and cannot contribute to changes in attitudes, behaviour, or enhance skills and understanding. While it can restrict, it provides no insight into how or what a young person is doing at home, in school or in the community. If a young person goes missing or breaks their restrictions, the tag will provide evidence of this but will not provide information on what they are up to. There are also legitimate concerns about the risks of labelling and stigmatising or that it will act as a badge of honour, glorifying the status of the young person as an offender. As a tag is difficult to conceal, anonymity and confidentiality may be limited.

Nonetheless, there is some evidence to suggest that the use of tagging may assist in imposing a structure to help break a cycle of very problematic behaviour or give decision makers the confidence to deal with a very serious offence in the community. It is generally agreed that tagging is most likely to be effective in conjunction with other positive social interventions and may buy time for other assistance to impact without recourse to secure accommodation or detention (Whitfield, 2001).

> What would you see as being advantages and disadvantages of electronic monitoring in Beni's case?

Early Canadian studies found no lasting negative impact in 50% of cases and 20% claimed positive benefits including bringing family members together (Mainprize, 1995). Elsewhere families have found themselves as unpaid warders, creating tension within family relations. Overall studies suggest the effect of tagging on offending is somewhat 'neutral' when compared with non-tagged groups (Mortimer, 2001; Nellis, 2006). At this stage there is simply too little rigorous research to indicate any precise benefits for young people and there is no helpful classification available to determine for whom tagging may be more or less suitable. Nonetheless commentaries and practitioners, even those initially sceptical or negatively disposed towards tagging, have suggested benefits in safeguarding young people by providing a reassuring means of allowing other work to be carried out in the community. For those with difficulties in dealing with authority or peer pressure the tag can provide an impersonal authority, avoiding clashes and loss of face by providing the young person with a rationale or excuse to resist peer pressure and to 'opt out' or avoid risky situations.

First-generation radio-controlled technology has been reliable but with obvious limitations. Manufacturers promise great potential from second- and third-generation GPS technology alongside the explosion of interpersonal communication technology such as mobile phones, microchips and electronic security, where satellite tracking will have greater scope for monitoring real-time activity. Several studies from around the world suggest that with adults high rates of compliance can be achieved but that this tends to decline over time (Whitfield, 2001).

Electronic monitoring may be useful in interrupting patterns of offending, helping to deal with peer pressure as a short-term control measure for up to around three months as an additional tool to monitor curfews or support compliance and provide reassurance, particularly to courts. At best tagging may create a window of opportunity for a supervisor to build a working relationship of trust and to assist in building motivation for dealing with more challenging change issues. If successful this can help shift the balance from control to help over time.

Conclusion

There is sufficient promising evidence to suggest that intensity of supervision needs to be graduated to fit the needs, risks and circumstances of the young person and the nature of their offending. It should be the minimum necessary to achieve the objectives set for the individual but in some instances this will be very intensive if operating as an alternative to removal from home or the community.

Intensive supervision in many jurisdictions has tended to be developed with the 'intensity' relating to the restriction and surveillance demands rather than to the intensity of assistance (Petersilia and Turner, 1992). Most effective programmes of intervention for those presenting greatest risk seem to combine intensive monitoring with constructive help aimed at changing behaviour.

Key questions

(1) What experience have you had of providing assistance and supervision to young people returning from different kinds of accommodation or institutions? What types seem to work best? How does your experience compare with findings from research?

(2) Thinking about the case of Beni, or a young person you have worked with, what challenges does returning to the community present for supervising social workers, for the young person, for their family and for the community?

(3) What kinds of situations might be most suitable for intensive involvement of 'natural' social network members and what kinds most suitable for intensive professional involvement?

(4) What resources are likely to be in the young person's home community that might be used to support and maintain positive change on return to the community?

(5) What steps can you take as a social worker to ensure the local authority fulfils its duties to young people and the community?

Practice exercise

Use the behaviour change analysis grid below to examine your own thinking about what Beni may be able to achieve at each stage of the change cycle discussed in Chapter Six (see Figure 6.1).

Behaviour change analysis

	What stage of the change cycle is the client in?	What are the agreed areas of concern?	What are the 'pros' for change at this stage?	What are the 'cons' against change at this stage?	What does this feel like for the young person?	What does this feel like for you, the super-visor?	What are likely to be the most effective methods to adopt?
Stage 1 Initial impressions							
Stage 2 Following first contact							
Stage 3 After a month: planning stage							
Stage 4 Review summary							

Further reading and resources

➲ Burt, M., Resnick, G. and Novick, E (1998) *Building Supportive Communities for At-risk Adolescents: It takes more than services*, Washington, DC: American Psychological Association.

➲ Petersilia, J. (1990) 'Conditions that permit intensive supervision programmes to survive', *Crime and Delinquency*, vol 36, no 1, pp 126–45.

➲ Weaver, A. (2008) *So You Think You Know Me?*, Sherfield: Waterside Press.

➲ Weibush, R., McNulty, B. and Le, T. (2000) 'Implementation of the intensive community-based aftercare program', *Juvenile Justice Bulletin*, www.ncjrs.gov/html/ojjdp/2000_7_1/contents.html

Maintaining and evaluating the change

Introduction

UK policy and associated children's legislation recognises the importance of shared or corporate responsibility in delivering integrated responses for troubled and troublesome children and young people. The concepts of corporate, shared and collective responsibility for provision, however, are under-developed in UK practice. The quality of provision is certainly not being evaluated and measured against a yardstick which has been suggested by some practitioners: that the services should 'be good enough for your own children' (STAF, 2006). Evidence of an effective corporate approach requires demonstration through practice evaluation that provision is being delivered towards staged, sequenced and maintained change.

Any plausible theory of change and change management should ideally attempt to incorporate and encompass the entire social 'ecology' in which the young person is located, including family, community, school and employment. This is particularly true for those making a transition back to the community from residential provision, secure accommodation and detention.

Few studies have focused sufficiently on the impact of significant life events on the performance of adolescent support networks (Cotterell, 1996) or on their views on what makes a difference to longer-term outcomes, including desistance from crime. While there is practice literature on maintaining positive change and supporting long-term desistance from crime with adults that is helpful for youth justice, the best practice evidence lies in research on throughcare with 'looked-after' and 'accommodated' young people. This chapter explores practice issues of maintaining change over time and the place of practice evaluation and evidence-led practice in supporting effective desistance from crime.

Vignette: reformed young person

Maqsood is just over 16. His legal supervision is completed and he has not committed any further offences in the last six months. You have been working with him and his family for a year.

Think about what factors you would want to address in a final review.

Throughcare: maintaining change over time

The importance of a sense of personal integrity reinforced by meaningful social integration is a key feature of healthy adolescence. Most young people under the age of 18 involved in serious or very persistent offending are likely to have been subject to some form of compulsory measures under children's and criminal legislation.

Young people in public care, including those involved in offending, are generally at high risk of social exclusion which has come to mean personal, social and material disadvantage and marginalisation (Hill et al, 2004). The most challenging and difficult young people tend to have multiple difficulties including poor educational achievement/qualifications, to be homeless, to experience unemployment and mental health problems, to have periods of dependency on benefits, to be likely to become young parents and to experience loneliness and social isolation; all in addition to offending and its consequences (Dixon and Stein, 2005). These difficulties can be further compounded for young people from minority ethnic backgrounds who may also experience identity problems derived from a lack of knowledge, or contact with family and community, as well as the direct impact of discrimination (Barn et al, 2005).

While it seems attractive at face value to adopt a social inclusion approach as a conceptual frame focusing on risk factors and poor life chances, this may mask differences between groups of vulnerable young people. The literature on looked-after young people along with literature on desistance from crime suggests that promoting personal resilience and social capital may prove more meaningful as a central organising concept than social inclusion (Schofield, 2001). Both social capital and personal resilience are 'developmental assets' that can improve a young person's ability to overcome personal difficulties and withstand stress, a key factor in adolescent coping (Gilligan, 2001; Daniel and Wassell, 2002).

The development or 'banking' of social capital has been highlighted as an important part of an effective response to helping young people access positive and durable support in their lives as and when they need it. It is important to recognise, however, that there can be negative features to social capital. Families, schools and communities, for example, can exclude as well as include and reinforce oppressive hierarchies of power within social networks based, for example, on age, gender, race and class. *Planned maintenance*, particularly throughcare or aftercare provision, can assist young people in acquiring life skills and further develop positive social networks and relationships, build self-esteem and experience a sense of personal control over their lives. Descriptive typologies tend to identify services supporting successful transition as including life skills, mentoring programmes, transitional housing, health and behavioural health services, education services and employment services (Courtney and Terao, 2002).

A 'corporate' model of practice is slowly emerging in the UK for looked-after and accommodated young people. A key to the model is a designated or lead professional carrying statutory responsibility for coordinating and directing the involvement of a range of agencies. This has been associated with a shift from informal interagency links to more formal agreements specified by needs assessment in order to establish 'pathways' geared to young people's requirements. There is always a danger in more formal approaches of underplaying the contribution that even fragmented or problematic families can bring to planning and ongoing support, given that they are likely to have an 'influence' whether practitioners like it or not. Their involvement should not represent an 'either/or' situation.

Finding the right blend of formal and informal supports is a challenge for practitioners. One guiding principle is that professional or formal provision should not attempt to do what informal networks can do either on their own or with professional support. In reality it is only informal supports that are likely to be active across a 24/7 spectrum of the young person's life or be available speedily in crisis or be there after 12 months' duration. The practical challenge is how to assist the young person in building positive informal social resources and to top these up if necessary. An important objective in sustaining change over time is to increase personal confidence and a sense of control by maximising natural resources. This will require new social opportunities, for example to contribute to their own community or by providing some assistance to other young people.

> How would you end your involvement with Maqsood as a social worker and reinforce the role of other parties who will be helping him from now on?

Research on young people leaving residential care has identified three distinctive groups of young people following transition to the community (Sinclair et al, 2005; Stein, 2005) – those who 'moved on' relatively successfully, 'survivors' and those described as 'victims'. The group who 'moved on' successfully often had some stability and continuity in their lives, including secure attachment relationships and a sense of their family relationship/care history; they had achieved some educational success; and their preparation had been graduated and planned.

Those viewed as 'survivors' had experienced a great deal of instability and disruption in their lives including further disruption when in residential or institutional care. They often had no qualifications; experienced instability in accommodation or homelessness; were able to attract only low-paid casual and unfulfilling work or experienced unemployment. They often experienced problems in their relationships through patterns of detachment and dependency. Many had a positive sense of self as having had to do things 'off my own back'. This sense of self-confidence had grown from the tendency to think that the many problems they faced had made them more grown up and self-reliant. This perception of self held even when contradicted by the reality of high degrees of agency dependency for assistance with accommodation and money and personal assistance.

Those young people classified as 'victims' were the most disadvantaged and had the most damaging pre-residential care family experiences which had not been compensated for by formal intervention or care experience. The associated disruption to their lives, especially in relation to their personal relationships and education, combined with a cluster of longstanding emotional and behavioural difficulties, problems at school and offending (Wade and Dixon, 2006). This group of young people were the least likely to have a positive relationship with a family member or carer. Their life chances were seen as very poor; they were likely to face unemployment, become homeless and have great difficulties in maintaining accommodation; to be lonely and isolated and to have mental health problems.

While the concept of 'victim' may not be an entirely helpful one, the characteristics of these young people leaving residential provision mirror many if not most of the characteristics of the most difficult young people involved in youth justice who have experienced out-of-home placements (Whyte, 2004). The greatest concern from these studies was the sense that existing models of throughcare and aftercare provision seemed unlikely to be able to help these young people overcome their very poor starting points.

The findings highlight the size of the challenge facing youth justice and childcare practitioners with responsibility for planning for the crucial transitional years of 15–18 and beyond. The evidence suggests that having personal and professional throughcare support can make a real difference, particularly in establishing a meaningful social network and stable accommodation, both of which are crucial to mental health and well-being (Dixon and Stein, 2005). There is evidence to suggest that buddying and mentoring, including peer mentoring, may assist in maintaining positive change by providing ongoing non-professional support (Osterling and

Hines, 2006). However, the empirical evidence remains equivocal and these should be used carefully as part of an integrated package of provision. Family network contacts, where they exist, provide a major source of support, but equally can prove very problematic for some young people as many families themselves need ongoing assistance to provide support for their young people (Sinclair et al, 2005).

Improving outcomes for young people involved in offending requires quite sophisticated staged responses and well-structured throughcare, aftercare and maintenance provision if they and their communities are to be safeguarded. This should include:

- opportunities for gradual transitions more akin to normative transitions;
- throughcare and aftercare support, especially for those with mental health problems and complex needs;
- good quality services to compensate for their damaging pre-admission experiences, in particular assistance to overcome educational deficits and to establish employment skills;
- family or social network assistance.

Nine quality indicators for best practice as identified by throughcare practitioners

1. Young people's active involvement in preparation and planning
2. Throughcare preparation as a long-term and continuous process
3. Assessment, planning and reviews that are well managed and independent
4. Accessible arrangements to meet the health and well-being needs of young people
5. A range of suitable accommodation options with appropriate support
6. Financial support during the transition to independence
7. Education, training and employment support and provision to achieve positive education outcomes and routes into education, training and employment
8. Management of risk – assessment, support, reviewing and monitoring of young people who may or may not be convicted offenders
9. Quality assurance and development of services as part of an integrated system for evaluating and ensuring quality (STAF, 2006, p 7).

Few would question the ambition in these principles. However, putting them into practice and resourcing them requires a corporate effort beyond the power of individual practitioners. Both anecdotal and empirical evidence suggests that, in reality, most young people are 'fitted into' existing services and what is available rather than into needs-led provision. As a consequence there is a tendency simply to 'allow' many of the most difficult young people to pass from childcare to justice provision, whether or not this is likely to be a more effective way of reducing their re-offending and safeguarding the community.

The interface between youth justice provision, children's services and adult justice provision needs to be improved if perverse 'incentives' to pass young people on to adult justice are to be reduced, for example where secure accommodation is paid for by local government and detention is paid for by central government. Practitioners' influence on their organisational context, in particular resource management, strategic planning and ultimately court and other decision making, is crucial. This can only be achieved by effective monitoring and evaluation which generates practice evidence to assist strategic planning and to establish more effective pathways tailored to individual needs and the presenting risks of young people involved in crime.

> For how long do you think aftercare and maintenance work with Maqsood should continue?
>
> What do you think Maqsood will expect and would prefer?

Monitoring and evaluation

There is a growing expectation that practitioners and managers will work to introduce a practice culture in which interventions are influenced by evidence-based evaluation. If evaluation is to become rooted in a culture of practice, it is important to build on the day-to-day ways in which practitioners review and make evaluative sense of their practice activities (Shaw and Shaw, 1997). This, in turn, requires a practical system whereby regular monitoring and reviewing of young people's needs and risks, individually and in aggregate form, can be used to provide data for service planning, delivery and for the development of service pathways.

Social work literature has always stressed the importance of evaluation as an essential ingredient of good practice. This should include basic feedback data from those in receipt of services through to data from systematic case reviews as a platform for continuous improvement. However, without good data, whether generated by internal self-assessment or rigorous and systematic external appraisal, there is no practical way to know if young people are being advantaged or disadvantaged by provision nor of identifying unmet needs and service gaps and shortfalls.

Data gathering can be improved by electronic means. This requires a major investment in technology and more importantly an investment in dedicated administrative or research support to maintain and interrogate systems. The development of comprehensive databases for core information and outcome data requires it to be captured in standardised formats to monitor it as part of routine practice. It is easy to say that all formal interventions should have in-built mechanisms for monitoring operations, whether through staff supervision or practice reviews, to enable service delivery to be adjusted when necessary. In real world practice these mechanisms have to exist and will only work if they assist practitioners in doing their job better.

Monitoring is primarily about processes and for verification purposes. It involves routine gathering of information in order to know what is happening. Monitoring data is essential for any process of quality assurance (QA) to embrace all the activities that go into producing an effective outcome. This requires data on inputs (the resources invested in a planned activity) and outputs (what the planned activity has done) and a practitioner and management commitment to gathering and using data at all levels of the organisation.

Agency monitoring should be integral to the design of planned intervention and may include a range of aspects that focus on:

- profiling information on young people who have accepted and those who have 'rejected' the planned activity;
- the adequacy of resources and services;
- whether interventions were delivered as planned by appropriately trained staff;
- attendance and completion rates;
- levels of participation or compliance;
- the methods used;
- adherence to activity or programme plans or manuals and planned style of delivery;
- whether the dynamic need and risk factors are matched by those targeted by the planned activity;
- staff continuity;
- staff selection, training, support and supervision.

Evaluation involves finding out whether the planned activity is achieving its objectives and involves measuring outcomes (the product of inputs and outputs). It is likely to require collecting non-routine information in addition to routine data and may require specially designed measurement tools.

The general expectation is that evaluation of effectiveness in youth justice will ultimately be judged by re-offending data. Re-offending rates, while important, are not straightforward measures and many intervening variables can influence outcomes. It is equally important to use interim and 'proxy' measures to demonstrate that the planned intervention is doing what is intended in meeting need and building the young person's resources (human capital). This will require providing evidence of the acquisition of knowledge, changes in understanding and attitudes and acquisition of skills as part of equipping young people for change. These measures can show change over time against stated aims and objectives and possibly impact on the perceived need and risk targeted by the planned activity.

There are a number of practical methods for gathering data routinely for evaluation that could provide evidence for practice reviews, including:

- changes in knowledge and understanding over time;
- attitude and behaviour changes (including skill development) which are linked to the approved activity's objectives;
- feedback from young people, family members and significant others where appropriate;
- feedback from the range of staff delivering services;
- service shortfall and unmet need;
- re-offending, re-referral or reconviction rates.

While most ongoing practice evaluation will be undertaken internally, as part of establishing progress with individual cases, the information, if made available in an aggregated form and shared between colleagues, can contribute to a process of continuous improvement and inform practice development over time. Local authorities have difficulties collecting up-to-date statistical information and outcome data. Despite this, many practice agencies and local authorities are actually awash with information, much of it never used to support continuous improvement because the purpose for gathering it is not necessarily clear in the first place. More importantly, data are seldom intended to be used simultaneously for individual case reviews and for strategic resource decision making. The contribution of a person to 'champion' evaluation has been established as crucial to programme integrity and to positive outcomes (Lispey, 1992) whatever their background – administrative, research or practitioner.

Evaluation is not value-free, and short- and long-term goals are inevitably directed and influenced by values and 'pressures' within the work environment. Practice in youth justice is subject to many value conflicts and is constantly open to political manipulation. Sound evaluation is only possible if practice or service aims and objectives are clear and measurable. Acronyms such as SMART (Specific, Measurable, Achievable, Relevant and Time-limited; see Talbot, 1996) or SMARTER (Specific, Measurable, Achievable, Relevant, Time-limited, Evaluated and Resourced) exhort practitioners to incorporate core and rigorous data gathering into their day-to-day practice. Some core criteria have to be set in advance to establish outcomes. It is also important to have a team or agency commitment to applying the same data standards to all aspects of work. It is a management responsibility to establish a realistic baseline for measuring progress to avoid a culture of blame.

Some government inspection reports have been guilty of noting deficits in practice – for example, 30% of supervision plans or assessment reports are unsatisfactory – without reference to any 'logic model' or strategic plan which connects baseline measures, priorities, inputs, outputs and outcomes to available staffing resources, skills, capacity, practice models and service demand. If the baseline is 100% satisfactory performance then a 30% shortfall is indeed a major deficit. If a realistic base measure is 50% then 30% poor performance could be seen as a success, particularly if it is better than planned. The development of national service standards can help. Paradoxically, they can equally support minimalist approaches if measurable objectives for provision are absent. Meeting minimum standards is often sufficient to ensure contact and to hold young people to account for supervision or 'responsibility' purposes but will seldom suffice in achieving change objectives. Effective change-related practice requires matching resources capable of achieving the outcomes set to resources that provide for relevant duration, intensity and sequencing of intervention(s).

Poor management practices can expose practitioners to external scrutiny without ever having established baselines for 'premium' change services or when minimal contact to meet 'standards' is expected. The comments are not intended to excuse practitioners but are simply recognition that in youth justice, the organisational context is as relevant to practitioners as the social context is to young people. Practitioners have to find ways of acknowledging the limitations of their agency and if possible to challenge them.

In an ideal world, following assessment, each young person would be directed along pre-defined service pathways in which the duration, intensity and sequencing of existing provision are then tailored to individual needs, as well as to levels of risk assessed. Information from standardised tools or other sources has rarely been used to generate aggregate data on interventions to provide information on the practice methods that are actually to be adopted, expected usage levels, likely service shortfalls/unmet need and the consequent requirements for service development. This gap in using data may reflect practitioner resistance or simply a disconnection between different organisational levels in youth justice – practitioners, middle/resource managers, strategic planners and senior managers. Middle/resource managers and strategists often lack experience of the potential uses for practice data for prioritising and responding appropriately to need and risk (Baker, 2005).

It is often not until standard data are being generated on young people's needs and analysed that it becomes clear how they can be used systematically to assist practice. All three levels – practitioner, middle/resource managers and strategic/senior managers – can operate in a self-occupying and autonomous manner without connecting 'intelligently' to other levels of the agency functioning. Effective data flow requires an understanding at each level of how each impacts on the other – 'what do I have to do to do my job well that will help others do theirs well, which in turn will help me do mine better?'.

Much has been written about 'top-down' or 'bottom-up' organisations. Professional organisations have to generate interdependent relationships, without which no one can perform their role effectively. In practical terms standardised assessment data on needs and risks should be used explicitly to establish action plans, at case reviews and at the same time harvested for managers and strategists to allow some indication of service demand and usage, practice achievements, services shortfall and gaps, on which new developments can be planned or realistic baseline standards set. In public services not everyone can be provided with a premium service. It is essential, however, that recipients know to what extent the services they are provided with are 'fit for purpose'.

Practice monitoring and evaluation can operate as the 'glue' to the integrity of individual interventions and agency provision. Practitioners cannot achieve this on their own. Equally, strategic planners cannot develop evidence or needs-led provision without data from practitioners. Middle/resource managers are the conduit through which the quality of practice data should be monitored and through whom data should flow to strategists. Achieving this in practice remains a major challenge for all service agencies.

Measuring change: what are good outcomes?

Ongoing evaluation of outcomes from practice is important for addressing basic questions such as 'can learning from research or experience be put into practice?', 'is it likely to work?', and if so, and most importantly, 'is it likely to make any positive difference to the life of a young person and their family?'.

Evaluation assumes that objectives for a given intervention or supervision programme can be specified – immediate, short and longer term – delivered as planned (programme integrity) and measured and aggregated in some way. The basic thinking that underpins an action plan is the same for service planning in general and tends to be directed by a common set of questions that require some defined ambition and a standard or measure that can be aggregated.

Questions for measuring success

What is the service intervention trying to do?

What difference is it trying to make?

What activity needs to be undertaken to achieve these outcomes?

With whom as partners and over what period of time?

What is the evidence that it can achieve these outcomes?

What resources are needed to do more or to do differently?

How will we know if it has made a difference?

What is needed in order to collect evidence about the difference intervention is making?

The evaluation 'gold standard' is claimed for randomised controlled trials and experimental designs where the effects of an intervention are assessed in relation to 'no intervention' or to a 'standard' approach and then a comparison made (see Chapter Three). This allows for a measure of the effect or impact of method A compared to method B; for example structured family group work compared to standard supervision (however defined), providing A and B are sufficiently different to have a differential effect.

Few practice evaluations in the UK meet this standard and it is not the intention here to suggest that practitioners can easily promote a randomised controlled trial approach in their day-to-day work. Nonetheless, familiarity with basic research methods can maximise the opportunities for data generation as part of meaningful day-to-day practice. What is important is that practice is 'intelligent' enough to generate data that allow some level of ongoing evaluation that can be shared with recipients and with colleagues in formal case reviews. At the same time, if these practice data can be presented in a format for aggregation, despite their limitations, they could be harvested and utilised to help establish patterns and trends to assist practitioners, managers and strategists to improve performance and service development. They can also be shared in some form with members of the community.

A detailed examination of research methods is beyond the scope or intention of this section. However, commonplace methodologies that could be used in practice, if the circumstances allow, might include:

1.   Follow–up (post-test) single case data on a group (caseload) of young people, which are useful as formative feedback to users and for supervision purposes, even though this will not produce rigorous outcome data.

2.   'Before and after' single case or group data, which will allow for some indication of 'distance travelled'. This is important in any change endeavour even though outcomes cannot be ascribed exclusively to the intervention.

3.   Post-test data: two groups or cohorts of young people using random allocation of young people to different interventions. This is unlikely to be very realistic in practice except possibly where there are waiting lists for a structured programme or specific intervention and 'standard' supervision or 'check in' is offered instead.

4.   Pre-test and post-test data using two groups (or two different caseloads) of young people as comparison groups; random allocation would be preferable.

5.   Repeated measures: two groups of young people randomly assigned the same intervention at different times.

6.   Time series measures on a group of young people, normally subject to multiple observations rather than formal tests, although could be both, over a period of time corresponding to statutory reviews.

7.   Single-subject experiments that require repeated measures of the same person before, during and after the intervention could be done on one caseload or on a team's workload.

A key aspect of practice crucial to the development of a culture of learning is the importance of engaging young people and their families in systematic evaluation of their own learning, change and progress. Relatively little research has been done on the views of recipients of services but the available studies suggest that, in addition to the value of the relationship itself, young people value being listened to and being actively involved in decision making and in communication that does not stress power differentials (Hill, 1999). Reviews, monitoring and evaluation provide opportunities for young people to have their say, to set priorities and to influence practice planning of services.

It is fairly commonplace to use tools or aids in practice whereby young people and family members are asked to complete some form or other before and after a session or sequence. Often, however, these contain free text that cannot be aggregated. Practitioners can utilise a continuum of measures ranging from a crude Likert scale (for example, rating 1-5 or 'smiley faces') that captures some measure of learning, interest, enjoyment and satisfaction with the experience through to completing systematic psychometric testing as part of a formal evaluation.

Young people can be supported to score themselves on completion of a case simulation or knowledge 'test'. If this can be done on a computer with a programme to generate an automatic individual score it can be used to feed an anonymous score to a database for group analysis. Yet so often this kind of practice data, even when gathered, are not in aggregate form or used for evaluation or planning purposes for individuals or for the service as a whole. To do so requires shared expectations across a team or agency and someone (an 'intelligence' or data champion) to gather the data regularly, analyse them and feed them down and up.

Translating information into Likert scores or similar numerical measures need not replace open text recording, nor be seen to reduce the purpose of practice to number counting. Nonetheless, it can generate, albeit crude, measures to assist practitioners and the agency in detecting patterns and trends of client change over time. It can also provide data on the possible effects of different types of provision without denying the limitations or over-stating the weight of the evidence produced.

For many practitioners, ongoing evaluation is likely to involve a single case approach. This can involve systematic observation as part of the practice process, setting up a notional baseline measure of a problem and providing a contextualised understanding of the nature of the problem in a young person's life, as part of an assessment and planning process. While this has its limitations, systematic observation is a valid evaluative method for the study of hidden or elusive domains, like motives, memories, thought processes, withheld actions, feelings and emotions that accompany overt behaviours. Structured tools such as Crime Pics II (Frude et al, 1998) can equally assist a young person in examining perceived changes overtime while providing scored data for the agency.

> In the case of Maqsood, what issues are likely to require maintenance?
>
> Who might help in this, if not you, the supervising social worker?

The use of behavioural approaches can proceed by counting and 'measuring' incidence, prevalence and patterns of problem behaviour such as offending.

However, case study evaluation can generate narratives and tell stories behind quantitative numbers, capture unintended impacts and effects and illuminate dimensions of desired outcomes that are difficult to quantify (Patton, 2002, p 152). User-led practice should result in outcome measures that pay attention to the client's view of service delivery that helps to understand them within their social context and reflects the impact of provision on their quality of life.

Simulations offer a rather different design solution for practice evaluation and an innovative method often already included in structured programmes (Turner and Zimmerman, 1994). Soft outcome measures, generated by practitioners, may not meet the 'gold standard' but they can capture what few studies do: those tiny changes in behaviour, like being able to look people in the eye and taking pride in appearance, which denote improvements in confidence and ability. For people who have suffered trauma and loss of ability, soft outcomes can be the building blocks towards 'harder' outcomes (DWP, 2003).

Intelligent social work

It is not so long ago that some commentators in the US (Fischer, 1993) were predicting that by the year 2000, empirically based practice – a new social work – would be the norm. It is certainly true that the empirical practice movement has advanced social work's long and laborious pursuit of the goal of creating a scientifically based profession. However, the gains achieved have been at best partial (Reid, 1994). In 2002, Reid remarked that 'within the profession, science remains on the cultural margins, struggling for a voice and a following'. He suggested that it makes sense to construe scientific practice as only one perspective on intervention, while giving importance 'to … ideas about measurement, data collection and the like that might not fit conventional research notions' (Kirk and Reid, 2002, p x).

It has to be recognised that there is seldom enough secure knowledge to support practice in any precise way other than to provide directionality. One possible solution to such problems is to produce a greater quantity of scientifically tested knowledge and to find ways of increasing its relevance to practice. However, the value and function of mainstream research and evaluation for practice has equally been challenged on epistemological grounds. Critics (Heineman, 1981; Witkin, 1991) have questioned whether or not conventional science is the best way to arrive at 'truth and meaning' in human services. The observation that much professional practice in reality is determined, at least initially, without the help of science is often cited to support such a critique.

The central tenet here is that practice knowledge is socially constructed through human narrative and discourse that is already routine in practice methods. For example, reports for courts or for other decision makers are often described in inspections as good at bringing alive the world of the subject – their thoughts, feelings and actions. Often the subject is the main respondent and source of information and evidence to be worked on. What is often lacking is a more 'objective' view, for example on how typical their criminality is in characteristic, in its operation in time, its enactment in geographical space or its social relationship (see page 33), or when set against local or national crime data; or what harm has actually been caused to victims or the community.

New technology is now creating means whereby additional local sources of information and evidence can be made more readily available to practitioners that may help provide a more 'objective' dimension to assessment and decision-making practice. Police can provide electronic geo-maps of crime – showing time, place and type of crime. This is often used to identify 'crime hotspots' and responses to them. This data if available locally can be used for the purpose of planning youth justice provision. In some European jurisdictions this has been taken a stage further and geo-mapping data on individuals are being used to highlight where and when a young person has been involved in further offending, with police data made available electronically, on a daily basis, to the social work supervisor.

In a study of restorative practices (Dutton and Whyte, 2006), data were generated on criminal activity which mapped youth crime against postcode and time of day. This highlighted that often an effective response to criminal activity in its social context may have less to do with youth justice practitioners and more to do with better school–family links during the day or the availability of street or community workers at crucial times at weekends. It is possible to add 'risk–need' scores from standardised tools to these maps to provide new ways of identifying needs and risks presented by cohorts of young people in a more meaningful social context to guide community and strategic planning. These data, at the same time, may assist practitioners 'make meaning' of individual criminal behaviour within a particular social setting, ensuring that individual crime-focused provision is not isolated from the need for wider crime prevention and community development activity aimed at dealing with structural issues.

Practice information can be used to direct individual responses and the development of better service 'pathways' and priorities rather than relying on ad hoc responses to need and risk. This is particularly important given the tendency to use scarce resources on those who need them least and sometimes to their detriment (net widening), or at times when less resource-demanding and less intrusive responses may achieve similar outcomes.

If effective intervention is to be sustained and evaluated, the practice agenda in youth justice has to operate somewhere in the interplay and application of science, art and values. This requires, among other things:

- a well-qualified workforce within which knowledge and experience are regularly updated by training courses that make regular reference to research both on the nature and development of social problems and on what is known at an empirical level about the effectiveness of different approaches designed to address them and how to evaluate them;
- qualifying courses which, as a matter of priority, address and review the literature on the effectiveness of services and equip students critically to appraise the results reported;
- a system of staff supervision that regularly draws upon research to inform decisions made about cases and projects, and where questions such as 'So, why are we proceeding in this way?' and 'On what evidence?' would be seen as routine professional enquiries and not as a personal threat;
- agency meetings that regularly include references to research on what has been tried elsewhere, locally, regionally, nationally and internationally, when services are being monitored or reviewed;
- a range of support facilities available to assist staff in their efforts to keep abreast of research relevant to their field, such as library facilities capable of delivering books and articles to enquirers, and able to distribute summaries of available evidence, with those in charge of them able to show that such services are regularly used;
- at an attitudinal level, practitioners who take some personal responsibility for acquainting themselves with the empirical evidence on service effectiveness, with a reasonably well-founded expectation of practical support from management;
- collaborative arrangements between practitioners and local and regional universities and research institutes, so that each tangibly influences the work of the other, and within which each group of staff might unexceptionally be encountered in the corridors of the other pursuing common purposes.

Conclusion

Effective practice in youth justice is intended, among other things, to support responsibility and autonomous decision making by young people. In compulsory situations where a young person's choice is generally 'restricted' (Barber, 1991), it is not sufficient to build a working alliance on the basis of 'trust me, I'm a social worker'. It is essential to engage young people and, where possible, their family in 'co-production' by establishing their views, informing them of existing evidence that might point to the most effective way forward, and providing them with ongoing evidence of change.

This approach requires practitioners to be 'intelligent', to have relevant knowledge and to be able to communicate this to a challenging 'user' group. Research over many years has suggested that if the client does not have a shared understanding of what they are involved in, the intervention may well fail (Mayer and Timms, 1970; Gambrill, 2003). Whatever directionality provided by current evidence, critical thinking and efforts to individualise intervention to the person and environment (including culture) of the client remain essential.

Key questions

(1) What features should be included in well-staged throughcare, aftercare and maintenance for the three distinctive groups of young people making transitions back to the community identified by Stein's research?

(2) What advantages and disadvantages are there of adopting a social inclusion approach to risk factors and poor life chances?

(3) The ASSET grid identifies the 'high' and 'medium' scores for 40 young people persistent in their offending.

ASSET domain	Total scoring 3 and 4	Typical service response?
Lifestyle	30	
Family and personal relationships	29	
Thinking and behaviour	34	
Attitude to offending	25	
Living arrangements	20	
Education	19	
Motivation to change	15	
Emotional and mental health	11	
Substance misuse	7	
Perception of self	11	
Neighbourhood	10	
Physical health	-	

Note: n=40.
Source: Adapted from Buist and Whyte (2004)

What do the patterns of scores suggest about the needs of this population in this youth justice team?

(4) Identify what you think a 'typical' or expected service response for those scoring 'high' on each ASSET domain might be; for example, how would you deal with a high score on 'lifestyle'?

Practice exercise

Using a case you are familiar with or any of the cases in this book, design a single case evaluation.

Further reading and resources

⮕   Stein, M. (1990) *Living out of Care*, Ilford: Barnardo's.
⮕   Stein, M. (2004) *What Works for Young People Leaving Care?*, Ilford: Barnardo's.

9

Towards integrated community justice and welfare

Introduction

A key theme underlying changes to youth justice in recent years has been the emphasis on 'responsibilising' young people who offend and holding them accountable for their offending. This theme has rather over-ridden the recognition that young people's ability to desist from crime is often constrained by acute levels of socioeconomic disadvantage and disruption. In practice government policies on child poverty, social exclusion and community regeneration aimed at combating the risks associated with social exclusion and facilitating reintegration have often had limited impact on young people entering the youth justice system. Indeed, youth justice agencies are slow to emphasise that, at best, their practitioners are often only working at the margins of young people's difficulties.

In the absence of clear practice models of shared and corporate responsibility, reintegration is often framed as solely the personal and moral responsibility of young people. This seems to place the onus on them to negotiate, individually or with the assistance of youth justice practitioners, the social risks involved in personal and social integration, with limited acknowledgement of the structural barriers that are posed by the unequal distribution of socioeconomic resources. This final chapter draws on previous chapters to examine case management and the requirements of reflective practice in the context of practice agencies as learning organisations whose aim is to promote social justice as a means of achieving rights and responsibilities.

Vignette: teenager with difficult family issues

Michael is 15. Most of his companions are involved in offending. He has been involved in theft from cars and from local shops and in assaults. His most recent offence involved stealing a car with his friends and 'joy riding', which resulted in crashing the car into a wall. No one was injured but the car was a 'write-off'.

Michael's parents separated when he was three. He and his two elder brothers live with his mother and her partner, who feel they have little control over him. Neither are employed; the partner has convictions for drug-related offences. Michael was seeing his birth father on occasional weekends until a year ago, when visits stopped for reasons that no one will discuss.

Michael's school attendance has been poor in the last year and he has a reputation for being disruptive in class. He is not expected to gain any educational qualifications.

What is important in establishing an effective working alliance with Michael and his family?

Rights and responsibilities

Youth crime is harmful and the objective of reducing criminality is a key priority for youth justice practice with young people who are at risk of poverty, low income and unemployment, education under-achievement, substance misuse, mental health problems and homelessness. Failure to progress or to stop offending presented in reports is often viewed, intentionally or unintentionally, as the result of individual shortcomings in the young person's compliance, attitude and behaviour, without recognition of the social context over which young people have limited influence. Failure to desist and to move towards better personal and social integration is seldom presented as service failure. State decision makers including courts, panel members and professionals have a responsibility to recognise the structural consequences in their decision making and not view practitioners who present these limiting factors as somehow excusing young people's offending or its consequences.

The wide range of initiatives provided or negotiated by youth justice, focusing on recreation, education, training, employment, substance misuse, accommodation and health with the aim of preventing youth crime and social inclusion, are crucial. However, youth justice provision is often disconnected from mainstream provision. Paradoxically, where social context issues are addressed, through partnership initiatives such as 'midnight football' run by the police, they tend to blur the boundaries between crime prevention and social inclusion policies and run the risk of the 'criminalisation of social policy' (Crawford, 1997). It has been argued that 'governing through crime' (Muncie et al, 2002) has the tendency to reinforce the criminal and underplay social inclusion and integration. In more practical terms those responsible for social provision as part of their mainstream responsibilities tend to get 'off the hook' of having to give meaningful expression to their corporate responsibility to the community and to young people who offend.

Over-focusing on individual need and risk factors detached from social risk factors and issues of social capital can confirm and amplify young people's difficulties without resolving them. Practice-related research using ASSET data (Baker et al, 2003) has suggested that initial practitioner assessments often rated individual risk factors as posing a higher risk to re-offending than social risks, despite strong evidence of severe personal and social disadvantage among young people.

Some commentators have suggested the need for a framework of social rights, legally enforceable, to ensure that the inclusion needs of young people who offend are addressed equitably in youth justice interventions. The search for 'transformative' social justice (Fraser, 1997, 2003) would require fundamental changes to the distribution of wealth and resources resulting in more equitable outcomes. The question of how to incorporate 'social justice' as a key driving force within youth justice interventions is often not answered by the critics and is certainly not a straightforward issue for practitioners.

Practitioners cannot postpone their work with young people until better social and structural opportunities are available. Nonetheless, the literature on reducing and ending offending suggests that young people become motivated to move away from crime as a result of changes in how they see themselves, their life chances and changes in the social context in which they make choices. Practice solutions are likely to lie in incorporating the evidence on desistance and personal and social integration within a rights-based agenda framed by UNCRC principles.

> **To what extent do the links between social capital, offending and desistance make sense in Michael's case?**

While these aspirations are likely to be shared by many if not most youth justice practitioners, a detailed debate on structural change is beyond the scope of this discussion (see Muncie and Goldson, 2007). Nonetheless, practitioners have a role to play in creating conditions in which the needs, risks and rights of young people who offend can be made transparent and incorporated into any policy discussion to set better universal targets on the standard of education, health, employment, leisure and recreational provision that young people who offend should have as a right (Scraton and Haydon, 2002, p 312). The task for youth justice practitioners is not simply to provide services, to monitor performance and broker access but also to interrogate the 'quality' of services and outcomes. They often uniquely hold the evidence of the shortfall between need and provision.

The United Nations Committee on the Rights of the Child (Harvey, 2002, p 4) criticised the UK government for its lack of a 'rights-based approach' to policy and practice development. While each UK jurisdiction is different, the drive for better integrated children services, outlined in ECM and GIRFEC, is disappointingly thin in its vision of children's rights. These seem to be assumed as achievable through the outcome of successful joined-up or integrated provision rather than explicitly through a rights-based framework modelled on UNCRC (Monaghan et al, 2003; Williams, 2004).

Recent legal judgments suggest that the same standards and principles as for practice with looked-after and accommodated children and young people should apply to all young people involved in crime. These stress the importance of locating practice within a social education paradigm driven by shared and corporate responsibility for personal and social integration rather than by crude 'responsibilitisation' that is often present in criminal justice practice. Research and policy formulations have highlighted a range of factors that can help vulnerable and risky young people subject to public care or criminal justice measures feel secure and valued, and which can help equip them to become more successful and individually responsible.

Factors that help young people feel secure and valued

- Social skills and a positive adult to turn to.
- Opportunities to experience activity, adventure and cultural, leisure and sports activities.
- Transition and/or pathway planning including ongoing support and practical help from family networks, foster or other carers, practitioners including residential staff, and mentors.
- Continuing support when in detention and on release.
- Staff awareness of financial resources available for further/higher education.
- Continuing financial and practical support while in education.
- Involving young people in decision-making processes.

Source: Adapted from Scottish Executive (2007, p 30); SWIA (2006)

It has been argued that the cost of wasted potential, including the cost of an extended criminal career and imprisonment and the associated costs to victims and the community, alongside the possibility of another generation of children in public care, is 'almost beyond comprehension' (Tapsfield and Collier, 2005, p 4). Government policy recognises that the success of various practice initiatives aimed specifically at individual young people can only be achieved as part of a wider strategy for better integrated services for children and young people. This requires local planning to provide 'more choices' and 'more chances' for those formerly classed as 'not in employment, education or training' (NEET), better quality assurance and joint inspections of services. All of these developments are crucial to give practical meaning in youth justice to the concept of corporate responsibility implied in policy directives.

Youth justice cannot ignore educational attainment as a crucial aspect of investing in young people's desistance from crime and longer-term change. Each step up the education ladder is associated with improvements in health, both mental and physical, employment, income, housing, family life and absence of addiction problems, and lower involvement with the criminal justice system (Jackson and Simon, 2005). This raises a range of key issues regarding education and social development that need to be tackled. A number of these challenges have already been identified in government publications, including:

- greater awareness of the education needs of these children and young people;
- the importance of stability and continuity within education and care settings and improved training for lead professionals, foster carers, residential workers, support workers and associated professionals across youth and adult justice;
- greater clarity on the role and responsibilities for a designated person within schools, residential establishments, secure accommodation and detention;
- the importance of providing flexible and appropriate support before, during and after transitions;
- the importance of physical, mental and emotional health and well-being in facilitating positive education outcomes;
- the need for good quality accommodation, which supports education, training or employment;
- the importance of clear advice and a range of emotional, practical and financial support as these young people make the transition to adulthood and independent living (adapted from Scottish Executive, 2007, p 4).

> How can Michael be expected or enabled to withdraw from
> relationships that seem to be associated with offending?

Joined-up services: case management and managing change

Inspection reports from all UK jurisdictions have been critical of the lack of holistic and integrated service approaches to disadvantage as well as to criminality. If interventions are to be multimodal and multi-systemic, involving different personnel within an agency and between agencies, then the practical difficulties of maintaining sufficient integrity across different aspects of the supervision process are likely to be considerable. This cannot be made into a simple process when implementing complex plans with young people who are reluctant, often damaged and sometimes dangerous, particularly when the multiple objectives can be in tension with one another.

The complexity of responding effectively to the needs and deeds of young people creates a management challenge for practitioners in trying to combine the necessary elements of a plan into a coherent programme of supervision that can support change towards desistance and personal and social integration as a whole. For this reason the term 'change management' is probably more accurate than the term 'case management'.

Effective relationships are at the crux of effective practice. Building an effective relationship or working alliance with the young person and all other 'interested' parties requires good communication and interpersonal skills. While change-supporting relationships lie at the heart of effective practice and are a necessary condition of it, they are not sufficient. Those relationships must be purposeful and used to influence and direct positive improvements in the young person's capacity for change – their human and social capital. The practitioner's role as change or case manager requires skills in assessment, planning, implementation and delivery, as well as monitoring and evaluation of progress.

The term 'case management' does not describe a single approach to supervision, but rather a family of related approaches in which resources should follow on from plans based on assessments of risks and needs. The concept generally implies one lead person with overall responsibility for deciding how planned objectives will be met and for ensuring that arrangements are in place to deliver the plan. At the same time others, often from different organisations or disciplines, are required or expected to deliver specific inputs to achieve some of the identified and measurable objectives. Collaborative case management formalises a process through which, in principle at least, the lead practitioner can work together with other providers to ensure a more coherent service and in which skeletal service pathways, ideally pre-established against need and risk requirements, can be activated or negotiated and brokered to complement direct face-to-face work undertaken by the change or case manager.

There is little brokerage a case manager can do if services do not exist or if they cannot be accessed easily. For a service pathway concept to be effective, it requires special access status for the case manager to housing, leisure, drug and mental health, education, careers and employment provision, which is seldom the reality at present. It is unlikely that this can be delivered without a community planning and strategic management framework and pre-established service pathways supported by protocols or service-level agreements. Agencies with corporate responsibility should be planning in advance against predicted 'demand' for the kinds of assistance required by these young people in ways that promote joint working and not simply 'pass-the-parcel' provision.

In reality integrated practice continues to prove very difficult to deliver with any consistency. Barriers to good case management are equally well documented as including:

- lack of time to build working alliances, to meet, to discuss and to contact the right people;
- over-burdened practitioners with work or caseloads that are too heavy;
- lack of resources and services themselves;
- lack of commitment on the part of partners to contribute despite protocols if these exist;
- differences in philosophical stances or ways of working with young people who offend;
- professional egos, attitudes and turf issues.

> **What might be the practical barriers to effective case management for Michael's case?**

A review of case management practices in probation (Partridge, 2004) provides a useful reference point for considering models for multidisciplinary provision in youth justice. Young people might be supervised in partnership with their parents, during the weekday by school staff and in the evenings and at weekends by youth justice or community education staff and, in more extreme cases, monitored electronically at night by others. All of this activity has to be pulled together into a meaningful whole by the supervisor if their work with the young person and family is to succeed.

Three useful models of case management were identified from the practice review: 'generic', 'specialist' and 'hybrid' models. Each had different benefits for different 'stakeholders' including management, practitioners and those involved in offending. Generic models involving a wide range of offenders offered greatest flexibility for senior management, particularly where staff resources were limited or spread across a rural or geographically dispersed area. Working with a mixed caseload seemed to enhance practitioner motivation. It supported continuity of contact and ensured staff retained a knowledge and overview of the various supervision stages, activities and processes.

A specialist model that attempted to separate out the different functions between different specialists provided some advantages for the coordination of service delivery and the targeting of specialist resources. It also allowed these to be better focused on key supervision stages, particularly with those considered the most 'risky'. Benefits included better monitoring of national standards, delivery of service priorities and increased professional accountability. Specialist approaches also created some efficiency gains by allowing different staff to concentrate on specific functions, using their specialist skills in relation to specific kinds of issues or types of offences. However, by separating tasks and responsibilities into specialist functions there were equally disadvantages such as boundary management and communication issues.

The important message for managing youth justice practice from this review was that the greater the level of task separation and fragmentation in a model, the more the client seemed confused by the range of different staff they saw at different stages of their supervision, about who was overseeing their order and who they should contact if they experienced a crisis. The client was, not surprisingly, more likely to build trust with a case manager if they saw the same person consistently over a period of time, particularly during the initial stages.

While it is the ideal for one supervisor to oversee a young person throughout their entire period of supervision, this is often impractical due to resource issues and staff turnover. Hybrid models attempt to compensate for this by providing a balance between generic and specialist elements, in order to maximise continuity of contact. Hybrid models tended to adopt a more integrated team approach, where at least one team member knows what is happening to an individual at each stage and is able to update other team members. The expectation is that hybrid approaches can help alleviate some of the effects of staff turnover, shortages and sickness absences by allowing regular contact with a small group or 'team' of people aware of the young person's circumstances and so create a consistent, familiar and supportive environment for them to learn, to be motivated and to complete their order. In a team setting, the named case manager was considered 'ultimately' responsible for assessment, progress, enforcement action and overall integration of the order. However, other team members were well used. The hybrid model may have use in a multidisciplinary youth justice context. Evidence, for example, from wraparound or intensive support models suggests that they are most effective when using a 'team' of concerned adults. Where the plan identifies when teachers or youth workers, care staff or any key person in the family network, in addition to the named supervisor, are routinely in a 'supervisory' role with young people, responsibilities can be shared as well as expectations on how they should communicate with the young person and with each other.

Whatever model is adopted, several helpful core principles emerge from the review that can be applied to improving engagement with and supervising young people.

Core principles for engaging with and supervising young people

■   Models need to acknowledge the young person's experiences and needs.

■   Continuity of contact with the same case manager and other staff is important to building confidence and rapport, particularly during the initial stages of supervision.

■   The greater the level of task separation, the more the confusion over the reasons for different elements of supervision, particularly where contact with the case manager is limited.

■   Face-to-face contact with a small case management team can be beneficial for both staff and the client.

■   Openness, flexibility and support are key motivating factors, exemplified by three-way meetings between case managers, practitioners and the client.

Some clear, although not necessarily very new, messages have emerged in managing effective change. These include the importance of using an holistic human service approach; enabling a single plan to be implemented and led by one professional where key stages are mapped on an end-to-end process, bound together by a case manager into a meaningful and coherent whole; enabling different resources and styles to be matched to different cases; and developing variable forms of teamwork and organisational support for multidisciplinary contributions to the core process of case management.

Case management can best be understood as consisting of key elements and tasks at different levels of an agency (see Table 9.1). These have been examined in some depth conceptually in relation to adult offenders and provide some possible lessons for practice approaches in youth justice (McNeill and Whyte, 2007). The three key elements of the case management process, 'management', 'supervision' and 'administration', are examined primarily from the viewpoint of a practitioner holding formal supervisory responsibility.

Management at the level of individual cases is the process in which legal authority, for example based on a compulsory order or sentence, is vested. This gives the plan its direction, order, pace and shape. It should imply a collaborative rather than an authoritarian form of responsibility. *Supervision* can be described as building a working alliance to support the sequencing of day-to-day, face to-face tasks and activities that are required in most cases to secure compliance, generate motivation, achieve cohesion and integration of the plan, and realise and maintain positive outcomes. Social modelling, participative planning and methods aimed at supporting individual change should be the foundation of good supervision. *Administration* involves the implementation of service standards and procedures required to meet objectives.

TABLE 9.1: Examples of case management tasks

Management	Supervision	Administration
Assess	Form and maintain trusting relationship	Begin data system and file
Plan	Model pro-social behaviour	Fix appointment as per standards and planned requirements
Allocate resources	Motivate	Monitor change and compliance
Ensure implementation	Negotiate, broker and provide services	Maintain records
Monitor progress	Prepare and support the young person's change	Deal with non-compliance
Review	Liaise with other providers	Arrange reviews and other meetings
Reassess need and risk	Coach	Collate data
Adjust plan	Gather data from other providers	
Evaluate and evidence progress and achievement	Prevent re-offending	
	Maintain change and close case	

Source: Adapted from NOMS (2005)

Lessons from research stress the importance of not allowing these elements to become too disaggregated, as this is likely to increase the risk of the plans going wrong. The intention of a 'single' plan approach is intended to overcome difficulties in contemporary social work practice created by a shift away from generic practice, where a single or lead person manages and delivers all aspects of the intervention, towards more specialist practice, where case management and programme delivery functions are typically shared. Effective case management has to achieve some of both. No one's interests are served by a system in which clients are conceived as 'portable entities' and in which staff engage in a 'pass-the-parcel' style of supervision (Robinson and Dignan, 2004).

The research evidence provides a compelling message that the task of managing interventions to promote and sustain desistance and personal change is not simply an administrative or bureaucratic one. It is important that the continuity of case management is maintained in order to harmonise multidisciplinary roles. These should operate with consistency across all aspects of supervision in order to ensure positive learning is consolidated through a shared commitment to helping the young person reduce their offending and acquire positive opportunities for change. The complex range of tasks outlined in Table 9.2 requires sophisticated management structures to support its operation.

A final important aspect of change management with young people who offend, given the often compulsory context and the nature of their behaviour that can place themselves and others at risk, is the issue of compliance and enforcement. This is an important aspect of supervision whether practice is cast in a social welfare, socioeducative or criminal context. While a criminal

TABLE 9.2: Framework for case management

Case management	Offending behaviour and other programmes
Structured assessment Targeting Supervision planning Risk management Coordination of service delivery Motivation Reinforcement Application Surveillance Compliance Enforcement Evaluation	Cognitive skills foundations Programmes targeted at specific offence or risk factors Programmes targeted at education and social development
	Associated personal factors Substance misuse Mental health Personal trauma Family and peer relationship
	Re-integration factors Basic life and social skills Education/employment Budgeting/debt counselling Accommodation

justice context often results in an over-emphasis on enforcement that can undermine positive change, equally the other contexts are often associated with under-playing positive authority with the same outcome.

In recent years, the political emphasis on punishment in the community has increased the demand for effective enforcement in order to 'reassure' communities that effective action is being undertaken. Although the language of 'enforcement' implies ensuring meaningful consequences or sanctions in the event of non-compliance, Bottoms (2001) has argued, in an adult context, that attempts to encourage or require compliance must adopt a creative mix of constraint-based mechanisms (those that somehow restrict) with instrumental mechanisms (related to incentives and disincentives) and normative mechanisms (related to beliefs, attachments and perceptions of legitimacy). These 'normative' mechanisms are likely to be crucial to the effectiveness of the case manager's role in supporting compliance.

The success of change management at the individual level will depend on the existence of the local strategic partnerships and service pathways that allow access to and coordination of appropriate services and resources. Even the best-designed, best-implemented and most research-based individual case plan will fail if the case manager cannot access the services and resources required to implement it. Equally the best-developed approach to securing compliance will fail unless organisational arrangements exist to underpin the worker's legitimate authority by delivering swift and proportionate responses that reward compliance and deal effectively with non-compliance.

Social justice for children and communities

While better personal and social integration for young people is generally an ambition of youth justice policy and practice, the reality is often some distance away from this ambition. There has been a resurgence of interest in the concept of social capital as a possible remedy for social problems on the assumption that individual problems lie in the weakening of civil society (see Chapter Six). The concept of social capital is not without its critics, nor its limitations. However, it provides potential as an over-arching concept to offer shape and direction for effective individualised practice.

Webster et al's (2006) study of repeat offenders and dependent drug users attempted to examine how social capital could help people cope with life in poor communities. Their findings suggest that achieving access into new networks and new social opportunities is not easy:

> Our informants' lack of access to wider networks makes individual or collective social mobility unlikely. Seldom did their networks of family and friends provide the sort of social capital that might assist

in transcending the limiting socio-economic conditions in which they lived. (Webster et al, 2006, p 13)

The lack of social capital effectively forced them back into destructive networks focused around their offending and/or drug use. In such circumstances strong community bonds might actually reinforce norms of criminal behaviour and low achievement (Field and Spence, 2000). This sadly captures the reality for many of the most difficult young people, particularly those returning from residential or institutional provision.

The practice implications are far reaching. At the individual level, without access to social resources and capital, it will be very difficult for a young person to sustain positive change or even to embark on it. If social capital is largely a product of community organisation and cohesion, it could be seen to be beyond the reach of youth justice practitioners. On the other hand, in the absence of effective community regeneration and inclusion strategies, practitioners have little choice, if they are not to abandon young people, but to seek to help them build positive social relationships and, where they exist, gain access to a family's or alternative social resources for practical and emotional support, as part of individual and offence-focused change. At the same time service planners should assist practitioners in their efforts by seeking to develop the education and employment prospects of young people and to explore the links between volunteering, mentoring, leisure opportunities and sustaining reduced offending.

> What types of social capital does Michael have, and what types does he not have access to?
>
> In what ways could Michael's 'social capital' be developed:
>
> ■ by working with his family origin or formation?
> ■ by working within his neighbourhood?

The process of social reintegration has to be two-way, whereby evidence of progress and personal change results in visible gains and rewards for the young person in their community. This is particularly true for young people whose family networks are at best diminished and at worst fragmented. In the past, intermediate treatment and social group work practice was accused of rewarding bad behaviour by providing outdoor activities and leisure opportunities in the absence of evidence of personal change. Practice in youth justice might run the risk of going too far the other way.

Probably the greatest challenge to youth justice practice is how to engage and relate to communities of interest including neighbours, employers, youth clubs and other agencies and to support them to contribute to the young person's development. The absence of an effective model of community social work and the success or failure sending signals to communities about the positive work undertaken may have major consequences for the capacity to generate wider social opportunities and the development of social capital.

There is a challenge for practitioners and agencies to generate a practical understanding of work within communities as a way of demonstrating that the best interests of the community and the best interests of the young person are not usually mutually exclusive. This is likely to mean engaging much more directly with members of 'vulnerable' communities as well as recruiting people from these communities, including young people, to contribute to the work than has previously been the case. The objective of youth justice practice should not be merely public protection through reduced re-offending but rather better community and social justice for young people and their communities (Nellis, 2001).

The reflective practitioner: combining art and science

Investment in planned interventions, structured programmes and other provision located within a more holistic practice approach requires the traditional skills of practitioners to nurture motivation to change and engagement (Morgan, 2003). Commentators emphasise the importance of the 'hands-on' involvement of the supervisor, who is 'not only the referrer, a broker and the enforcer' but also 'the motivator and the re-inforcer and the person who holds onto the longer-term aims of personal maturation, social re-integration and reducing re-offending' (Knott, 2004, p 23).

Despite encouraging findings from research on effective intervention, research on the characteristics of effective staff or the best staff practices to use in the delivery of interventions remains limited. This is, perhaps, because the meaning and understanding of generalised labels like 'counselling', 'one-to-one work', 'casework' and 'relationship-based work' are inherently vague, particularly to 'users'. Andrews and Kiessling (1980) identified five dimensions of effective practice skills mainly based on the social learning theory of criminal behaviour.

Five dimensions of effective practice

1.   Effective use of authority – a 'firm but fair' approach ensuring formal rules are made more visible, understandable and unambiguous.
2.   Modelling and reinforcing anti-criminal attitudes and behaviours through directive positive and/or negative reinforcement – promoting pro-social and anti-criminal attitudes through regular interactions with frontline staff.
3.   Concrete problem-solving skills – resolving the key obstacles that result in reduced levels of satisfaction and rewards for non-criminal pursuits.
4.   Effective use of community resources often referred to as advocacy/ brokerage.
5.   Relationship factors.

Essentially, they argued that the interpersonal influence exerted by practitioners is maximised under conditions characterised by open, warm and enthusiastic communication. An equally important consideration is the development of mutual respect between the client and practitioner. Dowden and Andrews (2004) developed these dimensions further and tested if 'core practices' could make a statistically significant independent contribution to outcomes of reduced re-offending over and above that contributed by the type of service. The results of their analysis showed that the following core practices did seem to enhance positive effects of human service provision, where they were relevant and directed by the principles of risk, need and general responsivity:

- quality of interpersonal relationships
- relationship factors
- effective use of community resources
- skills factors
- appropriate modelling and reinforcement
- effective use of authority
- effective reinforcement
- effective disapproval
- structured learning procedures
- problem solving.

This ranking of their statistical 'effect' supports the case that relationship characteristics are equally important as well-designed and structured learning programmes in effecting meaningful change, although these are likely to be mutually inclusive.

The business of reducing re-offending by supporting change involves a range of skills that go far beyond imposing control and monitoring or enforcing compliance, important though these activities are. The evidence points to the fact that modern practitioners need to combine human art with social science alongside the management of a series of 'levers' to ensure compliance and access to mainstream community services which may take many forms depending on the needs and risks presented. Effective delivery also requires investment in equipping practitioners with the key skills required and in creating a context for practice that provides them with realistic opportunities to exercise these skills.

Practising with integrity represents an immensely demanding responsibility for the reflective practitioner faced with a clientele whose social problems are widescale. Social problems are extraordinarily complex and resistant to intervention. The kind of solution or constellation of solutions developed to tackle a situation depends on the analysis of the problem in the first place, or, more subtly, whether the situation is deemed a problem, or more subtly still, whether it is deemed a problem that should be tackled (Joss, 1990). The issue of minimum and non-intervention principles and the likely impact of unnecessary intervention have to be factored into assessments and decision making.

Attempts to apply technical/rational or scientific models and problem-solving methods as opposed to punitive responses to the criminal behaviour of youth are generally presented as the most innovative approach to youth justice practice. At the same time, trying to resolve the problems that generate criminal behaviour by relying on an individualised problem-solving framework runs the risk of neglecting the key issues of problem identification, naming and framing, which are highly political and value-laden activities. Whose problems are practitioners trying to solve and are they likely to be explained in ways that conform to a predetermined set of affordable solutions? Inevitably, many practice solutions are resource-led rather than needs-led and often seem based on the premise that it is cheaper to manage the individual reactions to an adverse environment than it is to mend the environment itself (Gray, 2007).

Practitioners must learn how to frame and reframe situations in different ways and to engage in a process of questioning, improvisation, invention and testing strategies in response to individual circumstances. There is an art of problem framing, an art of implementation and an art of improvisation as well as an art of influencing and motivating individuals and systems (Schon, 1987). Even an appropriate technical 'solution' such as a structured group work programme with pre-set aims, measurable objectives and relevant content must be delivered in a way that matches the learning style of the individual participant and that allows them the opportunity to understand their circumstances and where possible take some control over them.

Each social problem is experienced by an individual as unique, open to many different explanations that cannot be resolved by the simplistic application of pre-formulated techniques. Research and practice principles and service pathways can provide direction for travel. Engagement with the young person and their family on the exact nature of provision and the journey to be travelled, on service shortfall and structural barriers, is crucial to effective practice. These are important characteristics of 'reflective' and critical practice. Many commentators have even greater expectations and distinguish the reflective from the reflexive practitioner whose characteristics are self-involvement and confrontation with the ethical basis and legitimacy of practice (Webb, 2006).

To think these practice expectations can be achieved without agencies nurturing and supporting practitioners lacks credibility. Young people can learn about themselves, others and their social context as they reflect on what they do. This same process is mirrored in learning by practitioners, when they, in turn, reflect on the young person's learning and achievement and on their own experience as change managers within their organisation. Learning by reflection has been defined as 'a process of internally examining and exploring an issue of concern triggered by experience, which creates and clarifies meaning in terms of self and results in a changed conceptual perspective' (Boyd and Fales, 1983, p 113).

Three types of learning are required to link theory and practice. These are factual knowledge, practice knowledge and experiential learning (Heron, 1981). In this context practitioners require what has been described as 'deep' as opposed to 'surface' learning, a duality of learning based on a deep understanding of theoretical principles, application of the rules of evidence, methods of enquiry and performance objectives and standards, combined with creativity. Deep learning is achieved when formal learning and personal experience are brought together within an agency learning environment (Entwhistle and Ramsden, 1983).

The task of promoting evidence-led practice must also involve getting professionals to stop doing things, where there is evidence of ineffectiveness, as well as promoting new practices based on promising evidence of effectiveness (Nutley et al, 2000, p 5). 'Unlearning' has been used to describe the need to ditch previously established but ineffective ways of doing things in order to be able to take on board new understanding. Why, for example, are so many young people criminalised or held in custody? Practitioners need to try and address this question in their team practice and understand what part they play in reinforcing or challenging these practices. The same has to be true for mainstream providers, in particular education, leisure and mental health services, who often fail to meet the needs of young people who offend. It often is left to youth justice to try to pick up the pieces.

Much more needs to be done to understand the theoretical and practical impact of interventionist as distinct from diversionary responses. Diversion is consistent with key international human rights instruments, which set the context, either through diversion with no action or diversion to a helping service, for more progressive practice (Buist and Whyte, 2004). Diversion from the criminal process has been shown to be an effective strategy in terms of youth crime prevention.

Practice agencies as learning organisations

Practitioners generally speaking are not autonomous actors. They operate and draw much of their power and authority from their agency context. Many observed management activities in the justice field seem to centre on carrying out procedures and requirements set by more senior managers with limited scope for 'deep' reflection and creativity (Skinner and Whyte, 2004). The prospect of dealing in innovation and research to direct practice can seem unreachable particularly if 'blame' as opposed to 'learning to take risks' dominates the practice culture.

Social learning theorists have emphasised the significance of observational learning in changing the behaviour of groups or individuals. The characteristics of social learning in its application to work with young people who offend is similar for agency change. It involves:

- a model for change;
- that the learning may take place without the specific intention of either the model to teach or the learner to learn;
- that specific behaviours and more general states can be learned in this way;
- that the consequences of the learning depend on the consequences of the change;
- that the characteristics of the model influence the learning which takes place (Bandura and Walters, 1963).

Much of the character of agency practice results from the social learning available to its staff through the behaviour of its significant members. This places an important responsibility on 'experienced' practitioners and those in leadership and senior management roles to demonstrate and value the kind of behaviour they want to encourage throughout the organisation. A culture of 'curiosity' and of learning from evidence and outcomes is needed if practitioners are to be supported in taking the risks involved in new and more effective ways of working.

Successful learning organisations empower all within them to take responsibility for the important aspects of the organisation's business, both internally and externally (Senge, 1992). They tend to have strong linkages between the three levels of activity – operations, strategy and policy – where operations inform and are informed by policy and strategy (Garratt, 1987). In Senge's model of change, staff are supported to evaluate their ongoing work and to use this knowledge and experience to contribute to continuous service improvement and to organisational development. These practices are similar to the model that practitioners should be applying with young people who offend.

Five learning disciplines within a learning organisation

- *Personal mastery:* an organisational climate which encourages its members to develop themselves towards the goals and purposes they choose.
- *Mental models:* reflecting on, continually clarifying and improving internal pictures of their world, and seeing how these shape actions and decisions.
- *Shared vision:* building a sense of commitment in a group, by developing shared images of the preferred future to be created, and the principles and guiding practices by which to get there.
- *Team learning:* transforming conversational and collective thinking skills, so that groups of people can reliably develop intelligence and ability greater than the sum of the individual members' talents.
- *Systems thinking:* a way of thinking about, and a language for describing and understanding, the forces and interrelationships that shape the behaviour of systems (Skinner and Whyte, 2004, p 377).

Conclusion

An evidence-led approach to practice development requires closer working relationships between agencies and independent academic institutions to ensure a two-way flow of information about policy and practice issues. Partnerships can provide practitioners with the opportunity to remain aware of the strengths and limitations of research and help support a sound empirical basis for learning that takes account of the changing needs of practice.

Establishing a climate of learning is not easy in a turbulent political context, in the face of scarce resources and increasing demands and expectations.

Yet it is the only way forward within existing structures if effectiveness and social justice is to be achieved for young people and communities.

Key questions

(1) To what extent is the young person's re-offending the product of a lack of social justice in his/her life?
(2) Which of the relationships that matter most to the young person are most likely to support desistance and why?
(3) What are some of the difficulties that practitioners might face in seeking to develop a young person's social capital?
(4) How can practitioners contribute to the 'five learning disciplines' to assist their agency to become a learning organisation?

Practice exercise

Using a youth justice case you are working on or are familiar with, discuss the role of the family and social network issues in the young person's desistance from offending.

As supervising social worker, what work might you attempt to support these?

Further reading and resources

➲ Reid, W. (1990) 'Change-process research: a new paradigm?', in L. Videka-Sjerman and W. Reid (eds) *Advances in Clinical Social Work Research*, Silver Spring, MD: NASW Press.
➲ Smale, G., Tuson, G. and Statham, D. (2000) *Social Work and Social Problems: Working towards Social Inclusion and Social Change*, Basingstoke: Macmillan.

References

Adler, R.M. (1985) *Taking Juvenile Justice Seriously*, Edinburgh: Scottish Academic Press.

ADSW (Association of Directors of Social Work) (2005) *Response to 21st Century Social Work Review*, Glasgow: ADSW.

Anderson, S., Kinsey, R., Loader, I. and Smith, C.G. (1994) *Cautionary Tales: Young People, Crime and Policing in Edinburgh*, Aldershot: Avebury.

Andrews, D. and Bonta, J. (1998) *The Psychology of Criminal Conduct*, Cincinnati, OH: Anderson.

Andrews, D. and Kiessling, J. (1980) 'Program structure and effective correctional practices: a summary of the CaVIC research', in R. Ross and P. Gendreau (eds) *Effective Correctional Treatment*, Toronto: Butterworth.

Andrews, D., Hollins, C., Raynor, P., Trotter, C. and Armstrong, B. (2001) *Sustaining Effectiveness in Working with Offenders*, Cardiff: The Cognitive Centre Foundation.

Andrews, D., Zinger, I., Hoge, R., Bonta, J., Gendreau, P. and Cullen, F. (1990) 'Does correctional treatment work? A clinically relevant and psychologically informed meta-analysis', *Criminology*, vol 28, no 3, pp 369-404.

Annison, J. (2006) 'Style over substance? A review of the evidence base for the use of learning styles in probation', *Criminology and Criminal Justice*, vol 6, no 2, pp 239-57.

Armstrong, T. (ed) (2003) *Intensive Interventions with High-Risk Youths: Promising Approaches in Juvenile Probation and Parole*, Monsey, NY: Criminal Justice Press.

Audit Commission (1999) *Children in Mind: Child and Adolescent Mental Health Services*, London: Audit Commission.

Ayers, C., Williams, J., Hawkins, J., Peggy, L. and Abbott, D. (1999) 'Assessing correlates of onset, escalation, de-escalation and desistance of delinquent behaviour', *Journal of Quantitative Criminology*, vol 15, no 3, pp 277-306.

Bailey, S. and Tarbuck, P. (2006) 'Recent advances in the development of screening tools for mental health in young offenders', *Current Opinion in Psychiatry*, vol 19, no 4, pp 373-7.

Bailey, W. (1966) 'Correctional outcome: an evaluation of 100 reports', *Journal of Criminal Law, Criminology and Police Science*, vol 57, no 2, pp 153-60.

Baker, K. (2005) 'Assessment in youth justice: professional discretion and the use of asset', *Youth Justice*, vol 5, no 2, pp 106-22 (http://yjj.sagepub.com/cgi/content/abstract/5/2/106).

Baker, K. (2007) 'Young people and risk', in M. Blyth, K. Baker and E. Solomon (eds) *Young People and Risk*, Bristol: The Policy Press.

Baker, K., Jones, S., Roberts, C. and Merrington, S. (2003) *Validity and Reliability of* ASSET, London: Youth Justice Board.

Baker, K., Pollack, M. and Kohn, I. (1995) 'Violence prevention through informal socialisation: an evaluation of the South Baltimore Youth Centre'. *Studies on Crime and Crime Prevention*, vol 4, no 1, pp 61-85.

Baker, R. and Mednick, B. (1984) *Influences on Human Development: A Longitudinal Perspective*, Boston, MA: Kluwer-Nijhoff.

Bandura, A. (1977) *Social Learning Theory*, London: Prentice-Hall.

Bandura, A. and Walters, R. (1963) *Social Learning and Personality Development*, London: Holt, Rinehart and Winston.

Barber, J. (1991) *Beyond Casework*, Basingstoke: Macmillan.

Barn, R., Andrew, L. and Mantovani, N. (2005) *Life After Care: A Study about the Experiences of Young People from Different Ethnic Groups*, York: Joseph Rowntree Foundation.

Baron, S., Field, J. and Schuller, T. (eds) (2000) *Social Capital: Critical Perspectives*, Oxford: Oxford University Press.

Barret, J. (1996) *A Review of Research Literature Relating to Outdoor Adventure and Personal and Social Development with Young Offenders and Young People at Risk*, Ravenglass: Foundation for Outdoor Adventure.

Barry, M. (2006) *Youth Offending in Transition: The Search for Social Recognition*, London: Routledge.

Barry, M. (2007) *Effective Approaches to Risk Assessment in Social Work: An International Literature Review*, Edinburgh: Scottish Government

Barton, C., Alexander, J.F., Waldron, H., Turner, C.W. and Warburton, J. (1985) 'Generalizing treatment effects of functional family therapy: three replications', *American Journal of Family Therapy*, vol 13, no 3, pp 16-26.

Bazemore, G. and Umbreit, M. (1994) *Balanced and Restorative Justice*, Washington, DC: Department of Justice, Office of Justice Programs.

Bazemore, G. and Umbreit, M. (2001) *A Comparison of Four Restorative Conferencing Models*, Washington, DC: US Department of Justice, Office of Juvenile Justice and Delinquency Prevention.

Becker, J. and Hicks, S. (2003) 'Juvenile sexual offenders: characteristics, interventions and policy issues', *Annals of the New York Academy of Sciences*, vol 989, pp 397-410.

Belsky, J., Vandell, D., Burchinal, M., Clarke-Stewart, A., McCartney, K. and Owen M. (2007) 'Are there long-term effects of early child care?', *Child Development*, vol 78, no 2, pp 681-701.

Berman, D. and Davis-Berman, J. (1999) 'Wilderness therapy for adolescents', in C. Schaefer (ed) *Innovative Psychotherapy Techniques in Child and Adolescent Therapy* (2nd edn), New York: John Wiley, pp 415-34.

Blackburn, R. (1994) *The Psychology of Criminal Conduct: Theory, Research and Practice*, Chichester: John Wiley.

Bonta, J. (2002) 'Offender risk assessment: guidelines for selection and use', *Criminal Justice and Behavior*, vol 29, no 4, pp 355-79.

Bonta, J., Rugge, T., Sedo, B. and Coles, R. (2004) *Case Management in Manitoba Probation*, Manitoba, Canada: Manitoba Department of Corrections.

Borduin, C., Mann, B., Cone, L., Henggeler, S., Fucci, B., Blaske, D. and Williams, R. (1995) 'Multi-systemic treatment of serious juvenile offenders: long-term prevention of criminality and violence', *Journal of Consulting and Clinical Psychology*, vol 63, no 4, pp 569-78.

Boswell, G. (1997) 'The backgrounds of violent young offenders: the present picture', in V. Varma (ed) *Violence in Children and Adolescents*, London: Jessica Kingsley Publishers.

Boswell, G. (1999) 'Young offenders who commit grave crimes: the criminal justice response', in H. Kemshall and J. Pritchard (eds) *Good Practice in Working with Violence*, London: Jessica Kingsley Publishers.

Bottoms, A. (1994) 'Environmental criminology', in M. Maguire, R. Morgan and R. Reiner (eds) *Oxford Handbook of Criminology*, Oxford: Clarendon Press.

Bottoms, A. (2001) 'Compliance and community penalties', in A. Bottoms, L. Gelsthorpe and S. Rex (eds) *Community Penalties: Changes and Challenges*, Cullompton: Willan Publishing.

Bottoms, A. and Dignan, J. (2004) 'Youth justice in Great Britain', in M. Tonry and A. Doob (eds) *Youth Crime and Youth Justice*, Chicago, IL: University of Chicago Press, p 1.

Bottoms, A. and McWilliams, W. (1979) 'A non-treatment paradigm for probation practice', *British Journal of Social Work*, vol 9, no 2, pp 160-201.

Bottoms, A., Shapland, J., Costello, A., Holmes, D. and Muir, G. (2004) 'Towards desistance: theoretical underpinnings for an empirical study', *The Howard Journal*, vol 43, no 4, pp 368-89.

Bourdieu, P. and Wacquant, L. (1992) *An Invitation to Reflexive Sociology*, Cambridge: Polity Press.

Boyd, E. and Fales, A. (1983) 'Reflective learning: key to learning from experience', *Journal of Humanistic Psychology*, vol 23, no 2, pp 99-102.

Braithwaite, J. (1989) *Crime, Shame, and Reintegration*, Cambridge: Cambridge University Press.

Braithwaite, J. (1999) 'Restorative justice: assessing optimistic and pessimistic accounts', in M. Tonry (ed) *Crime and Justice: A Review of Research*, Chicago, IL: University of Chicago Press.

Brantingham, P.J. and Brantingham, P.L. (eds) (1991) *Environmental Criminology* (2nd edn), Prospect Heights, IL: Waveland Press.

Brearley, P. (1982) *Risk in Social Work*, London: Routledge & Kegan Paul.

Brearley, P.C. with Hall, M.R.P., Jeffreys, P.M., Jennings, R. and Pritchard, S. (1982) *Risk and Ageing*, London: Routledge & Kegan Paul.

Brown, S. (2005) *Understanding Youth and Crime*, Maidenhead: Open University Press.

Bruns, E., Burchard, J. and Yoe, J. (1995) 'Evaluating the Vermont system of care: outcomes associated with community-based wraparound services', *Journal of Child and Family Studies*, vol 4, no 3, pp 321-39.

Buist, M. and Whyte, B. (2004) *International Research Evidence for Scotland's Children's Hearing Review: A Report for the Scottish Executive CRU*, Edinburgh: Scottish Executive.

Bunting, L. (2004) 'Parenting programmes: the best available evidence', *Child Care in Practice*, vol 10, no 4, pp 327-43.

Burnett, R. (2004) 'One-to-one ways of promoting desistance: in search of an evidence base', in R. Burnett and C. Roberts (eds) *What Works in Probation and Youth Justice*, Cullompton: Willan Publishing.

Burnett, R. and Appleton, C. (2004) *Joined-up Youth Justice: Tackling Youth Crime in Partnership*, Lyme Regis: Russell House.

Burns, B. (1999) 'A call for a mental health services research agenda for youth with serious emotional disturbance', *Mental Health Services Research*, vol 1, no 1, pp 5-20.

Burns, R. (1999) *Wilderness Therapy Programs for Troubled Youth: A Viable Alternative?*, cited in M. Ungar, C. Dumond and W. McDonald (2005) 'Risk, resilience, and outdoor programmes for at-risk children', *Journal of Social Work*, vol 5, no 3, pp 319–38.

Cameron, C. (2004) 'Social pedagogy and care: Danish and German practice in young people's residential care', *Journal of Social Work*, vol 4, no 2, pp 133-51.

Cannan, C., Berry, L. and Lyons, K. (1992) *Social Work and Europe*, London: Macmillan.

Carney, M. and Buttell, F. (2003) 'Reducing juvenile recidivism: evaluating the wraparound services model', *Research on Social Work Practice*, vol 13, no 5, pp 551-67.

Catalano, R., Berglund, M., Ryan, J., Lonczak, H. and Hawkins, J. (1998) *Positive Youth Development in the United States: Research Findings on Evaluations of Positive Youth Development Programs*, Seattle: Social Development Research Group.

Chamberlain, P. (1998) *Treatment Foster Care*, OJJDP Juvenile Justice Bulletin, Washington, DC: US Department of Justice.

Chamberlain, P., Leve, L. and DeGarmo, D. (2007) 'Multidimensional treatment foster care for girls in the juvenile justice system: 2-year follow-up of a randomized clinical trial', *Journal of Consulting and Clinical Psychology*, vol 75, no 1, pp 187-93.

Chapman, T. and Hough, M. (1998) *Evidence Based Practice: A Guide to Effective Practice*, London: Home Office.

Christie, N. (1993) *Crime Control and Industry*, London: Routledge.

Clifford, D. (1998) *Social Assessment Theory and Practice*, Aldershot: Ashgate.

Cloward, R. and Ohlin, L. (1960) *Delinquency and Opportunity*, New York: Free Press.

Coalter, F. with Allison, M. and Taylor, J. (2000) *The Role of Sport in Regenerating Deprived Areas*, Edinburgh: Scottish Executive Central Research Unit.

Coffield, F., Moseley, D., Hall, E. and Ecclestone, K. (2004) *Learning Styles and Pedagogy in Post-16 Learning*, London: Learning and Skills Research Centre.

Cohen, S. (1985) *Visions of Social Control*, New York: Plenum.

Coleman, J. (1988) 'Social capital in the creation of human capital', *American Journal of Sociology*, vol 94, supplement, pp 95-121.

Coleman, J. (1994) *Foundations of Social Theory*, Cambridge, MA: Harvard University Press.

Conduct Problems Prevention Research Group (1992) 'A developmental and clinical model for the prevention of conduct disorder: the FAST Track Program', *Development and Psychopathology*, vol 4, no 1, pp 509–27.

Cornish, D. and Clarke, R. V. (1998) 'Understanding crime displacement: an application of rational choice theory', in S. Henry and W. Einstadter (eds) *Criminology Theory Reader*, New York: New York University Press.

Cotterell, J. (1996) *Social Networks and Social Influences in Adolescence*, London: Routledge.

Coulshed, V. and Orme, J. (1998) *Social Work Practice: An Introduction*, London: Macmillan.

Courtney, M. and Terao, S. (2002) *Classification of Independent Living Services*, Chicago, IL: Chapin Hall Center for Children at the University of Chicago.

Crawford, A. (1997) *The Local Governance of Crime: Appeals to Community and Partnerships*, Oxford: Clarendon Press.

Crawford, A. and Newburn, T. (2003) *Youth Offending and Restorative Justice*. Cullompton: Willan Publishing.

Crisp, B., Anderson, M., Orme, J. and Lister, P. (2006) 'What can we learn about social work assessment from the textbooks?', *Journal of Social Work*, vol 6, no 3, pp 337-59.

Cross, N., Evans, J. and Minkes, J. (2003) 'Still children first? Developments in youth justice in Wales', *Youth Justice*, vol 2, no 3, pp 151-62.

Daly, K. (2003) 'Restorative justice: the real story', in G. Johnstone (ed) *A Restorative Justice Reader*, Cullompton: Willan Publishing.

Daly, K. and Hayes, H. (2001) 'Restorative justice and conferencing in Australia', *Trends and Issues*, no 186, Canberra: Australian Institute of Criminology.

Daniel, B. and Wassell, S. (2002) *Adolescence: Assessing and Promoting Resilience in Vulnerable Children*, London: Jessica Kingsley.

Deater-Deckard, K. and O'Connor, T. (2000) 'Parent–child mutuality in early childhood: two behavioral genetic studies', *Developmental Psychology*, vol 36, no 5, pp 561-70.

Dembo, R. and Walters, W. (2003) 'Innovative approaches to identifying and responding to the needs of high risk youth', *Substance Use and Misuse*, vol 38, no 11/13, pp 1713-38.

DePanfilis, D. (2006) *Child Neglect: A Guide for Prevention, Assessment, and Intervention*, Washington, DC: US Department of Health and Human Services (www.childwelfare.gov/pubs/usermanuals/neglect/neglect.pdf).

Devlin, A. and Turney, B. (1999) *Going Straight: After Crime and Punishment*, Winchester: Waterside Press.

DfES (Department for Education and Skills) (2007) *Aiming High for Children: Supporting Families*, London: HM Treasury.

DH (Department of Health) (2004) *Standards for Better Health*, London: DH.

Dingwall, R. (1989) 'Some problems about predicting child abuse and neglect', in O. Stevenson (ed) *Child Abuse: Public Policy and Professional Practice*, Hemel Hempstead: Harvester Wheatsheaf.

Dixon, J. and Stein, M. (2005) *Leaving Care, Throughcare and Aftercare in Scotland*, London: Jessica Kingsley.

Dodge, K. (1993) 'The future of research on the treatment of conduct disorder', *Development and Psychopathology*, vol 5, no 1–2, pp 311-19.

Dowden, C. and Andrews, D.A. (1999) 'What works for female offenders: a meta-analytic review', *Crime and Delinquency*, vol 45, no 4, pp 438-52.

Dowden, C. and Andrews, D. (2004) 'The importance of staff practice in delivering effective correctional treatment: a meta-analytic review of core correctional practice', *International Journal of Offender Therapy and Comparative Criminology*, vol 48, no 2, pp 203-14.

Dreyfoos, J.G. (1990) *Adolescents at Risk*, New York: Oxford University Press.

Duff, A. (2001) *Punishment, Communication and Community*, New York: Oxford University Press.

Duff, A. (2003) 'Probation, punishment and restorative justice: should altruism be engaged in punishment?', *The Howard Journal*, vol 42, no 1, pp 181-97.

Dumbrill, G.C. (2006) 'Parental experience of child protection intervention: a qualitative study', *Child Abuse and Neglect*, vol 30, no 1, pp 27-37.

Dutton, K. and Whyte, B. (2006) *Implementing Restorative Justice within an Integrated Welfare System: The Evaluation of Glasgow's Restorative Justice Service, Interim Summary Report*, Edinburgh: Criminal Justice Social Work Development Centre for Scotland (CJSWDC).

DWP (Department for Work and Pensions) (2003) *A Practical Guide to Measuring Soft Outcomes and Distance Travelled*, Cardiff: Welsh European Fund Office.

EC (European Commission) (2005) *Report by Mr Alvaro Gil-Robles Commissioner for Human Rights on his visit to the United Kingdom*, Geneva: European Commission.

Emsley, C. (1997) 'The history of crime and crime control institutions', in M. Maguire, R. Morgan and R. Reiner (eds) *The Oxford Handbook of Criminology* (3rd edn), Oxford: Oxford University Press.

Entwhistle, N. and Ramsden, P. (1983) *Understanding Student Learning*, London: Croom Helm.

Epstein, R. (1999) 'Mindful practice', *Journal of the American Medical Association*, vol 282, no 9, pp 833-9.

Erikson, E. (1995) *A Way of Looking at Things: Selected Papers from 1930-1980*, New York: W.W. Norton.

Farrall, S. (2002) *Rethinking What Works with Offenders: Probation, Social Context and Desistance from Crime*, Cullompton: Willan Publishing.

Farrall, S. (2004) 'Supervision, motivation and social context: what matters most when probationers desist?', in G. Mair (ed) *What Matters in Probation*, Cullompton: Willan Publishing.

Farrall, S. and Bowling, B. (1999) 'Structuration, human development and desistance from crime', *British Journal of Criminology*, vol 17, no 2, pp 252-67.

Farrington, D. (1989) 'Early predictors of adolescent aggression and adult violence', *Violence and Victims*, vol 4, no 2, pp 79–100.

Farrington, D. (1996) *Understanding and Preventing Youth Crime*, York: Joseph Rowntree Foundation.

Farrington, D. (2002) 'Developmental criminology and risk-focused prevention', in M. Maguire, R. Morgan and R. Reiner (eds) *The Oxford Handbook of Criminology* (3rd edn), Oxford: Oxford University Press.

Farrington, D. and Tarling, R. (eds) (1985) *Prediction and Criminology*, New York: State University of New York Press.

Farrington, D. and Welsh, B.C. (2003) 'Family-based prevention of offending: a meta-analysis', *The Australian and New Zealand Journal of Criminology*, vol 36, no 2, pp 127-51.

Feld, B. (1998) 'Juvenile and criminal justice systems' responses to youth violence', in M. Tonry and M. Moore (eds) *Youth Violence: Crime and Justice, A Review of Research*, vol 24, pp 186-293.

Felson, M. (1998) *Crime and Everyday Life* (2nd edn), Thousand Oaks, CA: Pine Forge Press.

Ferguson, J.L. (2002) 'Putting the "what works" research into practice: an organizational perspective', *Criminal Justice and Behavior*, vol 29, no 4, pp 472-92.

Field, J. and Spence, L. (2000) 'Social capital and informal learning', in F. Coffield (ed) *The Necessity of Informal Learning*, Bristol: The Policy Press.

Fischer, J. (1993) 'Empirically-based practice: the end of an ideology?', *Journal of Social Service Research*, vol 18, no 1, pp 19-64.

Flood-Page, C., Campbell, S., Harrington, V. and Miller, J. (2000) *Youth Crime: Findings from the 1998/99 Youth Lifestyles Survey*, Home Office Research Study 209, London: Home Office.

Fortune, A. and Reid, W. (1998) *Research in Social Work*, New York: Columbia University Press.

Franklin, J. (ed) (1998) *The Politics of Risk Society*, Cambridge: Polity Press.

Fraser, M. and Galinsky, M.J. (1997) 'Toward a resilience-based model of practice', in M. Fraser (ed) *Risk and Resilience in Childhood: An Ecological Perspective*, Washington, DC: NASW Press.

Fraser, N. (1997) *Justice Interruptus: Critical Reflections on the 'Post Socialist' Condition*, New York: Routledge.

Fraser, N. (2003) 'Social justice in the age of identity politics: redistribution, recognition, and participation', in N. Fraser and A. Honneth (eds) *Redistribution or Recognition? A Political-Philosophical Exchange*, London: Verso.

Frude, N., Honess, T. and Maguire, M. (1998) *CRIME-Pics Manual*, Cardiff: Michael and Associates.

Furlong, A. and Cartmel, F. (1997) *Young People and Social Change: Individualisation and Risk in Late Modernity*, Buckingham: Open University Press.

Gambrill, E. (2003) 'Evidence-based practice: sea change or the emperor's new clothes', *Journal of Social Work Education*, vol 39, no 1, pp 3-23.

Garfat, T. (ed) (2003) 'A child and youth care approach to family work', *Child and Youth Services*, vol 25, no 1/2, pp 1-6.

Garland, D. (1997) 'Of crime and criminals: the development of criminology in Britain', in M. Maguire, R. Morgan and R. Reiner (eds) *The Oxford Handbook of Criminology* (3rd edn), Oxford: Oxford University Press.

Garratt, B. (1987) *The Learning Organisation*, London: Fontana.

Garrett, C. (1985) 'Effects of residential treatment on adjudicated delinquents: a meta-analysis', *Journal of Research in Crime and Delinquency*, vol 22, no 4, pp 287-308.

Gelsthorpe, L. (2003) *Exercising Discretion: Decision Making in Criminal Justice*, Cullompton: Willan Publishing.

Gendreau, P. and Ross, R. (1979) 'Effectiveness of correctional treatment: bibliotherapy for cynics', *Crime and Delinquency*, vol 25, no 4, pp 463-89.

Gendreau, P. and Ross, R. (1981) 'Offender rehabilitation: the appeal of success', *Federal Probation*, vol 45, no 4, pp 45-8.

Gendreau, P and Ross, R. (1987) 'Revivification or rehabilitation: evidence from the 1980s', *Justice Quarterly*, vol 4, pp 349-407.

Gendreau, P., Cullen, F. and Bonta, J. (1994) 'Intensive rehabilitation supervision: the next generation in community corrections?', *Federal Probation*, vol 58, no 4, pp 72-8.

Gendreau, P., Little, T. and Goggin, C. (1996) 'Meta-analysis of the predictors of adult offender recidivism: what works?', *Criminology*, vol 34, no 4, pp 575-607.

Gilligan, R. (2001) *Promoting Resilience: A Resource Guide on Working with Children in the Care System*, London: British Agencies of Adoption and Fostering.

Goldson, B. (2002a) 'New punitiveness: the politics of child incarceration', in J. Muncie, G. Hughes and E. McLaughlin (eds) *Youth Justice: Critical Readings*, London: Sage Publications.

Goldson, B. (2002b) *Vulnerable Inside: Children in Secure and Penal Settings*, London: Children's Society.

Goldson, B. (2008) *Dictionary of Youth Justice*, Cullompton: Willan Publishing.

Gordon, D. (2002) 'Intervening with families of troubled youth: functional family therapy and parenting wisely', in J. McGuire (ed) *Offender Rehabilitation: Effective Programmes and Policies to Reduce Re-offending*, London: Wiley.

Gordon, M. (2005) *Roots of Empathy: Changing the World Child by Child*, Toronto: Thomas Allen Publishers.

Gorsuch, K., Steward, M., Van Fleet, R. and Schwartz, I. (1992) *Missouri Division of Youth Services: An Experience in Delinquency Reform, in Missouri and Hawaii: Leaders in Youth Correction Policy*, Ann Arbor, MI: Center for the Study of Youth Policy.

Gottfredson, S. and Hirschi, T. (1990) *A General Theory of Crime*, Palo Alto, CA: Stanford University Press.

Gottfredson, S. and Gottfredson, D. (1986) 'Accuracy of prediction models', in E. Blumstein, J. Cohen, J. Roth and C. Visher (eds) *Criminal Careers and Career Criminals*, vol 2, Washington, DC National Academy Press, pp 212-90.

Graham, J. (1998) *Schools, Disruptive Behaviour and Delinquency: A Review of Research*, London: Home Office.

Graham, J. and Bowling, B. (1995) *Young People and Crime*, Home Office Research Study 145, London: HMSO.

Gray, P. (2007) 'Youth justice, social exclusion and the demise of social justice', *The Howard Journal*, vol 46, no 4, pp 401–16.

Griffin, H. and Beech, A. (2004) *An Evaluation of the AIM Framework for the Assessment of Adolescents who Display Sexually Harmful Behaviour*, London: Youth Justice Board.

Grisso, T., Vincent, G. and Seagrave, D. (eds) (2005) *Mental Health Screening and Assessment in Juvenile Justice*, London: Guildford Press.

Grubin, D. and Wingate, S. (1996) 'Sexual offence recidivism: prediction versus understanding', *Criminal Behaviour and Mental Health*, vol 6, no 4, pp 349–59.

Gurney, A. (2000) 'Risk management', in M. Davies (ed) *The Blackwell Encyclopaedia of Social Work*, Oxford: Blackwell.

Hagel, A. (1998) *Dangerous Care: Reviewing the Risk to Children from their Carers*, London: Policy Studies Institute and the Bridge Child Care Trust.

Hagel, A. and Newburn, T. (1994) *Persistent Young Offenders*, London: Policy Studies Institute.

Halpern, D. (2001) 'Moral values, social trust and inequality – can values explain crime?', *British Journal of Criminology*, vol 41, no 2, pp 236–51.

Hämäläinen, J. (2003) 'The concept of social pedagogy in the field of social work', *Journal of Social Work*, vol 3, no 1, pp 69–80.

Harrington, R. and Bailey, S. (2004) 'Prevention of antisocial personality disorder: mounting evidence on optimal timing and methods', *Criminal Behaviour and Mental Health*, vol 14, no 2, pp 75–81.

Harvey, R. (2002) 'The UK before the UN Committee on the Rights of the Child', *ChildRIGHT*, October, issue no 190, pp 9–11.

Heidensohn, F. (2002) 'Gender and crime', in M. Maguire, R. Morgan and R. Reiner (eds) *The Oxford Handbook of Criminology* (3rd edn), Oxford: Oxford University Press.

Heineman-Pieper, M. (1985) 'The future of social work research', *Social Work Research and Abstracts*, pp 3–11.

Henggeler, S., Melton, G., Smith, L., Schoenwald, S. and Hanley, J. (1993) 'Family preservation using multi-systemic treatment: long-term follow-up to a clinical trial with serious juvenile offenders', *Journal of Child and Family Studies*, vol 2, pp 283–93.

Henry, B., Caspi, A., Moffitt, T.E. and Silva, P. (1996) 'Temperamental and familial predictors of violent and non-violent criminal convictions: from age 3 to age 18', *Development Psychopathology*, vol 32, no 4, pp 614–23.

Heron, J. (1981) 'The role of reflection in a co-operative inquiry', in P. Reason and J. Rowan (eds) *Philosophical Bases for a New Paradigm in Human Inquiry: A Source Book of New Paradigm Research*, Chichester: Wiley.

Heyman, B. (1997) *Risk, Health and Health Care: A Qualitative Approach*, London: Edward Arnold.

Higham, P.E. (2006) *Social Work: Introducing Professional Practice*, London: Sage Publications.

Hill, M. (1999) 'What's the problem? Who can help? The perspectives of children and young people on their well-being and on helping professionals', *Journal of Social Work Practice*, vol 13, no 2, pp 135-45.

Hill, M., Davis, J., Prout, A. and Tidsall, K. (2004) 'Moving the participation agenda forward', *Children and Society*, vol 18, no 2, pp 77-96.

Hill, M., Lockyer, A. and Stone, F. (eds) (2006) *Youth Justice and Child Protection*, London: Jessica Kingsley.

Hirschi, T. (1969) *Causes of Delinquency*, Berkeley, CA: University of California Press.

HM Treasury (2003) *Every Child Matters*, Cm 5860, London: The Stationery Office.

Hodges, K. (1994). *Child and Adolescent Functional Assessment Scale*, Ypsilanti, MI: Eastern Michigan University.

Hollins, C. (ed) (2001) *Handbook of Offender Assessment and Treatment*, Chichester: Wiley.

Hollins, C. (2002) 'Psychological theories', in M. Maguire, R. Morgan and R. Reiner (eds) *The Oxford Handbook of Criminology* (3rd edn), Oxford: Oxford University Press.

Hollins, C., McGuire, J. and Palmer, E. (2004) *Pathfinder Programmes in the Probation Service: A Retrospective Analysis*, London: Home Office Research, The Environmental Sciences Division (ESD).

Honess, T., Seymour, L. and Webster, R. (2000) *The Social Context of Underage Drinking*, London: Home Office.

Honey, P. and Mumford, A. (2000) *The Learning Styles Helper's Guide*, Maidenhead: Peter Honey Publications.

Horsefield, A. (2003) 'Risk assessment: who needs it?', *Probation Journal*, vol 50, no 4, pp 374-9.

Houchin, R. (2005) *Social Exclusion and Imprisonment in Scotland: A Report*, Glasgow: Glasgow Caledonian University.

Hudson, B. (1997) 'Social control', in M. Maguire, R. Morgan and R. Reiner (eds) *The Oxford Handbook of Criminology* (3rd edn), Oxford: Oxford University Press.

infed.org (2005) *Infed Social Pedagogy* (www.infed.org/biblio/b-socped. htm).

Irvine, A., Biglan, A., Smolkowski, K. and Ary, D. (1999) 'The value of the Parenting Scale for measuring the discipline practices of parents of middle-school children', *Behaviour Research and Therapy*, vol 37, no 2, pp 127-42.

Izzo, R. and Ross, R. (1990) 'Meta-analysis of rehabilitation programs for juvenile delinquency', *Criminal Justice and Behaviour*, vol 17, no 1, pp 134-42.

Jackson, S. (2000) 'Reducing risk and promoting resilience in vulnerable children', *Journal of Social Work*, vol 4, no 4 (www.bemidjistate.edu/academics/publications/social_work_journal/issue04/articles/jackson.html).

Jackson, S. and Simon, A. (2005) 'The costs and benefits of educating children in care', in E. Chase, S. Simon and S. Jackson (eds) *In Care and After: A Positive Perspective*, London: Routledge.

Jaeger, C., Renn, O., Rosa, E. and Webler, T. (2001) *Risk, Uncertainty and Rational Action*, London: Earthscan Publications.

Jamieson, J., McIvor, G. and Murray, C. (1999) *Understanding Offending Among Young People*, Edinburgh: Scottish Executive.

Jones, P.R. (1996) 'Risk prediction in criminal justice', in A. Harland (ed) *Choosing Correctional Options that Work*, Thousand Oaks, CA: Sage Publications.

Jones, P.R., Harris, P., Fader, J. and Grubstein, L. (2001) 'Identifying chronic juvenile offenders', *Justice Quarterly*, vol 18, no 3, pp 479-507.

Joss, R. (1990) 'Competency-led assessment', Unpublished paper, Bristol: Brunel University.

Juby, H. and Farrington, D. (2001) 'Disentangling the link between disrupted families and delinquency', *British Journal of Criminology*, vol 41, no 1, pp 22-40.

Kane, J., Lloyd, G., McCluskey, G., Riddell, S., Stead, J. and Weedon, E. (2006) *Restorative Practices in Three Scottish Councils*, Edinburgh: SEED.

Kemshall, H. (1996) *Reviewing Risk: A Review of Research in the Assessment and Management of Risk and Dangerousness*, London: Home Office.

Kemshall, H. (1998) *Risk in Probation Practice*, Aldershot: Ashgate.

Kemshall, H. (2002) *Risk, Social Policy and Welfare*, Buckingham: Open University Press.

Kemshall, H. (2003) *Understanding Risk in Criminal Justice*, Buckingham: Open University Press.

Kemshall, H. (2007) 'Risk, social policy and young people', in J. Wood and J. Hine (eds) *Work with Young People: Developments in Theory, Policy and Practices*, London: Sage Publications.

Kemshall, H. and Pritchard, J. (eds) (1997a) *Good Practice in Risk Management 1*, London: Jessica Kingsley.

Kemshall, H. and Pritchard, J. (eds) (1997b) *Good Practice in Risk Management 2: Protection, Rights and Responsibilities*, London: Jessica Kingsley.

Kirby, B. (1954) 'Measuring effects of treatment of criminals and delinquents', *Sociology and Social Research*, vol 38, no 3, pp 368-74.

Kirby, M. and Fraser, M. (1998) *Risk and Resilience in Childhood: An Ecological Perspective*, Washington, DC: NASW Press.

Kirk, S. and Reid, W.J. (2002) *Science and Social Work*, New York: Columbia University Press.

Knott, C. (2004) 'Evidence-based practice in the national probation service', in R. Burnett and C. Roberts (eds) *What Works in Probation and Youth Justice: Developing Evidence-Based Practice*, Cullompton: Willan Publishing.

Kohlberg, L. (1981) *The Philosophy of Moral Development: Moral Stages and the Idea of Justice*, London: Harper & Row.

Lab, S. and Whitehead, J. (1988) 'An analysis of juvenile correctional treatment', *Crime and Delinquency*, vol 34, pp 60-83.

Lahey, B., Moffitt, T. and Caspi, A. (2003) (eds) *Causes of Conduct Disorder and Juvenile Delinquency*, New York: Guilford Press.

Latessa, E., Cullen, F. and Gendreau, P. (2002) 'Beyond correctional quackery – professionalism and the possibility of effective treatment', *Federal Probation*, vol 66, no 2, pp 43-9.

Latimer, J., Dowden, C. and Muise. D. (2005) *The Effectiveness of Restorative Justice Practices: A Meta-Analysis*, Washington, DC: Department of Justice.

Laub, J. and Sampson, R. (2003) *Shared Beginnings, Divergent Lives: Delinquent Boys to Age Seventy*, Cambridge, MA: Harvard University Press.

Laybourn, A. (1986) 'Traditional strict working class parenting – an undervalued system', *British Journal of Social Work*, vol 16, no 6, pp 625-44.

Liddle, M. and Solanki, A.R. (2002) 'Persistent young offenders: research on individual backgrounds and life experience', *Research Briefing No 1*, London: Nacro.

Limandri, B. and Sheridan, D. (1995) 'Prediction of intentional interpersonal violence: an introduction', in J. Campbell and J. Conte (eds) *Assessing the Risk of Dangerousness: Potential for Further Violence of Sexual Offenders, Batterers and Child Abusers*, Newbury Park, CA: Sage Publications.

Lin, A.C. (2000) *Reform in the Making: The Implementation of Social Policy in Prison*, Princeton, NJ: Princeton University Press.

Lipsey, M. (1992) 'Juvenile delinquency treatment: a meta-analytic inquiry into the viability of effects', in T. Cook, H. Cooper, D. Cordray, H. Hartmann, L. Hedges, R. Light, T. Louis and F. Mosteller (eds) *Meta-Analysis for Explanation*, New York: Russell Sage.

Lipsey, M. (1995) 'What do we learn from 400 research studies on the effectiveness of treatment with juvenile delinquents?', in J. McGuire (ed) *What Works? Reducing Reoffending*, New York: John Wiley.

Lipsey, M. (1999) 'Can intervention rehabilitate serious delinquents?', *Annals of the American Academy*, July, pp 142-66.

Lipsey, M. and Cullen F. (2007) 'The effectiveness of correctional rehabilitation: a review of systematic reviews', *Annual Review of Law and Social Science*, vol 3, December, pp 1–24.

Lipsey, M. and Derzon, J. (1998) 'Predictors of violent or serious delinquency in adolescence and early adulthood: a synthesis of longitudinal research', in R. Loeber and D. Farrington (eds) *Serious and Violent Juvenile Offenders: Risk Factors and Successful Interventions*, Thousand Oaks, CA: Sage Publications.

Lipsey, M. and Wilson, D. (1998) 'Effective intervention for serious juvenile offenders: a synthesis of research', in R. Loeber and D. Farrington (eds) *Serious and Violent Juvenile Offenders: Risk Factors and Successful Interventions*, Thousand Oaks, CA: Sage Publications.

Loeb, S., Bridges, M., Fuller, B. and Rumberger, R. (2007) 'How much is too much? The influence of preschool centres on children's social and cognitive development', *Economics of Education Review*, vol 26, no 1, pp 52–66.

Loeber, R. and Farrington, D.P. (eds) (1998) *Serious and Violent Juvenile Offenders: Risk Factors and Successful Interventions*, London: Sage Publications.

Loeber, R. and Farrington, D. (2000) *Child Delinquents: Development, Intervention and Service Needs*, Thousand Oaks, CA: Sage Publications.

Loeber, R. and LeBlanc, M. (1990) 'Toward a developmental criminology'. in M. Tonry, and N. Morris (eds), *Crime and Justice: A Review of Research, vol 12*, Chicago, IL: University of Chicago Press, pp 415–34.

Logan, C. (1972) 'Evaluation research in crime and delinquency', *Journal of Criminal Law, Criminology and Police Science*, vol 63, no 3, pp 378–87.

Longo, R. (2003) 'Emerging issues, policy changes, and the future of treating children with sexual behaviour problems', *Annals of the New York Academy of Sciences*, vol 989, pp 502–14.

Loucks, N., Power, K., Swanson, V. and Chambers, J. (2000) *Young People in Custody in Scotland*, Occasional Paper Series No 3, Edinburgh: Scottish Prison Service.

McAra, L. and McVie, S. (2007) 'Youth justice? The impact of system contact on patterns of desistance from offending', *European Journal of Criminology*, vol 4, no 3, pp 315–45.

McCold, P. (2004) 'Paradigm muddle: the threat to restorative justice posed by its merger with community justice', *Contemporary Justice Review*, vol 7, no 1, March, pp 13–35.

McCulloch, P. (2005) 'Probation, social context and desistance: retracing the relationship', *Probation Journal*, vol 52, no 1, pp 8–22.

McGarrell, E. (2001) 'Restorative justice conferences as an early response to young offenders', *Office of Juvenile Justice and Delinquency Prevention Juvenile Justice Bulletin*, August, Washington, DC: US Department of Justice.

McGarrell, E., Olivares, K., Crawford, K. and Kroorand, N. (2000) *Returning Justice to the Community: The Indianapolis Juvenile Restorative Justice Experiment*, Indianapolis: Hudson Institute Crime Control Policy Center.

McGuire, J. (2000) *An Introduction to Theory and Research: Cognitive Behavioural Approaches*, London: Home Office.

McIvor, G., Jamieson, J. and Murray, C. (2000) 'Study examines gender differences in desistance from crime', *Offender Programs Report*, vol 4, no 1, pp 5-9.

McNeece, C. and Thyer, B. (2004) 'Evidence-based practice and social work', *Journal of Evidence-Based Social Work*, vol 1, no 1, pp 7-25.

McNeill, F. (2006) 'A desistance paradigm for offender management', *Criminology and Criminal Justice*, vol 6, no 1, pp 39-62.

McNeill, F. and Whyte, B. (2007) *Reducing Reoffending: Social Work and Community Justice in Scotland*, Cullompton: Willan Publishing.

Maguin, E. and Loeber, R. (1996) 'Academic performance and delinquency', in M. Tonry (ed) *Crime and Justice: A Review of Research*, vol 20, Chicago, IL: University of Chicago Press.

Mainprize, S. (1995) 'Social, psychological, and familial impacts of home confinement and electronic monitoring: exploratory research findings from British Columbia's pilot project', in K. Schulz (ed) *Electronic Monitoring and Corrections: The Policy, the Operation, the Research*, Burnaby, BC: Simon Fraser University.

Mair, G. and May, T. (1997) *Offenders on Probation*, Home Office Research Study No 167, London: Home Office.

Marshall, K. (2007) 'The present state of youth justice in Scotland', *Scottish Journal of Criminal Justice Studies*, vol 13, no 1, pp 4-19.

Marshall, W. and Serran, G. (2004) 'The role of therapists in offender treatment', *Psychology, Crime and Law*, vol 10, no 3, pp 309-20.

Martinson, R. (1974) 'What works? – questions and answers about prison reform', *The Public Interest*, vol 35, no 1, pp 22-54.

Martinson, R. (1979) 'New findings, new views: a note of caution regarding sentencing reform', *Hofstra Law Review*, vol 7, pp 243-58.

Maruna, S. (2000) 'Desistance from crime and offender rehabilitation: a tale of two research literatures', *Offender Programs Report*, vol 4, no 1, pp 1-13.

Maruna, S. (2001) *Making Good*, Washington, DC: American Psychological Association.

Matsueda, R. and Braithwaite, J. (2000) 'Social reaction', in R. Paternoster and R. Bachman (eds) *Explaining Criminals and Crime: Essays in Contemporary Criminological Theory*, Maryland, MD: Roxbury Publishing.

Maxwell, G.M. and Morris, A. (1993) *Families, Victims and Culture: Youth Justice in New Zealand*, Wellington: Department of Social Welfare and Institute of Criminology.

Mayer J. and Timms, N. (1970) *The Client Speaks*, London: Routledge.

MDJJ (Maryland Department of Juvenile Justice) (1997) *Maryland Department of Juvenile Justice Recidivism Analyses: A Program By Program Review of Recidivism Measures at Major Facilities for Department of Juvenile Justice Youths*, Baltimore, MD: MDJJ.

Mearns, D. (2003) *Developing Person-Centred Counselling* (2nd edn), London: Sage.

Mendel, R. (2000) *Less Hype More Help. Reducing Youth Crime: What Works and What Doesn't?*, Washington, DC: American Youth Policy Forum.

Mental Health Foundation (1999) *Bright Futures: Promoting Children and Young People's Mental Health*, London: Mental Health Foundation.

Mental Health Foundation (2002) *The Mental Health of Young Offenders. Bright Futures: Working with Vulnerable Young People*, London: Mental Health Foundation.

Merton, R. (1957) *Social Theory and Social Structure*, London: Collier-Macmillan.

Miller, W. and Rollnick, S. (eds) (2002) *Motivational Interviewing: Preparing People to Change* (3rd edn), New York: Guilford Press.

Milner, J. and O'Byrne, P. (2002) *Assessment in Social Work* (2nd edn), Basingstoke: Macmillan.

Moffitt, T. (1993) 'Life-course-persistent and adolescence-limited anti-social behaviour: a developmental taxonomy', *Psychological Review*, vol 100, no 4, pp 674–701.

Monaghan, G., Hibbert, P. and Moore, S. (2003) *Children in Trouble: Time for Change*, Ilford: Barnardo's.

Monahan, J. (1981) *Predicting Violent Behavior: An Assessment of Clinical Techniques*, Beverley Hills, CA: Sage Publications.

Moran, P., Ghate, D. and van der Merwe, A. (2004) *What Works in Parenting Support? A Review of the International Evidence*, Research Report 574, London: The Stationery Office.

Morawska, A. and Sanders, M. (2006) 'A review of parental engagement in parenting interventions and strategies to promote it', *Journal of Children's Services*, vol 1, no 1, pp 29–40.

Morgan, R. (2003) 'Foreword', in *HMIP Annual Report 2002/2003*, London: Home Office.

Morris, A. and Maxwell. G. (1998) 'Restorative justice in New Zealand: family group conferences as a case study', *Western Criminology Review*, vol 1, no 1 (http://wcr.sonoma.edu/v1n1/morris.html).

Morris, K. (ed) (2008) *Social Work and Multi-agency Working*, Bristol: The Policy Press.

Morris, K., Barnes, M. and Mason, P. (2009: forthcoming) *Children, families and social exclusion: Developing understandings*, Bristol: The Policy Press.

Mortimer, E. (2001) 'Electronic monitoring of released prisoners: an evaluation of the home detention curfew scheme', *Home Office Findings No 139*, London: Home Office.

Moss, P. and Petrie, P. (2002) *From Children's Services to Children's Spaces*, London: Routledge/Falmer.

Muncie, J. and Hughes, G. (2002) 'Modes of youth governance: political rationalities, criminalization and resistance', in J. Muncie, G. Hughes and E. McLaughlin (eds) *Youth Justice: Critical Readings*, London: Sage Publications.

Muncie, J. and Goldson, B. (2007) *Comparative Youth Justice: Critical Issues*, Oxford: Blackwell Publishers.

Muncie, J., Hughes, G. and McLaughin, E. (eds) (2002) *Youth Justice: Critical Readings*, London: Sage Publications.

NACRO (2003) *A Failure of Justice: Reducing Child Imprisonment*, London: NACRO.

NCH Scotland (2002) *Factfile 2002: Facts and Figures about Scotland's Children*, Glasgow: NCH Scotland.

Nellis, M. (2001) 'Community penalties in historical perspective', in A. Bottons, L. Gelsthorpe and S. Rex (eds) *Community Penalties: Change and Challenges*, Cullompton: Willan Publishing.

Nellis, M. (2004) 'Electronic monitoring and the community supervision of offenders', in A. Bottoms, S. Rex and G. Robinson (eds) *Alternatives to Prison: Options for an Insecure Society*, Cullompton: Willan Publishing.

Nellis, M. (2006) 'Surveillance, rehabilitation, and electronic monitoring: getting the issues clear', *Criminology and Public Policy*, vol 5, no 1, pp 103-8.

Neustatter, A. (2002) *Locked in Locked Out*, London: Calouste Gulbenkian Foundation.

Newburn, T. (2002) 'The contemporary politics of youth crime prevention', in J. Muncie, G. Hughes and E. McLaughlin (eds) *Youth Justice: Critical Readings*, London: Sage Publications.

Newman, T. and Blackburn, S. (2002) *Transitions in the Lives of Children and Young People: Resilience Factors*, Edinburgh: Scottish Executive.

NOMS (National Offender Management Services) (2005) *Working Together to Reduce Reoffending*, London: Home Office.

Nutley, S., Davis, H. and Tilley, N. (2000) 'Getting research into practice', *Public Money and Management*, October-December, pp 3-6.

O'Donnell, J., Hawkins, J.D., Catalano, R.F., Abbott, R.D. and Day, L.E. (1995) 'Preventing school failure, drug use and delinquency among low income children: long-term intervention in elementary schools', *American Journal of Orthopsychiatry*, vol 65, no 1, pp 87-100.

Olweus, D. (1997) 'Bully/victim problems in school: facts and intervention', *European Journal of Psychology of Education*, vol 12, no 4, pp 495-510.

Osborn, S.G. and West, D.J. (1978) 'The effectiveness of various predictors of criminal careers', *Journal of Adolescence*, vol 1, no 2, pp 101-17.

Osher, T. and Huff, B. (2006) *Working with Families of Children in the Juvenile Justice and Corrections Systems*, Washington, DC: National Evaluation and Technical Assistance Center for the Education of Children and Youth Who are Neglected, Delinquent, or At Risk (NDTAC).

Osterling, K. and Hines, A. (2006) 'Mentoring adolescent foster youth: promoting resilience during developmental transitions', *Child and Family Social Work*, vol 11, no 3, pp 242-53.

Palmer, T. (1974) 'The Youth Authority's community treatment programme', *Federal Probation*, March, pp 3-14.

Palmer, T. (1992) *The Re-emergence of Correctional Intervention*, Newbury Park, CA: Sage Publications.

Parker, J. and Bradley, G. (2003) *Social Work Practice: Assessment, Planning, Intervention and Review*, Exeter: Learning Matters.

Parsloe, P. (ed) (1999) 'Risk assessment in social care and social work', *Research Highlights in Social Work No 36*, London: Jessica Kingsley.

Parton, N. (1996) 'Social work, risk and "the blaming system"', in Parton, N. (ed) *Social Theory, Social Change and Social Work*, London: Routledge.

Partridge, S. (2004) *Examining Case Management Models for Community Sentences*, Home Office Online Report, London: Home Office.

Patterson, G.R. (1996) 'Some characteristics of a developmental theory for early-onset delinquency', in M. Lenzenweger and J. Haugaard (eds) *Frontiers of Developmental Psychopathology*, New York: Oxford University Press.

Patterson, G.R. and Yoerger, K. (1997) 'A developmental model for late-onset delinquency', in D.W. Osgood (ed) *Motivation and Delinquency: Nebraska Symposium on Motivation*, vol 44, Lincoln, NE: University of Nebraska Press, pp 119-77.

Patterson, G.R., Reid, J.B. and Dishion, T.J. (1992) *Antisocial Boys: A Social Interactional Approach*, vol 4, Eugene, OR: Castalia.

Patton, M. (2002) *Qualitative Research and Evaluation Methods*, Thousand Oaks, CA: Sage Publications.

Pawson, R. and Tilley, P. (1997) *Realistic Evaluation*, London: Sage.

Pearson, C. and Thurston, M. (2006) 'Understanding mothers' engagement with antenatal parent education services: a critical analysis of a Sure Start service', *Children and Society*, vol 20, no 5, pp 348-59.

Petersilia, J. and Turner, S. (1992) 'An evaluation of intensive probation in California', *Journal of Criminal Law and Criminology*, vol 83, no 3, pp 610-58.

Petras, D., Massat, C. and Essex, E. (2002) 'Overcoming hopelessness and social isolation: the ENGAGE model for working with neglecting families toward permanence', *Child Welfare*, vol 81, pp 225-48.

Petrie, P. (2001) 'The potential of pedagogy/education for work in the children's sector in the UK', *Social Work in Europe*, vol 8, no 3, pp 23-5.

Petrie, P. (2004) 'Pedagogy: a holistic, personal approach to work with children and young people across services: European models for practice, training, education and qualification', Unpublished paper, London: Thomas Coram Research Unit, Institute of Education, University of London.

Pfohl, S.J. (1985) *Images of Deviance and Social Control: A Sociological History*, New York: McGraw-Hill.

Pollock, N., McBain, I. and Webster, C. (1989) 'Clinical decision making: the assessment of dangerousness', in K. Howells, and C. Hollin (eds) *Clinical Approaches to Violence*, Chichester: John Wiley.

Poulin, F., Dishion, T. and Haas, E. (1999) 'The peer influence paradox: friendship quality and deviancy training within male adolescent friendships', *Merrill-Palmer Quarterly*, vol 1, no 1, pp 42-61.

Prior, D. and Paris, A. (2006) 'Preventing children's involvement in crime and anti-social behaviour: a literature review', Paper produced for the National Evaluation of the Children's Fund Institute of Applied Social Studies Research, Report No 623, Birmingham: DfES Publications.

Prochaska, J. and Di Clemente, C. (1982) 'Transtheoretical therapy: towards a more integrative model of change', *Psychotherapy: Theory, Research and Practice*, vol 19, no 3, pp 276-88.

Pullmann, M.D., Kerbs, J., Koroloff, N., Veach-White, E., Gaylor, R. and Sieler, D. (2006) 'Juvenile offenders with mental health needs: reducing recidivism using wraparound', *Crime and Delinquency*, vol 52, no 3, pp 375-97.

Putnam, R. (2000) *Bowling Alone: The Collapse and Revival of American Community*, New York: Simon and Schuster.

Quinsey, V., Harris, G. and Rice, M. (1998) *Violent Offenders: Appraising and Managing Risk*, Washington, DC: American Psychological Association.

Raynor, P. (1985) *Social Work, Justice and Control*, Oxford: Blackwell.

Raynor, P. (1997) 'Some observations on rehabilitation and justice', *Howard Journal of Criminal Justice*, vol 36, no 3, pp 248-62.

Raynor, P. and Vanstone, M. (1994) 'Probation practice, effectiveness and the non-treatment paradigm', *British Journal of Social Work*, vol 24, no 4, pp 387-404.

Reid, W. (1994) 'The empirical practice movement', *Social Service Review*, vol 68, no 2, pp 165-88.

Rex, S. (1999) 'Desistance from offending: experiences of probation', *Howard Journal of Criminal Justice*, vol 36, no 4, pp 366-83.

Rice, M. and Harris, G. (1995) 'Violent recidivism: assessing predictive validity', *Journal of Consulting and Clinical Psychology*, vol 63, no 5, pp 737-48.

Righthand, S., Prentky, R., Knight, R., Carpenter, E., Hecker, J. and Nangle, D. (2005) 'Factor structure and validation of the juvenile sex offender assessment protocol (J-SOAP)', *Sexual Abuse: A Journal of Research and Treatment*, vol 17, no 1, pp 13–30.

Roberts, C. (2004) 'Offending behaviour programmes: emerging evidence and implications for practice', in R. Burnett and C. Roberts (eds) *What Works in Probation and Youth Justice*, Cullompton: Willan Publishing.

Robinson, G. (2003) 'Risk assessment', in W.-H. Chui and M. Nellis (eds) *Probation: Theories, Practice and Research*, Harlow: Pearson Education.

Robinson, G. and Dignan, J. (2004) 'Sentence management', in A. Bottoms, S. Rex and G. Robinson (eds) *Alternatives to Prison: Options for an Insecure Society*, Cullompton: Willan Publishing.

Rock, P. (1997) 'Sociological theories of crime', in M. Maguire, R. Morgan and R. Reiner (eds) *Oxford Handbook of Criminology* (2nd edn), Oxford: Oxford University Press.

Rollnick, S. and Miller, W.R. (1995) 'What is motivational interviewing?', *Behavioural and Cognitive Psychotherapy*, vol 23, no 3, pp 325–34.

Ross, R.R., Fabiano, E. and Ewles, C. (1988) 'Reasoning and rehabilitation', *International Journal of Offender Therapy and Comparative Criminology*, vol 32, no 1, pp 29–35.

Rowe, D. (2002) *Biology and Crime*, Los Angeles, CA: Roxbury.

Rowe, W. (2002) *A Meta-analysis of Six Washington State Restorative Justice Projects: Accomplishments and Outcomes*, Washington, DC: Office of Juvenile Justice.

Rumgay, J. (2004) 'Scripts for safer survival: pathways out of female crime', *Howard Journal of Criminal Justice*, vol 43, no 4, pp 405–19.

Russell, M.N. (1990) *Clinical Social Work: Research and Practice*, Newbury Park, CA: Sage

Rutter, M., Giller, H. and Hagel, A. (1998) *Antisocial Behavior by Young People*, New York: Cambridge University Press.

Sampson, R. (2004) 'Networks and neighbourhoods: the implications of connectivity for thinking about crime in the modern city', in H. McCarthy, P. Miller and P. Skidmore (eds) *Network Logic: Who Governs in an Interconnected World?*, London: Demos.

Sampson, R. and Laub, J. (1993) *Crime in the Making: Pathways and Turning Points through Life*, Cambridge, MA: Harvard University.

Sampson, R., Raudenbush, S. and Earls, F. (1997) 'Neighbourhoods and violent crime: a multilevel study of collective efficacy', *Science*, vol 277, no 5238, pp 918–24.

Sarri, R., Shook, J., Ward, G., Creekmore, M., Alberston, C., Goodkind, S. and Chih Soh, J. (2001) *Decision Making in the Juvenile Justice System: A Comparative Study of Four States. Final Report to the National Institute of Justice*, Ann Arbor, MI: Institute for Social Research.

Scarr, S. (1992) 'Developmental theories for the 1990s: development and individual differences', *Child Development*, vol 63, no 1, pp 1-19.

Schiff, M. (1998) 'The impact of restorative justice interventions on juvenile offenders', in L. Walgrave and G. Bazemore (eds) *Restoring Juvenile Justice: Repairing the Harm of Youth Crime*, Monsey, NY: Criminal Justice Press.

Schinke, P., Orlandi, M. and Cole, K. (1992) 'Boys and girls clubs in public housing developments: prevention services for youth at risk', *Journal of Community Psychology*, Special Issue, vol 20, no 1, pp 118-28.

Schmidt, S., Liddle, H. and Dakof, G. (1996) 'Changes in parenting practices and adolescent drug abuse during multidimensional family therapy', *Journal of Family Psychology*, vol 10, no 1, pp 12-27.

Schofield, G. (2001) 'Resilience and family placement: a lifespan perspective', *Adoption and Fostering*, vol 25, no 3, pp 6-19.

Schon, D. (1987) *Educating the Reflective Practitioner*, San Francisco, CA: Jossey-Bass.

Schumacher, M. and Kurz, G. (2000) *The 8% Solution*, Thousand Oaks, CA: Sage Publications.

Schur, E. (1973) *Radical Non-intervention: Rethinking the Delinquency Problem*, Englewood Cliffs, NJ: Prentice-Hall.

Schweinhart, L. and Weikart, D. (1997) *Lasting Differences. The High/Scope Preschool Curriculum Comparison Study Through Age 23*, Ypsilanti, MI: High/Scope Educational Research Foundation.

Scottish Executive (2004) *Getting it Right for Every Child*, Edinburgh: Scottish Executive.

Scottish Executive (2006) *Reconvictions of Offenders Discharged from Custody or Given Non-Custodial Sentences in 2002/03, Scotland*, Edinburgh: Scottish Executive.

Scottish Executive (2007) *Looked After Children and Young People: We Can and Must Do Better*, Edinburgh: Scottish Executive.

Scraton, P. and Haydon, D. (2002) 'Challenging the criminalization of children and young people: securing a rights-based agenda', in J. Muncie, G. Hughes and E. McLaughlin (eds) *Youth Justice: Critical Readings*, London: Sage Publications.

Senge, P. (1992) *The Fifth Discipline: The Art and Practice of the Learning Organization*, London: Century Business.

Shaw, I. and Shaw, A. (1997) 'Keeping social work honest: evaluating as profession and practice', *British Journal of Social Work*, vol 27, no 6, pp 847-69.

Shaw, M. and Hannah-Moffat, K. (2004) 'How cognitive skills forgot about gender and diversity', in G. Mair (ed) *What Matters in Probation*, Cullompton: Willan Publishing.

Sheldon, B. (1994) 'Social work effectiveness research: implications for probation and juvenile justice services', *Howard Journal of Criminal Justice*, vol 33, no 3, pp 218-35.

Sherman, L. and Strang, H. (2007) *Restorative Justice: The Evidence*, London: Smith Institute.

Sherman, L., Gottfredson, D., MacKenzie, D., Eck, J., Reuter, P. and Bushway, S. (1997) *Preventing Crime. What Works, What Doesn't, What's Promising*, National Criminal Justice Reference Series, Washington, DC: US Department of Justice, Office of Justice Programs (www.ncjrs.org).

Sherman, L., Strang, H. and Woods, D. (2000) *Recidivism in the Canberra Re-integrative Shaming Experiments (RISE)*, Canberra: Centre for Restorative Justice (www.aic.gov.au/rjustice/rise/recidivism/index.html).

Silber, K. (1965) *Pestalozzi: The Man and his Work*, London: Routledge & Kegan Paul.

Sinclair, I., Baker, C., Wilson, K. and Gibbs, I. (2005) *Foster Children: Where They Go and How They Get On*, London: Jessica Kingsley.

Siporin, M. (1975) *Introduction to Social Work Practice*, New York: Macmillan.

Skinner, K. and Whyte, B. (2004) 'Going beyond training: theory and practice in managing learning', *Social Work Education*, vol 23, no 4, August, pp 365-81.

Smith, D. (1997) 'Ethnic origins, crime and criminal justice', in M. Maguire, R. Morgan and R. Reiner (eds) *Oxford Handbook of Criminology* (2nd edn), Oxford: Oxford University Press.

Smith, D. (2002) 'Crime and the life course', in M. Maguire, R. Morgan and R. Reiner (eds) *The Oxford Handbook of Criminology* (3rd edn), Oxford: Oxford University Press.

Smith, D. (2004) *Parenting and Delinquency at Ages 12 to 15*, The Edinburgh Study of Youth Transitions and Crime (www.law.ed.ac.uk/cls/esytc/findings/digest3.pdf).

Smith, D. (2005) 'The effectiveness of the juvenile justice system', *Criminal Justice*, vol 5, pp 181-95.

Smith, D. and McAra. L. (2004) *Gender and Youth Offending*, Edinburgh: Edinburgh Study of Youth Transitions.

Smith, M. and Whyte, B. (2008) 'Social education and social pedagogy: reclaiming a Scottish tradition in social work', *European Journal of Social Work*, vol 11, no 1, pp 15-28.

Smith, D., McVie, S., Woodward, R., Shute, J., Flint, K. and McAra, L. (2001) *Edinburgh Study of Youth Transitions and Crime: Key Findings at Ages 12 and 13*, Edinburgh: University of Edinburgh.

Social Exclusion Unit (2002) *Reducing Re-offending by Ex-prisoners*, London: Social Exclusion Unit.

Spratt, T. and Callan, J. (2004) 'Parents' views on social work interventions in child welfare cases', *British Journal of Social Work*, vol 34, pp 199-224.

STAF (Scottish Throughcare and Aftercare Forum) (2006) *How Good are your Throughcare and Aftercare Services? Quality Indicators for Best Practice*, Edinburgh: STAF.

Stalker, K. (2003) 'Managing risk and uncertainty in social work: a literature review', *Journal of Social Work*, vol 3, no 2, pp 211-33.

Stein, M. (2005) *Resilience and Young People Leaving Care: Overcoming the Odds*, York: Joseph Rowntree Foundation (www.jrf.org.uk/bookshop/eBooks/185935369X.pdf).

Sutherland, E. and Cressey, D. (1970) *Criminology*, Philadelphia, PA: Lippincot.

SWIA (Social Work Inspection Agency) (2005) *Review of the Management Arrangements of Colyn Evans by Fife Constabulary and Fife Council*, Edinburgh: Scottish Executive (www.swia.gov.uk).

SWIA (2006) *Extraordinary Lives*, Edinburgh: SWIA.

Talbot, C. (1996) *Realising Objectives in the Probation Service: A Workbook*, London: Home Office Probation Unit.

Tapsfield, R. and Collier, F. (2005) *The Cost of Foster Care: Investing in our Children's Future*, London: BAAF and TFN.

Taylor, J. and Daniel, B. (2000) 'The rhetoric vs the reality in child care and protection: ideology and practice in working with fathers', *Journal of Advanced Nursing*, vol 31, no 1, pp 12-19.

Taylor, P., Crow, I., Irvine, D. and Nicholls, G. (1999) *Demanding Physical Activity Programmes for Young Offenders under Probation Supervision*, London: Home Office.

The Community Resources Cooperative (1993) 'Intensive wraparound implementation', Paper presented at training meeting conducted at the wraparound services training, Pittsburgh, PA.

Tierney, J., Grossman, J. with Resch, N. (1995) *Making a Difference: An Impact Study of Big Brother's Big Sisters*, Philadelphia, PA: Public/Private Ventures.

Tonnies, F. (1912) *Gemeinschaft und Gesellschaft* (2nd edn), Leipzig: Fues's Verlag.

Tonry, M. and Doob, A. (eds) (2004) *Youth Crime and Youth Justice*, Chicago, IL: University of Chicago Press, p 1.

Trotter, C. (2006) *Working with Involuntary Clients: A Guide to Practice*, (2nd edn), London: Sage.

Tuckman, B. (1965) 'Developmental sequence in small groups', *Psychological Bulletin*, vol 63, no 6, pp 384-99.

Tuckman, B. and Jensen, M. (1977) 'Stages of small group development revisited', *Group and Organizational Studies*, vol 2, no 4, pp 419-27.

Tunstill, J., Aldgate, J. and Hughes, M. (2007) *Improving Children's Services Networks: Lessons from Family Centres*, London: Jessica Kingsley.

Turner, M. and Zimmerman, W. (1994) 'Acting for the sake of research', in J. Wholey, H. Hatry and K. Newcomer (eds) *Handbook of Practical Program Evaluation*, San Francisco, CA: Jossey-Bass.

UK Children's Commissioners (2008) *Report to the UN Committee on the Rights of the Child* (www.sccyp.org.uk/).

Ungar, M. (2004) *Nurturing Hidden Resilience in Troubled Youth*, Toronto: University of Toronto Press.

Ungar, M. (2006) 'Resilience across cultures', *British Journal of Social Work*, Research Note, pp 1–18.

Utting, D. and Vennard, J. (2000) *What Works with Young Offenders in the Community?*, Ilford: Barnardo's.

Wade, J. and Dixon, J. (2006) 'Making a home, finding a job: investigating early housing and employment outcomes for young people leaving care', *Child and Family Social Work*, vol 11, no 3, pp 199–208.

Wain, N. (2007) *The ASBO: Wrong Turning, Dead End*, London: Howard League.

Walker, M., Barclay, A., Malloch, M., McIvor, G., Kendrick, A., Hunter, L. and Hill, M. (2006) *Secure Accommodation in Scotland: Its Role and Relationship with 'Alternative' Services*, Edinburgh: Scottish Executive Education Department.

Ward, T. and Maruna, S. (2007) *Rehabilitation: Beyond the Risk Assessment Paradigm*, London: Routledge.

Warner, F. (1992) *Risk: Analysis, Perception and Management: Report of a Royal Society Study Group*, London: Royal Society.

Weatherburn, D. and Lind, B. (1997) *Social and Economic Stress, Child Neglect and Juvenile Delinquency*, Sydney: NSW Bureau of Crime Statistics and Research, Attorney-General's Department.

Webb, S. (2006) *Social Work in a Risk Society: Social and Political Perspectives*, London: Palgrave Macmillan.

Webster, C., MacDonald, R. and Simpson, M. (2006) 'Predicting criminality? Risk factors, neighbourhood influence and desistance', *Youth Justice*, vol 6, no 1, pp 7–22.

Webster-Stratton, C. and Hancock, L. (1998) 'Parent training for young children with conduct problems: content, methods, and therapeutic processes', in C. Schaefer (ed) *Handbook of Parent Training*, New York: John Wiley & Sons.

Whitfield, D. (2001) *The Magic Bracelet: Technology and Offender Supervision*, Winchester: Waterside Press.

Whyte, B. (2004) 'Responding to youth crime in Scotland', *British Journal of Social Work*, vol 34, no 4, April, pp 395–411.

Whyte, B. (2007) 'Restoring "stakeholder involvement" in justice', in P. Richie and S. Hunter (eds) *Co-Production and Personalization in Social Care*, Research Highlights, London: Jessica Kingsley.

Williams, F. (2004) 'What matters is who works: why every child matters to New Labour. Commentary on the DfES Green Paper *Every child matters*', *Critical Social Policy*, vol 24, no 3, pp 406-27.

Wilson, J. and Hernstein, R. (1985) *Crime and Human Nature*, New York: Simon & Schuster.

Wilson, J. and Kelling, G. (1982) 'Broken windows', *The Atlantic Monthly*, vol 269, no 3, pp 29-38.

Wilson, S.J., Lipsey, M.W. and Derzon, J.H. (2000) 'Wilderness challenge programs for delinquent youth: A meta-analysis of outcome evaluations'. *Evaluation and Program Planning*, vol 23, no 1, pp 1-12.

Wilson, W.J. (1987) *The Truly Disadvantaged: The Inner City, the Underclass and Public Policy*, Chicago, IL: University of Chicago.

Witkin, S. (1991) 'Constructing our future', *Social Work*, vol 44, no 1, pp 5-9.

Worling, J. (2004) 'The estimate of risk of adolescent sexual offence recidivism (ERASOR): preliminary psychometric data', *Sexual Abuse: A Journal of Research and Treatment*, vol 16, no 3, pp 235-54.

Yatchmenoff, D. (2005) 'Measuring client engagement from the client's perspective in non voluntary child protective services', *Research on Social Work Practice*, vol 15, no 2, pp 84-96.

YJB (Youth Justice Board) (2004) *National Evaluation of the Restorative Justice in Schools Programme*, London: YJB for England and Wales.

YJB (2005a) *Risk and Protective Factors*, London: YJB.

YJB (2005b) *Mental Health Needs and Effectiveness of Provision for Young Offenders in Custody and the Community*, London: YJB.

YJB (2007) *1 -Month ISSP*, London: YJB.

Young, J. (1994) 'Recent paradigms in criminology', in M. Maguire, R. Morgan and R. Reiner, *The Oxford Handbook of Criminology* (2nd edn), Oxford: Clarendon Press.

Index

A

action-oriented methods 49, 51
action plans 91-3
actuarial risk assessment 78-9, 81-2
adjourning 136, 137
Adler, R.M. 2
Adolescent Transition Programme 139
age-crime curve 34
age of criminal responsibility 2, 7, 9
age of onset 100-3
age thresholds 12
Anderson, S. 35
Andrews, D. 53, 54, 55, 56, 61, 65, 135,
    136, 200-1
anomie 25
anti-social behaviour 100-1, 103-4
ASBOs (Anti-Social Behaviour
    Orders) 11
assessment 71, 72-3, 94
    combined need and risk assessment
    80-3
    developing an action plan 91-3
    dynamic need-risk factors 79-80
    holistic and integrated 86-7
    and predicting re-offending 75-8
    risk assessment methods 78-9
    specialist 87-91
    standardised assessment tools 83-5
ASSET 83-4, 132, 159, 162, 189

B

Baker, K. 84
Baron, S. 125
Barret, J. 144
Barry, M. 128
base rates 81

Bazemore, G. 113
Beijing Rules 7, 67
biogenetic theories 22-3
bonding social capital 127
Bonta, J. 54
Bottoms, A. 15-16, 57-8, 198
Bourdieu, P. 125-6
Bowling, B. 35, 37, 129
Braithwaite, J. 113, 115
bridging social capital 127
British Association of Social Workers
    (BASW) 2-3
Bulger case 6
bullying 118, 141
Burns, R. 144

C

Callan, J. 109
Canada 163
Canberra 116
Cannan, C. 68
capital 125-6
    see also human capital; social capital
case management 192-8
change 61, 63
    maintaining over time 169, 170-4
    measuring 178-82
    monitoring and evaluation 174-8
    motivational interviewing 131-3
change management 91-3, 192-8
Chapman, T. 63
Chicago School of Criminology 23,
    34
Child and Adolescent Functional
    Assessment Scale 158
Child and Adolescent Mental Health
    Services (CAMHS) 90

child welfare 2, 99
children or offenders first 3-5
   practice approaches 1-3
Children Act 1989 9-10
civic engagement 127
Clarke, R.V. 26
clinical assessment 78-9, 82
Coalter, F. 143
coercion model 103
Coffield, F. 63
cognitive behavioural practice 49, 51,
   66-7, 135, 137
cognitive behavioural theory 26-7, 29
Cohen, S. 25
Coleman, James 126, 127-8
Columbia University 141-2
Commission of Human Rights 10-11
common assessment framework (CAF)
   86, 159
communities 40, 46
   interventions 63, 141-5
   protecting 103-4
   and social education 68
   social justice 199-200
   wraparound provision 157-61
Communities that Care 142-3
competence 3
compliance theories 58
Cornish, D. 26
Coulshed, V. 72
Crawford, A. 117
credence 51
credibility 51
Cressey, D. 27
crime
   theories 22-35
   see also youth crime
criminogenic need principle 62
cultural capital 126

D

Daly, K. 114
deep learning 203
defensibility 82-3
Derzon, J. 101, 102
desistance 34-5, 42, 129
   effective practice 46
   and gender 36-7
desistance paradigm 16, 17
Di Clemente, C. 61, 131
Directing Principles of Riyadh 7-8
diversion 2, 19n, 100
Dowden, C. 201
Dunedin study 103
Durkheim, Émile 25
Dutton, K. 116
dynamic risk factors 79-80, 88

E

early intervention 100, 103-4, 118-19
early onset 100-3
early years preventive practice 105-9
ecological theories 23-5
economic capital 125-6
economy 51
Edinburgh Study of Youth Transitions
   and Crime 36
education 18, 40, 46, 87, 191
   school-based programmes 140-1
   and social capital 126
   see also social education
effective practice 45, 46-7, 67-8, 123,
   184-5
  directing principles 61-7
evidence-based practice 47-51
   intelligent social work 182-4
   reflective practitioners 200-4
   what does not seem to work 56-8
   what should direct practice 58-61
   what works 51-5

electronic monitoring 163-4
empowerment 51
England and Wales
    age of criminal responsibility 2
    assessment 86
    separation of family and youth
        courts 12
environmental criminology 24-5, 26
ethics 51
ethnicity 30
European Convention on Human
    Rights (ECHR) 6, 10-11
evaluation 174-82
Every Child Matters (ECM) (HM
    Treasury) 12-13, 99, 190
evidence-based practice (EBP) 47-51
Ewles, C. 66

F

Fabiano, E. 66
families 39, 46
    early years preventive practice
        105-9
family group conferences 114-15, 116
    interventions 137-40
    and secure accommodation 155-6
    wraparound provision 157-8
Farrall, S. 46, 130
Farrington, D. 32-3
Feld, B. 155
feminist theories 30-1
Flood-Page, C. 37
forming 136
Fortune, A. 51
foster care 140
Fraser, M. 110
functional family therapy (FFT) 139

G

Galinsky, M.J. 110
Garrett, C. 53

gender
    and desistance 36-7, 129
    and responsivity 63
    and theories of crime 30-1
Gendreau, P. 54, 65
genetic theories 22-3
Germany 68
Getting it Right for Every Child
    (GIRFEC) (Scottish Executive)
    12-13, 99, 190
Glasgow 116, 161
Gordon, D. 108
Gottfredson, M. 24
Graham, J. 35, 37, 129
group work 135-7
Gurney, A. 74, 75

H

Hagel, A. 37-8, 80
Havana Rules 7, 8, 12
Henry, B. 103
Heyman, B. 81
Hirschi, T. 24, 29-30
holistic and integrated assessment
    86-7
Hollins, C. 135
Houchin, R. 104
Hough, M. 63
housing 40
Howard League for Penal Reform 9-
    10, 13
human capital 18, 47, 68, 123, 124-5
human dignity 3
hybrid models 194-5

I

Indianapolis 116
integrated theories 32-5
integration *see* joined-up approaches
integrative paradigm 17
integrity 3

intelligent social work 182–4
intensive intervention 149, 150–2, 164
Intensive Probation Supervision (IPS)
    162–3
Intensive Supervision and Monitoring
    Scheme (ISMS) 161
Intensive Supervision and Surveillance
    Programme (ISSP) 161–2
interdisciplinary practice *see* joined-up
    approaches
intervention 123, 146–7, 164
    community-based approaches 141–5
    community-based wraparound
    provision 157–61
    electronic monitoring 163–4
    family-based approaches 137–40
    from action plan to intervention
    128–30
    intensive 149, 150–2
    intensive support services 161–3
    motivational interviewing 130–3
    pro-social modelling 133–4
    residential and institutional
    approaches 145–6
    school-based approaches 140–1
    secure accommodation 152–7
    structured programme approaches
    135–7
    see also early intervention
Irvine, A. 139
Izzo, R. 67

J

Jaeger, C. 74
Jamieson, J. 36, 129
joined-up approaches
    assessment 86–7
    case management and managing
    change 192–8
    practice 11–17
justice 2
    see also youth justice

K

Kane, J. 118
Kiessling, J. 200–1
Kilbrandon approach 87

L

lead professional 13–14, 87
learning 203
learning organisations 204–5
learning styles 62–3
left realism 33–4
life course theories 27–9
Lipsey, M. 55, 56, 101, 102, 144, 145
Loeb, S. 106
looked-after children 12–13
low base rates 81

M

McAra, L. 31
McGarrell, E. 116
McNeill, F. 16, 17
McWilliams, W. 15–16
Marshall, T.F. 113
Martinson, R. 52
Maruna, S. 21, 34
Maryland 146
maturational change theories 34
Maxwell, G. 117
men
    desistance 36–7, 129
    theories of crime 30–1
Mendel, R. 155
mental health problems 90–1
mentoring 142
meta-analysis 52–5, 56, 59, 81–2
    intensive intervention 150
    restorative practice 116–17
    structured programme approaches
    135

Milwaukee 158-60
Minnesota 146
minority ethnic groups 30
Missouri 146
modality principle 64
Moffitt, T. 28
monitoring 175
Morris, A. 117
motivational interviewing (MI) 130-3
movement restriction conditions
    (MRCs) 161
multi-agency public protection
    arrangements (MAPPAs) 89
multi-systemic family therapy (MST)
    139-40
multidisciplinary provision see joined-
    up approaches

N

Nacro 104
narrative data 48
narrative theory 34
need 4, 8, 54-5, 65
    criminogenic need principle 62
    and social education 17-19
need assessment 11, 71
    methods 79
    and predicting re-offending 75-8
    and risk assessment 80-3
    standardised assessment tools 83-5
neighbourhood communities see
    communities
Nellis, M. 58
net widening 7
New Zealand 5, 114
Newburn, T. 37-8, 117
non-treatment paradigm 15-16
norming 136
Norway 141

O

Ohio 162-3
Orme, J. 72
Ottawa 141
outdoor adventure programmes 143-5

P

Palmer, T. 53-4
paramountcy principle 3-5, 11-12
parenting
    early years preventive practice 105-9
    interventions 138-9
    and youth crime 39
Parenting Adolescents Wisely 139
PATHE Project 140
Patterson, G.R. 28, 103
performing 136
Perry Pre-school Programme 105-6
persistence 28, 37-9, 42
    and restorative practice 115-18
planned maintenance 171
poverty 23
practitioners
    in learning organisations 204-5
    reflective 200-4
pro-social modelling 133-4
problem analysis triangle 27
Prochaska, J. 61, 131
programme integrity principle 64-5
protective mechanisms 111
psychodynamic theories 26
punishment 57-8
Putnam, Robert 126, 127-8

Q

qualitative data 48
quantitative data 47

R

R v Secretary of State 9–10
randomised controlled trials 47, 48
rational choice theory (RCT) 26
Raynor, P. 16–17
re-integrative shaming 113, 116
Re-integrative Shaming Experiments
    (RISE) 116
re-offending *see* persistence
realist criminology 33–4
reflective practitioners 200–4
reflexivity 21
Reid, W. 51
relational principle 64
residential training schools 145–6
resilience 41, 110–12, 170
responsibilities 187, 188–92
responsivity principle 62–3, 65
Restorative Justice Conferencing
    Experiment 116
restorative practice 5, 112–18, 119
    ecological influences 25
    intelligent social work 183
revised paradigm 16
Rex, S. 134
rights 188–92
risk 40–2, 73–5, 94
    dynamic risk factors 79–80
risk factors 54–5
risk assessment 11, 71, 73–4
    methods 78–9
    and need assessment 80–3
    and predicting re-offending 75–8
    specialist 88
    standardised assessment tools 83–5
risk management 74, 75, 83, 89, 91–3
risk, need and responsivity (RNR) 65
risk principle 61–2, 83
Riyadh Guidelines 7–8
Roots of Empathy 107
Ross, R. 54, 65, 66, 67
routine activity theory (RAT) 26–7

Rumgay, J. 37
Russell, M.N. 56
Rutter, M. 111

S

school *see* education
science as knowledge 50
science as method 49
Scotland
    age of criminal responsibility 2
    assessment 86
    Kilbrandon approach 87
    looked-after children 13
    UNCRC 1
    welfare-based system 11–12
    youth courts 12
secure accommodation 149, 152–7
Senge, P. 205
service to humanity 3
Sheffield 141
Sheldon, B. 56
Sherman, L. 116, 117–18
single assessment plan (SAP) 86
Smith, D. 28, 31, 36
social bonding theory 29–30, 34
social capital 18, 25, 47, 125–8, 170–1
    and communities 198–9
    and social education 68
    Tokyo Rules 8
social cohesion 25
social constructionism 48
social control theories 23–4
social development theories 32–4
social disorganisation theories 24–5
social education 17–19, 29, 67–8
    interventions 135–6, 147
social justice 3, 189, 198–200
social learning theory 29, 124
    interventions 49, 51, 135
    practice agencies 204
social maps 24–5
social networks 127

social pedagogy *see* social education
social reaction theories 25
social strain theories 25
socioeconomic theories 23-5
specialist assessment 87-91
sports 143-5
Spratt, T. 109
standardised assessment tools 83-5
static risk factors 78, 88
statistical fallacy 81
storming 136
Strang, H. 117-18
sub-cultural delinquency 27
substance abuse 40, 87, 101, 104
supervision *see* intervention
Sutherland, E. 27

T

tagging 163-4
Taylor, P. 145
Think First 137
throughcare 170-4
Tokyo Rules 7, 8
Tonnies, F. 23
Triple-P Positive Parenting
    programme 106
Tuckman, B. 136-7
Tunstill, J. 106-7

U

Umbreit, M. 113
Ungar, M. 76
United Nations 7-8
United Nations Committee on the
    Rights of the Child vii, 9, 190
United Nations Convention on the
    Rights of the Child (UNCRC) vii,
    1, 6-7, 8-9, 152
    age thresholds 12
    children or offenders first 3-5
    social education 18, 67

United Nations Declaration on
    Basic Principles on the Use of
    Restorative Justice Programmes in
    Criminal Matters 113
US
    assessment 88
    centre-based childcare 106
    early onset 101
    functional family therapy 139
    intensive support services 162-3
    residential training schools 146
    RNR approach 65
    wraparound provision 157-60
Utting, D. 144

V

Vanstone, M. 16-17
Venables v Crown 6
Vennard, J. 144
Venture Trust 143
victimisation 109-10
Vienna Guidelines 7, 8

W

Wales *see* England and Wales
Webster, C. 198-9
Webster-Stratton programmes 106-7
welfare 2
    see also child welfare
what works? paradigm 16-17
Whyte, B. 116
Wilson, D. 144
women
    desistance 36, 37, 129
    responsivity 63
    theories of crime 30-1
Wraparound Milwaukee 158-60
wraparound provision 157-61

Y

Young, J. 33
youth crime 21, 42
   families, schools and communities
    39-40
   nature 35-9
   risk and resilience 40-2
youth justice 2
   benchmarks for practice 6-11
   children or offenders first 3-5
   converging practice 11-12
   directing principles of effective
    practice 45-69
   future directions 12-14
   paradigm for practice 14-17
   practice approaches 1-3
   restorative practice 112-18

ASBO nation
The criminalisation of nuisance
Edited by Peter Squires

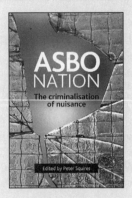

"The social construction of 'anti-social behaviour', together with the extension and dispersal of interventions, sanctions and, ultimately, punishments targeted at the 'anti-social', comprise some of the most controversial policy developments of the New Labour era. This timely volume critically illuminates the origins, applications and impact of such phenomena. It makes essential reading for researchers, students, policy-makers and practitioners alike."
Barry Goldson, Professor of Criminology and Social Policy, University of Liverpool

Anti-social behaviour (ASB) has been a major preoccupation of New Labour's project of social and political renewal, with ASBOs a controversial addition to crime and disorder management powers. Thought by some to be a dangerous extension of the power to criminalise, by others as a vital dimension of local governance, there remains a concerning lack of evidence as to whether or not they compound social exclusion.

This collection, from an impressive panel of contributors, brings together opinion, commentary, research evidence, professional guidance, debate and critique in order to understand the phenomenon of anti-social behaviour. It considers the earliest available evidence in order to evaluate the Government's ASB strategy, debates contrasting definitions of anti-social behaviour and examines policy and practice issues affected by it.

Contributors ask what the recent history of ASB governance tells us about how the issue will develop to shape public and social policies in the years to come. Reflecting the perspectives of practitioners, victims and perpetrators, the book should become the standard text in the field.

PB £24.99 US$45.00 **ISBN** 978 1 84742 027 5
HB £65.00 US$99.00 **ISBN** 978 1 84742 028 2
234 x 156mm 392 pages June 2008

Children and young people in custody
Managing the risk
Edited by Maggie Blyth, Chris Wright and Robert Newman

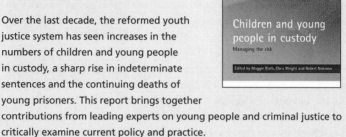

Over the last decade, the reformed youth justice system has seen increases in the numbers of children and young people in custody, a sharp rise in indeterminate sentences and the continuing deaths of young prisoners. This report brings together contributions from leading experts on young people and criminal justice to critically examine current policy and practice.

PB £14.99 US$29.95 **ISBN** 978 1 84742 261 3
245 x 170mm 128 pages November 2008

Prevention and youth crime
Is early intervention working?
Edited by Maggie Blyth and Enver Solomon

The 2008 UK government Youth Crime Action Plan emphasises prevention and early intervention in different aspects of work with young people who offend or are considered to be 'at risk' of offending. Through contributions from leading experts on youth work and criminal justice, this report takes a critical look at early intervention policies.

PB £14.99 US$29.95 **ISBN** 978 1 84742 263 7
245 x 170mm 144 pages November 2008

Young people and 'risk'
Edited by Maggie Blyth, Enver Solomon and Kerry Baker

Alongside the current media public preoccupation with high-risk offenders, there has been a shift towards a greater focus on risk and public protection in UK criminal justice policy. Much of the academic debate has centered on the impact of the risk paradigm on adult offender management services; less attention has been given to the arena of youth justice and young adults. Yet, there are critical questions for both theory – are the principles of risk management the same when working with young people? – and practice – how can practitioners respond to those young people who cause serious harm to others? – that need to be considered.

The distinguished contributors to *Young people and 'risk'* consider risk not only in terms of public protection but also in terms of young people's own vulnerability to being harmed (either by others or through self-inflicted behaviour). One of the report's key objectives is to explore the links between these two distinct, but related, aspects of risk.

PB £14.99 US$29.95 **ISBN** 978 1 84742 000 8
245 x 170mm 128 pages September 2007

Youth crime and youth justice
Public opinion in England and Wales
Mike Hough and Julian V. Roberts

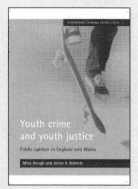

This report presents the findings from the first national, representative survey of public attitudes to youth crime and youth justice in England and Wales.

Significantly, it highlights that most people are demonstrably ill-informed about youth crime and youth justice issues. It also carries clear policy implications in relation to both public education and reform of the youth justice system.

Youth crime and youth justice is essential reading for academics, researchers, policy makers and practitioners in the fields of criminal justice, criminology, social policy, social work and probation.

PB £14.99 US$25.00 **ISBN** 978 1 86134 649 0
245 x 170mm 80 pages November 2004

To order copies of this publication or any other Policy Press titles please visit **www.policypress.org.uk** or contact:

In the UK and Europe:
Marston Book Services, PO Box 269, Abingdon, Oxon, OX14 4YN, UK
Tel: +44 (0)1235 465500
Fax: +44 (0)1235 465556
Email: direct.orders@marston.co.uk

In the USA and Canada:
ISBS, 920 NE 58th Street, Suite 300, Portland, OR 97213-3786, USA
Tel: +1 800 944 6190
(toll free)
Fax: +1 503 280 8832
Email: info@isbs.com

In Australia and New Zealand:
DA Information Services,
648 Whitehorse Road Mitcham,
Victoria 3132, Australia
Tel: +61 (3) 9210 7777
Fax: +61 (3) 9210 7788
E-mail: service@dadirect.com.au